I0031799

Everard F. Im Thurn

The Botany of the Roraima Expedition of 1884

Everard F. Im Thurn

The Botany of the Roraima Expedition of 1884

ISBN/EAN: 9783337324834

Printed in Europe, USA, Canada, Australia, Japan

Cover: Foto ©Andreas Hilbeck / pixelio.de

More available books at **www.hansebooks.com**

2nd Ser. BOTANY.]   [VOL. II. PART 13.

THE

TRANSACTIONS

OF

THE LINNEAN SOCIETY OF LONDON.

THE BOTANY OF THE RORAIMA EXPEDITION OF 1884.

By E. F. IM THURN.

(Communicated by SIR J. D. HOOKER, K.C.S.I.)

L O N D O N:

PRINTED FOR THE LINNEAN SOCIETY

BY TAYLOR AND FRANCIS, RED LION COURT, FLEET STREET.

SOLD AT THE SOCIETY'S APARTMENTS, BURLINGTON-HOUSE, PICCADILLY, W.,

AND BY LONGMANS, GREEN, AND CO., PATERNOSTER-ROW.

July 1887.

XV. *The Botany of the Roraima Expedition of* 1884; *being Notes on the Plants observed, by* EVERARD F. IM THURN; *with a list of the Species collected, and Determinations of those that are new, by* Prof. OLIVER, *F.R.S., F.L.S., and others.* (*Communicated by* Sir J. D. HOOKER, *K.C.S.I., F.R.S., F.L.S., &c.*)

(Plates XXXVII.–LVI.)

[Read 15th April, 1886.]

I. *Notes on the Plants observed during the Roraima Expedition of* 1884.
By EVERARD F. IM THURN.

AS was expected, the plants collected on the way to Roraima, and especially about that mountain itself, during the recent expedition and first ascent to its summit, have proved of great interest, now that they have been examined and catalogued at Kew. Several specialists have most kindly lent their aid in examining and determining these plants. While Professor Oliver undertook the bulk of the collection, Mr. J. G. Baker, besides determining a few of the Petaloid Monocotyledons, has, with Mr. G. S. Jenman of British Guiana, worked out the Ferns, Mr. H. N. Ridley, of the British Museum, the Orchids and Cyperaceæ, and Mons. E. Marchal the Araliaceæ, Dr. Engler has described a new *Moronobea*, Mr. E. Brown a new Aroid, and Mr. Mitten has named the Muscales; lastly, Dr. Maxwell Masters has supplied a note on two Passifloræ, perhaps new, but imperfectly represented. In all, fifty-three new species and three new genera have been described by these various workers.

The number of species collected would probably have been greater but for the extreme difficulty of drying plants in so excessively damp a climate as that of Roraima, and also for the fact that the other very serious labours inseparable from the direction of such an expedition greatly curtailed the time I was able to devote to the preparation of botanical specimens. As regards the number of new generic and specific forms collected, great as it is, it would undoubtedly have been much greater but for the fact (unfortunate in this respect) that my collection was made at exactly the same period of the year [November and December] at which such collecting as had been done before about Roraima had been accomplished by Sir Robert and Dr. Schomburgk and by Karl Appun*.

* The list of visitors to Roraima, other than natives, is as follows :—Sir ROBERT SCHOMBURGK, then at the head of a boundary commission, was there in 1838, and again, with his brother, Dr. RICHARD SCHOMBURGK, the present director of the Adelaide Botanical Gardens, in 1842. Both made considerable botanical collections, which were distributed, I believe, mainly between the Herbaria at Kew, the British Museum, and at Berlin. KARL APPUN was at Roraima in 1864 ; his collections are chiefly at Kew. C. B. BROWN, then the geological surveyor of British Guiana, was there in 1869 ; two Englishmen, FLINT and EDDINGTON, were there in 1877 ; and two others, M'TURK and

Probably no district of equally small size, after such brief and cursory exploration, has yielded greater, or as great, botanical results as has Roraima; still more probable is it that few small districts are so distinctly marked off from the country immediately surrounding them by such great and remarkable peculiarities in their vegetation. In brief, the district of Roraima is, from a botanical point of view, chiefly interesting as an oasis clothed with a vegetation distinct from that of the country which immediately surrounds it, and at the same time, also in a very marked degree, peculiar either to this special district or to this in common with a few other almost equally isolated, but widely separated districts.

I cannot devote these prefatory remarks (in which I have the privilege of introducing the list and description of my collection, so kindly prepared by the authorities above mentioned) to a better purpose than to make as emphatic a statement as I can *of the isolated character, botanically, of the Roraima district, of the probable botanical relation to certain other possibly similar districts, and of the general appearance of the very peculiar and distinct vegetation of these districts* *.

The whole area known under the name of Guiana may be likened to a wedge driven into the north-eastern shoulder of South America. Geographically, it is thus placed between Brazil on the south and Venezuela on the north; for our present purpose it will, however, be better to describe its position somewhat differently. The artificially formed political divisions of the continent for obvious reasons correspond very closely with the tracts naturally differentiated each by its own river-system. As it is along the river-systems that the migration of animals and plants chiefly occur, the customary and convenient names of these divisions therefore really correspond somewhat closely with the natural and important differences in flora and in fauna, which distinguish the narrow river-basins. Thus, as Venezuela is essentially the tract drained by the great river Orinoco, and as the northern part of Brazil is essentially the tract drained by the great river Amazon, and as Guiana, intermediate between these two, consists essentially of the parallel tracts drained by comparatively smaller rivers (of which the Essequibo, the Demerara, the Berbice, the Corentyn, the Saramacca, and the Maroni may be

---

BODDAM WETHAM, in 1878. None of these made botanical collections. DAVID BURKE, an English orchid-collector, was there in 1881, and brought home interesting living plants, among others, the South-American pitcher-plant (*Heliamphora nutans*), which has, I believe, since been distributed by Messrs. Veitch & Sons. HENRY WHITELY, an English collector of bird-skins, was there on several occasions between 1879 and 1884, and is, I believe, again there ta the present moment, but he has collected no plants. SIEDEL, a German orchid-collector, was there in April 1884, and again, with us, in December of the same year. He brought back only living plants, especially the magnificent *Cattleya Lawrenceana*, which have since been distributed by Mr. H. Sander. Of these Siedel, the only traveller with an eye for plants who has been at Roraima except in the last months of the year, assures me that the abundance of flower was much greater there in April than in December. But in the latter month the natives' Cassava-fields are in full bearing, and provision is therefore much more easily attainable.

* I use the phrase "Roraima district" as including not only the mountain of that name, but the whole of the small group of similar sandstone mountains of which Roraima is the best known, and at present the only explored member.

mentioned), so Venezuela, Guiana, and North Brazil therefore represent tracts which are really more or less differentiated from one another in their flora and fauna.

Now, as the whole of the tract under consideration (that drained by the Orinoco, the Amazon, and the intermediate rivers) rises gradually, or, more generally, by step-like ascents, from the sea-level on its east toward the tableland on its west (*i. e.* the centre of the continent), it is, of course, on this tableland that the rivers take their origin. And as, owing to the irregularity of the surface of this tableland, and still more that of its slope toward the eastern sea, it follows that each of these rivers collects its head-waters from unusually widely separated localities, so it often happens that two or more of these rivers draw some portion of their head-waters from unusually contiguous localities. Thus it is conceivable, and even probable, that any peculiar animal or vegetable forms, which may originate at one of these localities which supplies water to very divergent river-systems may distribute themselves over very wide areas by passing along the courses of the various rivers thence arising.

It happens that the rock-pillars of the Roraima group, rising some 5000 feet over the general level of the tableland. itself at that part some 3000 feet above the level of the sea, pour down from their summits streams which go to swell the Orinoco, the Essequibo, and the Amazon—in other words, the three rivers respectively of Venezuela, Guiana, and Brazil. Now, as has been already mentioned, the flora of Roraima is of a very remarkably peculiar character. A most interesting question still awaits solution, namely, the relation of the flora of Roraima to the floras of Venezuela, Guiana, and Brazil.

No answer, I say, has yet been attempted to this question; nor can I pretend to suggest any. I am, however, able here to offer, as data to be considered in the question, some very general account of the flora of Guiana, and a rather more special account of the flora of Roraima in its relation to that of Guiana.

Guiana, as has been said, rises gradually from the east toward the high tableland of the interior of the continent. Instead, however, of thus placing ourselves in imagination on its sea-coast and looking westward up its gradual slope, let us imagine ourselves on the tableland on Roraima, and that we are looking eastward down toward the sea. Were such a bird's-eye view really possible, we should find that the tableland, or savannah, as it is there called, is an open treeless country, its elevated surface hardly anywhere level, but swelling up in many hills, and even into some mountain-ranges. We find that only along the courses of the rivers, or in the other lower parts where water has accumulated in some form, are there more or less extensive belts of trees, and that, on the savannah itself, even these trees are, considering that we are in the tropics, of no great size. Further eastward, on the lower part of the slope toward the sea, where the rivers have already grown wider and approached each other more nearly, the trees are more numerous and larger. Still further eastward, lower down the slope, the belts of trees, each pertaining to its own river, have widened with the rivers, till they have approached and then joined each other; here the trees are of yet larger size. At last, at the bottom of the slope, between its foot and the still far distant sea-waves, the wide tract of alluvial soil which has been deposited, having either been brought down by the rivers or cast up from the sea, is virtually entirely occupied by the omnipresent forest of trees, which have there attained their true gigantic tropical size.   If we except certain small patches of very swampy open land within this forest of the alluvial tract, locally called "wet savannahs," all is forest except the very narrow strip of land actually washed by the waves, and not even that toward the north.

Very different and distinct floras characterize the parts of Guiana thus variously conditioned, though, naturally, a certain number of species are common to all three.

Where the narrow sea-washed strip has been artificially disafforested, a generally dwarf and weed-like flora prevails, very rarely consisting of non-indigenous plants.

Within the forest, after the generally great height of the trees and often the abundance of palms, perhaps the most noteworthy features of the vegetation, are in the first place, the great scarcity of mosses, herbage, and low-growing plants, especially of any with conspicuous flowers, and the consequent barrenness of the soil, which is relieved by only a few scattered ferns, ginger-worts, Caladiums and other aroids, Dieffenbachias, Cyperaceæ, and other shade-loving plants; and, in the next place (though this is hardly discernible from below), the abundance of the flowering creepers and epiphytes spread over the matted tops of the dense and lofty trees.   The representatives of the low-growing flowering plants of the thinner, lighter woods of temperate climates have here, in this dense shade of the tropical forest, to send their immensely long, flowerless, creeping stems up some one or even two hundred feet, to reach above the highest tree-branches, before they can break into bloom.   Only as semiaquatics along the river-side there are a few showy-flowered dwarf plants.

Quite different again is it on the savannahs, where, among the grasses which naturally form the chief vegetation, are scattered a considerable number of bright-flowered dwarf plants; though even here the abundance of bloom very rarely reaches the extraordinary development which it often does in the meadows of temperate climates.   Rather striking, too, is it that on these savannahs many of the bright-flowered plants, unlike those of temperate meadows, are here also true climbing-plants, leguminous chiefly, and various species of *Echites*, though their stems, instead of climbing far and high over giant trees, here only ramble weakly over the short grasses.

In each of these distinct floras of the coast, the forest, and of the savannah, the number of species is of course great; but in each separate district the species characteristic of it are, as a rule, remarkably widely and evenly scattered throughout its extent. For example, within the forest-district probably by far the larger number of species have an unbroken distribution throughout its extent, and of the remaining species most have an unbroken distribution throughout the district from north to south; though they may be limited from east to west, according, that is, to the greater or less distance from the sea or to the higher or lower position on the general upward slope of the country.   On the savannah, the level of which probably corresponds more or less closely with the general level of the main tableland of that part of the continent, the distribution of the main species is still more even and universal.   On almost every part of the savannah certain grasses, dwarf shrubs, and herb-like plants, form the dominant vegetation. Yet a few remaining parts are marked by the occurrence of certain distinct and, so to speak, localized species, which are scattered more or less widely among the more ordinary forms. Again, a very few other parts are still more distinctly marked, and made very distinct areas, by the more or less complete absence of the ordinary forms, and the substitution there of an entirely new and generally very distinct set of species. These areas with a few localized species, several of which were passed by us on our way to Roraima, and still more these areas of distinct vegetation, of which the Kaieteur savannah which we traversed, and especially Roraima itself, are remarkably fine examples of the utmost botanical interest.

A few notes must first be given of the species here described as localized. It is to be remembered that these notes were made during a single walk, long as it was, through a country otherwise almost absolutely unknown; so that though these species were noticed by me because I saw them either only in one spot, or at least in very few spots—*i. e.* I passed through either only one distinct group or through very few such groups of them—yet it is, of course, impossible to assert that many other such distinct groups do not occur wherever the requisite soil and other circumstances permit.

A considerable number of such localized species occur on tracts where the soil is of so peculiar a nature as to have earned a special name for such places from the natives, who call them *Eppellings*. This name is applied by the Arekoonas to certain tracts in which the underlying very soft sandstone is overlaid by a coating of hard dense and dry mud, or, in some other cases, of hard conglomerate. Wherever, as is often the case, this hard-mud surface is unbroken, it resembles an asphalt pavement, or, perhaps, rather a floor made of hard-beaten earth. But this curious earth-surface overlies hill and dale alike—is, therefore, not often level. Wherever, then, there has been the slightest crack in its surface, rain-water gathers, and, having once obtained a lodgment, eats away and enlarges the crack. The result is an eppelling surface, which, instead of being like an asphalt pavement, is like a pavement formed of irregularly-shaped and scattered flag-stones. But, again, the mud-layer which overlies the eppelling being by no means thick, whenever this has once been indented, as just described, by many cracks enlarged by water, these cracks are soon engraved through the mud-layer down to the soft sandstone below; and, when this has once occurred, the sandstone thus exposed, which yields to the action of the water even more readily than does the hard mud, is rapidly worked out. In this way the eppelling is made to assume the form of a number of blocks of sandstone, often pillar-like. Each of such blocks is capped and protected by a patch of the original hard earth, or, in other cases, of the original conglomerate. (See woodcut, fig. 1, p. 254.)

Now, where the original eppelling surface is unbroken, in which state we have compared it to an asphalt pavement, it is as entirely devoid of vegetation as such an artificial pavement would be. But where the surface of the eppelling has reached its furrowed stage, a few plants find lodgment, chiefly certain orchids and other such plants, of which the roots are of such a nature that, in the dry season, when the furrows are waterless, the whole plant shrinks into complete rest, and even in some cases loses its roothold, and is blown about on the surface of the eppelling until the next rains come, when it again throws out anchor-like roots into some new furrow.   One orchid of this wandering tendency is a *Catasetum* (*C. cristatum* ? [No. 148]); another is the new and very beautiful *Oncidium*, named and described by Mr. Ridley in the appended list as *O. orthostates* [No. 12].   Sometimes, too, in this same state of the eppelling, especially where such ground occurs on the brows of exposed hills, shrubs of considerable size find anchorage in the furrows and flourish.   One such hill-top which we passed was made very beautiful in this way by a large and isolated patch of the large rosy-flowered *Bonnetia sessilis*, Benth. [No. 11].   In another similar place we passed through a distinct patch of the compact *Stifftia condensata*, Baker [No. 110]. And more than one such place was distinguished by thickets of *Gomphia guianensis* [No. 15].

Fig. 1.

Rock-pillars on the summit of Roraima.

Lastly, as regards the eppellings where the furrows of these places have been worked down into the sandstone, and have been much enlarged, the deep ravines and pits of all sizes thus formed, though bare of vegetation wherever the process of water-washing still continues in violent action, where this action has ceased owing to the stoppage of the outlet, or has become much moderated, are comparatively thickly clothed with vegetation.

Another remarkable localized plant, though not occurring on an eppelling, was the beautiful *Aphelandra pulcherrima* ? [No. 14].   It has already been said that, even on the otherwise open savannahs, more or less extensive belts of forest often clothe the sides of the narrower parts of the valleys through which the rivers run.   One such place we came to, where, after crossing the Ireng river and the low watershed which there separates that river from its tributary, the Karakanang, we were descending toward the level of the last-named river.   It was here that, in a somewhat extensive wood of which most of the trees were common species of *Cassia*, we found the dense, shrubby underwood to consist almost entirely of this beautiful scarlet-flowered *Aphelandra*.

Throughout a small tract on either side of the Ireng river, where the ground was almost entirely covered by a gravelly layer of shattered conglomerate, a very beautiful herb, with flowers of an intense violet-blue—a very rare colour in Guiana—was common, and pleasantly reminded me of an English "viper's bugloss." It was *Stachytarpheta mutabilis*, Vahl [No. 1], which seems to me to correspond to my description of a localized species.

Again, between the Ireng and the Cotinga rivers, there grew in abundance, and evidently as a native, a plant [*Furcræa gigantea*] which, common enough near the coast of Guiana in cultivation, and even as an evident escape from cultivation, is nowhere else, as far as I have seen in many wanderings, wild in that colony.

Lastly, as regards localized species, I would mention several dwarf bamboos, none of which, unfortunately, did I succeed in finding in flower. One of these, a wonderfully graceful species, appears to me peculiar, in that it grows in dense thickets on the open savannah. This was on the Ireng river, and more sparingly onward from there toward the Cotinga. Another of these bamboos (*Chusquea* [sp. ?], No. 18), I think the most graceful plant I ever saw, occurred sparingly, and only in one spot, on the Arapoo river close to the village of Tooroiking. A third bamboo, a climbing form (*Guadua*) [No. 359], occurred to me first on the same river, but is much more common on Roraima itself, and should perhaps be spoken of in connection with the vegetation of that mountain.

Turning next to the areas of distinct vegetation, the first to be mentioned is that of the Kaieteur savannah [*]. This is certainly a very remarkable place, with an equally remarkable vegetation. It is an open space, some two miles long by one across, in the heart of the ordinary dense forest, and some four days' journey on foot from the nearest open country. It has been said that the descent from the tableland of the interior toward the sea is not a gradual slope, but occurs chiefly in a series of step-like descents. These descents are generally of no great individual height; but that of the Kaieteur takes the form of an almost abrupt cliff—at the Kaieteur fall itself it is an actual cliff—of between seven and eight hundred feet in height. The Potaro river, rising apparently from the neighbourhood of, but not actually on, Roraima, after an unknown upper course of considerable length, runs along one side of the almost perfectly level Kaieteur savannah, and precipitates itself, at the east end of that savannah, down the sheer descent of 800 feet. The savannah itself is virtually a flat exposed rock, many parts of which are as absolutely bare as a London pavement. This rock is sandstone, which, as in the eppellings (indeed it probably is one, but of unusually unbroken surface) is capped by a harder material, a layer of conglomerate. Just as the hard surface of the eppellings cracks, and eventually affords roothold in the fissures thus made for plants, so the hard conglomerate covering of the Kaieteur savannah has cracked, and in many of the fissures thus produced has given harbourage for plants. Some of these latter fissures have gradually been filled up by the accumulation of vegetable matter; others remain still open. On this savannah, however, the fissures are larger than is commonly the case in the eppellings—are, in fact, often very long but generally narrow fissures. Many of these are now entirely occupied by shrubs and dwarf trees. The lines of these masses of vegetation, necessarily following the direction of the fissures,

* Some excellent "Remarks on the aspect and flora of the Kaieteur Savannah" were published by my friend Mr. G. S. Jenman in 'Timehri' vol. i. (1882) p. 229.

present, in most remarkable degree, the appearance of the well-marked designs laid out by a landscape-gardener; the whole effect is like that of an artificial garden, with regular groups of shrubs separated by wide paths and roads of clean bare rock. Moreover, it is not only in the fissures that plants grow on this savannah. As on the eppellings, so here too, a certain number of plants find sufficient foothold in the vegetable accumulations in the slight depressions in the conglomerate sheet before these have¸been engraved deeply enough to leave the sandstone exposed and to make regular fissures.

But not only is the arrangement of the vegetation of the savannah thus very remarkable; the plants composing this vegetation are also individually of great interest. As might be expected, very few of them occur in the forest which everywhere, and for a great distance, surrounds this strange open space. Much more remarkable is it that very few of these plants occur on the nearest savannah, nor, indeed, on the general savannah-land of the interior. And, most noteworthy of all is it, a very large number of these peculiar plants of this isolated savannah occur, often with slight but interesting differences, on Roraima.

By far the most striking, as it is also the most abundant, plant on the Kaieteur savannah is a huge aloe-like Bromeliaceous plant, *Brocchinia cordylinoides*, Baker, which was gathered there by Mr. Jenman and myself some years ago, but which was, until the Roraima expedition, unknown elsewhere. This gigantic plant, so striking as to compel notice even from the most unobservant traveller, is ranged in enormous numbers on the Kaieteur savannah, and indeed makes, to a large extent, the strangeness of that strange scene. There the height of a full-grown specimen, under favourable circumstances, is about 14 feet, and, in the older specimens at least, the crown of leaves is supported on a tall bare stem. It seems also there to flower abundantly. We shall see that the plant occurs, but with slightly different characters, on Roraima. Moreover, at the Kaieteur, in the axils of the leaves of this *Brocchinia*, and only in that position, grows a very remarkable and beautiful *Utricularia* (*U. Humboldtii*, Schombk.), with flower-stems 3 or 4 feet long, supporting its many splendidly large violet flowers. This plant too we found on Roraima, and with slightly different characters from those which it exhibits at the Kaieteur. Another remarkable and distinct plant on the Kaieteur savannah is a low-growing *Brocchinia* (*B. reducta*, Baker), also previously known only from there, and may be roughly described as resembling three or four sheets of yellowish-grey foolscap paper rolled loosely one round the other, the whole standing on one end of the roll. This plant I did not observe on Roraima, though I feel convinced that it will one day be found there; but I did see it, in very considerable quantity, in one small district about halfway between the Kaieteur and Roraima. Only one other plant common, but with a difference of form, to the two districts can be mentioned here. Mr. Jenman found at the Kaieteur a very striking new *Moronobea* (*M. Jenmani*, Engl.); and I found on Roraima another very remarkable congener (*M. intermedia*, Engl., No. 337), of which its describer says that it is intermediate between *M. riparia* and *M. Jenmani*.

In short, the Kaieteur savannah and Roraima may be regarded as two isolated areas marked by a very peculiar vegetation, which vegetation is, however, to a noteworthy extent, common to the two.

Before referring to the district of Roraima, I may mention that, if I may judge from the reports of the natives, and of the one or two white men who have been there, savannahs occur curiously like this very remarkable example at the Kaieteur (1) above Amailah fall on the Curichrong river, a tributary of the Potaro, (2) above Orinidouie fall on the Ireng river, and (3) above a certain very large fall which exists (I have myself heard the roar of its waters) on the Potaro, about two days' boat journey above the Kaieteur. In each of these places the large and not easily mistakable *Brocchinia cordylinoides* is credibly said to occur; and it seems highly probable that with this some of the other, but less conspicuous, plants of the Kaieteur occur also on these other savannahs. In short, it may very probably be that each of these reported fall-savannahs is a distinct area, parallel and similar in vegetation to the Kaieteur savannah and to Roraima. In passing it may also here be noted that apparently a *Brocchinia*, similar to *B. cordylinoides*, occurs on the Organ Mountains, near Rio, in Brazil, reached by Gardner in 1837, and that in the axils of its leaves occurs a *Utricularia* (*U. nelumbifolia*, Gard.) which, to judge from Gardner's passing descriptions, must be strikingly similar to *U. Humboldtii* as it occurs on the Kaieteur savannah. Possibly

Fig. 2.

View of the south-east face of Roraima, showing the waterfall and ledge of ascent.

the Organ Mountains, too, resemble in some of their vegetable features the Kaieteur savannah and Roraima *.

* Gardner's description of the vegetation of the Organ Mountains (see his 'Travels in Brazil,' London, 1849, pp. 50-52, 102-103) reads extraordinarily like an account of the vegetation of Roraima. The height of the two elevations is about the same, but the Organ Mountains consist almost exclusively of granite, not, as Roraima does, of sandstone.

Let us now pass to the consideration of Roraima itself as an area of distinct vegetation ; and in so doing a few words must first be said as to the physical features of the mountains.

Roraima is one (certainly the best known, perhaps really the most remarkable) of a group of pillar-like sandstone mountains capped with hard conglomerate, which group is, it seems to me, identical in nature and origin with the groups of sandstone pillars, capped with conglomerate or hardened mud, of the eppellings already described. In short, Roraima and its fellow mountains seem to be an eppelling on a gigantic scale. Some notion of how large this scale is may be gathered from the fact that Roraima itself, one pillar of the group, is almost exactly four miles wide along its south-eastern face, and is apparently seven or eight miles long from south to north, and that its height is some 5000 feet above the general level of the plain from which it rises.

This 5000 feet of height, it must be explained, is made up of a sloping base, the pediment of the pillar, of about 3000 feet, which is surmounted by the more strict pillar-like portion, 2000 feet in height. The plateau on top of the pillar is a very slightly, almost imperceptibly, hollowed basin, four miles wide by some seven or eight long, over which are scattered innumerable single rocks and piles of rocks, the largest of which are apparently some eighty or ninety feet in height. The sloping basal part of the mountain is, everywhere but toward the south-east, covered by dense, but not lofty forest; while on the south-east a considerable portion of it (which portion does not, however, extend up to the foot of the actual cliff) is treeless and grass-covered. The cliff itself is bare, but for a comparatively few mosses, ferns, grasses, and trailing plants clinging closely to the rougher parts of its surface, especially where the many waterfalls trickle down the rock-face, and for the dwarf shrubs, ever dwarfer and more alpine in character toward the top, which have found a lodgment on the few transverse ledges which break the evenness of the surface. The hollow basin at the top of the pillar is, wherever a little soil has accumulated in the depressions of the bare rock which constitutes the greater part of its surface, clothed with a dwarf herb-like vegetation of most remarkable appearance, consisting largely of various species of *Pæpalanthus*, a *Drosera*, a few terrestrial orchids (these not very conspicuous in flower), a remarkable low-growing aloe-like *Abolboda* of which I shall have more to say hereafter, various ground-clinging shrubs of alpine *Vaccinium*-like character, and of a very few single shrubs, all of one species (*Bonnetia Roraimæ*, Oliv., n. sp. [No. 330]), of larger growth, even though this is but some three feet high.

Nor in this brief sketch of the physical features of Roraima in their bearing on the vegetation is it possible to avoid mention of the great moisture of the atmosphere which surrounds the mountain. The shallow basin of the upper plateau always holds much water, and probably at times is almost full ; the sides of the cliff are ever moistened by the innumerable rills and streams poured down from the plateau above on to the sloping base ; and this basal portion itself is, on the more level undulating parts of its exposed surface, a mere spongy swamp, while in its forested parts it is traversed by almost innumerable rills hastening down to join the large rivers of the plain below.

When dealing with the vegetation along our line of march to Roraima I pointed out that I could only pretend to speak of the plants actually along that line ; in now dealing with the vegetation of Roraima itself I can only speak of that of the south-eastern side of this mountain, which alone I was able to examine closely. We spent nearly a month on this side, where it is treeless, savannah-like, and swampy, and we climbed to the top of the mountain by a ledge running obliquely up the south-eastern face of its cliff (see fig. 2, p. 257).

It was not till we reached the top that we saw the most remarkable features in the wonderful plant-life of this very distinct area of vegetation. Even while only approaching the base of the mountain (which for convenience of description I will take to be marked on the south-eastern side by the bed of the Kookenaam river), and while we were still far off, we met for the first time with plants which we afterwards found commonly on Roraima, the outposts, as it were, of the remarkable group of plant-forms centred on Roraima. From the moment when the first of these distinctive plants of the mountain was met with till the moment, some weeks later, when we reached the top, we ever travelled onward into a more and more peculiar flora.

Our discovery, on the savannahs a full day's journey from Roraima, of the first outpost of the vegetation of that mountain was a very distinct event. We found a well-marked dense patch, perhaps some 40 yards in diameter, of *Abolboda Sceptrum*, Oliver, nov. sp. [No. 312], a compact and dwarf, yucca-like plant, with a rosette, perhaps a foot and a half in diameter, of most acutely needle-pointed leaves. This plant appeared again in patches once or twice before we reached Roraima, and formed much of the turf, as it were, both of the savannah slope of the base of that mountain and also of the top. It was, whenever it appeared, a constant source of annoyance and of danger, not only to the naked feet of my Indian companions, but also to my own canvas-clad feet. Luckily a rumour which in some way spread among us that these rosettes of vegetable bayonets were poisonous, after causing some rather comic alarm, proved groundless. Where we first found the plant, as also on the sloping base of the mountain, it was out of flower and, though its withered flower-stems were already extant, was already seedless; but on the top we found it in full and striking flower. From the centre of the rosette of leaves rises a single stem, perhaps 18 inches in height, crowned by a very regularly formed whorl of dependent yellow flowers. The general appearance—the facies, to use a term recognized, I believe, by botanists—was remarkably like that of the yellow form of the Crown Imperial (*Fritillaria imperialis*). For the botanical description of this interesting plant, as indeed of all the other new plants of which I shall attempt to describe the facies, I must refer to the list carefully worked out at Kew *.

After passing the first station of *Abolboda Sceptrum* till we reached the actual foot of Roraima, at the bed of the Kookenaam river, we continued through a country over which, though it was still furnished chiefly with the ordinary savannah vegetation, were scattered a few, indeed as we advanced an ever-increasing number of new plants. Across this tract, about halfway between the station of *Abolboda* and the Kookenaam, runs the Arapoo river, which, falling down from Roraima, has its course marked in a pronounced

* It may here be mentioned that three volumes of admirable original sketches of British Guiana plants by (Sir Robert?) Schomburgk exist in the Herbarium of the British Museum. Among these sketches are to be found many Roraima plants, and among others *Abolboda Sceptrum*.

way by plants characteristic of that mountain, such as *Marcetia taxifolia* [No. 68],
Cassia Roraimæ, Benth. [No. 71], *Dimorphandra macrostachya*, Benth. [No. 39], *Meissneria microticioides*, Naud. [No. 174], *Calea ternifolia*, Oliv. [No. 27]. To me the most
interesting plant on this river was a very beautiful little slipper-orchid (*Selenipedium
Klotzschianum*, Reichb. f. [No. 31]), which grew in the moist gravel of the river-bed, where
the plant must frequently be under water. This plant we also found in great abundance
on an island in the Cotinga river, on another in the Roraima river, and on a small creek,
called Aroie, a tributary of the Cotinga. Naturally the Arapoo river, as are its fellows
flowing from Roraima, is an artery allowing of the dissemination of the plants of that
mountain.

At last we reached the Kookenaam river, at the village of Teroota, at the base, that
is, of Roraima. Even beyond the bed of the river, for some distance up the slope
of the mountain, the tract of ordinary savannah vegetation still continues, its characteristic plants ever becoming more and more mingled with plants belonging to the
Roraima flora, till the very distinctly marked zone of strictly Roraima vegetation is
reached.

The course of the Kookenaam river, where it flows through the tract of neutral
vegetation—vegetation, that is, not yet deprived of ordinary savannah plants, and not
yet composed exclusively of Roraima plants—is, as was the course of the Arapoo river
already described, very well defined by the large number of Roraima plants clustering
on its banks. Among these may be mentioned various shrubs, *Ilex Maconcoua*, Pers.
[No. 75], *Dipteryx reticulata*, Benth. ? [No. 73], *Myrcia Roraimæ*, Oliv. [No. 74], and
another species close to *M. Kegeliana*, Berg [No. 82]) which in places fringe the banks of
this stream, and are also characteristic of the upper, proper flora of the mountains.
Along the banks of this river, after its emergence from the mountain, grows in the peaty
soil at the water's edge a very beautiful and sweet-scented white orchid (*Aganisia alba*,
Ridley [No. 360]), and on the more rocky parts of the bank a very remarkable red
passion-flower [No. 84], with panicles of many pendent flowers, each panicle having the
appearance—the *facies*, to use that ugly but convenient term again—of a spray of fuchsia-
blossom *. It was here, too, in the deep cuttings made by the river and half filled up
with huge blocks of stone which are now overgrown with gnarled trees and shrubs, that
one of the most famous of all Roraima plants grows—*Cattleya Lawrenceana*, Reichb. f.
[No. 80].

This *Cattleya* is doubtless the one collected by the Schomburgk brothers, and enumerated
by Richard Schomburgk as *C. pumila*; for it appears to be the only representative of this
genus occurring on this side, at least, of Roraima, and this was the only side visited by
the Schomburgks. It grows apparently not high up on the mountain, but on the gnarled
tree-trunks, close to the water, in the clefts through which the Kookenaam and some of
its small tributary streams flow, at a height of about 3700 to 4000 feet above the sea. At
the time of our visit, Mr. Siedel, an orchid collector, having set the natives to work
to collect this plant for him, I have seen ten or twelve of these people come into

* This passion-flower is well figured in Schomburgk's drawings, of which mention has already been made.

camp, afternoon after afternoon, each laden with a basket (a good load for a man) full of these lovely plants, many of them then in full flower.   One day I myself, having gone down to the Kookenaam to bathe, gathered, just round the small pool I chose for that purpose, two most glorious clumps of this orchid, the better of the two having five spikes of flower, of which one bore nine, each of the others eight, blossoms—in all forty-one of some of the largest and finest-coloured *Cattleya*-flowers ever seen, on a single small plant, the roots of which easily lay on my extended hand [*].

Before now dealing with the plants actually of Roraima, it will be convenient to say a few more words as to the form of this south-eastern face of the mountain (woodcut, fig. 2).

From the bed of the Kookenaam at Teroota (3751 feet) the mountain slopes, somewhat gradually though of course not evenly, upward for a distance of about three miles, till a height of 5000 feet is attained. This last-mentioned point is that to which a considerable number of the plants belonging to the ordinary savannah vegetation of Guiana ascend [†]. From this point the mountain rises, at first somewhat more abruptly and then again more gradually, so as to form, as it were, a terrace about midway up the slope. The upper level of this terrace, which lies at a height of about 5400 feet, is almost everywhere swampy, though here and there a few rocks crop out. This is the place so enthusiastically described by Dr. Schomburgk, on account of the extraordinary richness of its vegetation, as a "botanical Eldorado;" and it was here too, just within the forest which edges this swamp, that we built our house and made our headquarters. It is to this point that the open savannah extends; for above it all is more or less densely forested. Between this swamp, lying along its terrace, is a ravine, and again, beyond this ravine, in which it must be remembered that the forest begins, the mountain slopes up very abruptly to a height of about 6500 feet, to the base, that is, of the actual cliff. In the accompanying diagram (woodcut, fig. 2, p. 257) all up to the ravine is distinguished as the savannah-slope; all above, to the base of the cliff, as the forest-slope. It should also be noted that the forest-slope is not uniformly clad with trees. The lower part is densely wooded, covered, as it were, by dense jungle; next comes a belt of bush, rather than of jungle; while still higher, just under the cliff, the masses of rock which have fallen from above lie like a moraine, on which are scattered sparse trees, the low, wide-spreading branches of which interlock in a remarkable way [‡]. The actual face of the cliff is, of course, bare; but wherever ledges run up for any distance these are often tree- or bush-clad; and the one ledge which runs right up to the top, the one by which we ascended, is bush-clad to a point about two-thirds up, then bushless but plant-covered.

In the ascent from Teroota up to about 5000 feet (nearly up, that is, to the commencement of the El Dorado swamp) we met with many plants new to me scattered among the

[*] Full descriptions of this *Cattleya* have been given in the 'Gardeners' Chronicle,' 1885. vol. xxiii. pp. 374, 375, and vol. xxiv. p. 168.

[†] The most conspicuous of the few plants of the ordinary plain which ascend above this point are :—*Polygala hygrophila*, H. B. K.; *P. longicaulis*, H. B. K.; *P. variabilis*, H. B. K.; *Sida linifolia*, Cav.; *Drosera communis*, A. St.-Hil.; *Pleroma Tibouchinum*, Triana; *Sipanea pratensis*, Aubl.; *Pectis elongata*, H. B. K.; *Cnephalium spicatum*, Lam.; and *Centropogon surinamensis*, Presl.

[‡] This moraine-like part of the slope is curiously like the well-known "Wistman's Wood" on Dartmoor.

usual savannah plants.   Conspicuous among these were three orchids, two growing on
bare pebble-covered ground, the third on the huge boulders scattered over the slope.   The
two former were *Cyrtopodium parviflorum*, Lindl. [No. 55], with its handsome spike,
often eighteen inches high, of many yellow and purple flowers, and the delicately beautiful
white-flowered *Kœllensteinia Kellueriana*, Reichb. f. [No. 61], which latter grows also on
the Kaieteur savannah.   The third of the above-mentioned orchids was the curious *Masda-
vallia brevis*, Reichb. f. [No. 286], with flowers more remarkable than beautiful.   Another
striking new plant also growing on the boulders of this part of the slope was a remarkably
handsome and large *Puya* (?) [No. 45], with flowers of a magnificently deep indigo-blue—
a colour so rare in the tropics.   This *Puya*, Mr. Baker tells me, is probably a new and
interesting species, but the dried specimens of it which I deposited at Kew are unfortunately not sufficient for its determination.   I have, however, some fine young living plants
of the species.

I come now to the description of the El Dorado swamp, for the place is really so
remarkable botanically as to be worthy of distinction under this name.   It is worth, also,
another effort to give some picture of the appearance of the place.   The swamp (botanists
will understand that the rather dismal suggestions of this word are often, as certainly in
this case, undeserved) lies on a terrace midway up the mountain.   Its surface is very
uneven, and it is consequently much wetter in some parts than in others—its flatter parts
and its hollows so saturated with wet that the foot of one who walks there sinks often up
to the ankle; its higher parts islands, rarely of any great size, of dry ground scattered
through the swamp.   Often from these dry islands considerable groups of rocks
crop out and sometimes rise to a considerable height.   In the wetter parts the grass,
which, of course, forms the main vegetation, is everywhere high, rank, and coarse; on
the islands of drier ground the grass is finer and even turf-like; from the actual rocks
grass is absent.   Each of these two aspects of the swamp, wet ground and dry rocky
island, presents a distinct vegetation, of which almost the only common feature is distinction from the vegetation outside this El Dorado.

Mingling and vying in height with the rank grass * of the wet parts, their flowers
mingling with the blossom of the grasses, are plants of wonderful beauty.   The ever lovely
violet-flowered *Utricularia Humboldtii*, Schombk. [No. 43], is there, growing, not, as on
the Kaieteur savannah, as an epiphyte, but with independent roots in the ground; but of
this I shall have more to say presently.   The *Abolboda* is there too, in a form slightly
larger and much less compact than is natural to it when growing on drier ground.   The
flag-leaved, yellow-flowered *Xyris setigera*, Oliver [No. 62], and the small pink-flowered
Begonia tovarensis, Klotzsch [No. 141], are also there.   A very few plants of *Brocchinia cordylinoides*, Baker, just two or three single specimens, are there; but of this
I shall have more to say presently.   Various ferns are there, especially the magnificent
Cycad-like *Lomaria Boryana*, Willd. (*L. Schomburgkii*, Klotzsch); also many orchids;
a "lady's slipper" (*Selenipedium Lindleyanum*, Reichb. f. [No. 53]), with huge-branched
flower-stems, each bearing many blooms, the whole plant, flower, leaf, and stem alike, all

---

* The grasses chiefly noticed at this place were:—*Paspalum stellatum*, Flügge; *Panicum nervosum*, Lam.; *Arundinella brasiliensis*, Raddi.

velvety in texture, and of various shades of one colour, the colour of sunlight as it falls through green young beech-leaves; the beautiful *Zygopetalum Burkeii*, Reichb.f.[No. 50]*, with flowers seeming like gigantic, pale-coloured "bee orchises" (*Ophrys apifera*, Huds.), but far sweeter in scent; in great abundance the rosy-flowered *Pogonia parciflora*, Reichb. f. [No. 115], which recalls in habit our English wild tulip (*Tulipa sylvestris*, L.); and, to mention but one more among many, *Epidendrum elongatum*, Jacq. [No. 42], its stems varying in height from one to eight feet, its verbena-like clusters of flowers varying in colour in different plants, some pale yellow, some fawn-colour, many pure rich pink, dark purple, and even mauve. This last-mentioned orchid, it may be noted in passing, is one of a group to which I shall presently refer.

The effect of the whole is as of an Alpine meadow, coloured in early summer by innumerable flowers of the brightest and most varied tints.

If this tall vegetation be anywhere parted by the hand of the curious traveller, underneath it is seen a carpet of other, low-growing, plants—*Papalanthus Schomburgkii* [No. 33] and *P. flavescens*, Körw. [No. 60], *Drosera communis*, A. St.-Hil. ? [No. 313], a pretty little orchid, *Spiranthes bifida*, Ridley [No. 342], ferns, Lycopodiums, and sphagnum-like mosses.

One, perhaps the most remarkable, plant of the swamp has not yet been noticed. It is the South-American Pitcher-plant, *Heliamphora nutans*, Benth. [No. 258], which grows in wide-spreading, very dense tufts in the wettest places, but where the grass happens not to be long. Its red-veined pitcher-leaves, its delicate white flowers raised high on red-tinted stems, its sturdy habit of growth, make it a pretty little picture wherever it grows. But it attains its full size and best development, not down here in this swamp, but up on the ledges on the cliff of Roraima, and even on the top.

The vegetation of the drier, rocky patches is very different. A few shrubs of from four to eight feet in height, a very few stunted and gnarled trees are there, a few single specimens of the one Roraima palm (*Geonoma Appuniana*), which, as will presently be told, is much more abundant higher up; but more abundant are very dwarf shrubs of curiously Alpine aspect, such as *Gaultheria cordifolia*, H. B. K. [No. 105], and various trailing plants, such as a blackberry (*Rubus guianensis*, Focke [No. 106]), a passion-flower [No. 110], and a few orchids and ferns.

Of the orchids the most noteworthy is *Oncidium nigratum*, Lindl. [No. 114], its delicately thin, but wiry and much-branched stems, five feet high or more, seeming to float in the air a crowd of innumerable, tiny, butterfly-like flowers of cream-colour and black; but two others (*Zygopetalum Burkeii* and *Epidendrum elongatum*), which we have already seen in rank luxuriance in the wetter parts of the swamp, grow also on these drier parts, but are here much reduced in general habit, though with larger and brighter-coloured flowers. Of the ferns the most striking are a beautifully delicately cut *Schizæa* (*S. dichotoma*, Sw. [No. 100]) and a very remarkable *Gymnogramme* (*G. elaphoglossoides*, Baker, [Nos. 101 & 215]), of which more hereafter.

Again, the tiny coppices which are on the swamp and the forest which bounds it—

---

* This is represented on the Organ Mountains by *Z. Mackaii*, Hook.

which forest, it must be remembered, covers on the other faces of the Roraima slope what is here swamp—are full of interesting trees. One with vast numbers of large magnolia-like white flowers is *Moronobæa intermedia*, Engler [No. 337], the new species already alluded to as very closely allied to a second new species, *M. Jenmani*, Engl., which occurs in corresponding circumstances on the Kaieteur savannah. Another abundant tree represents an entirely new genus, *Crepinella gracilis*, Marchal [No. 162]; another is a new species of *Sciadophyllum* (*S. coriaceum*, March. [No. 128]). Another common, and strikingly beautiful, tree is a variety of *Byrsonima crassifolia*, H. B. K. [No. 130], with leaves the under surfaces of which are tinted with so deep and rich a violet as to impart a very striking violet shade to the whole tree, even when it is seen from a distance. Under the shade of these and the hosts of other trees ground-shrubs and tree-trunks alike are swathed in thick green mosses. There, too, but half clinging to the tree-trunks, are various species of *Psammisia* [Nos. 56 & 49], woody-stemmed creepers, the innumerable drop-like crimson flowers of which, as they catch the tiny gleams of light striking down between the thick leaves of the forest-roof, glow with intense colour. In these shady, moss-covered, quiet places stand erect many tree-ferns [Nos. 92, 270, 87, 37] and a very beautiful new aroid (*Anthurium roraimense*, N. E. Brown [No. 264]), its huge heart-shaped leaves and large arum-like flowers of purest white carried high on a slender but stiff stem. There, too, are innumerable ferns of wonderful interest, and many, but not showy, orchids—especially of the latter family, many of those tiniest and most delicate species which, if seen under a powerful magnifying-glass, would rival the most showy and graceful of their kindred of our hothouses.

We must now pass to the forest-slope, which, as has been said, consists of three fairly distinct belts or zones, which I have called respectively, beginning from the lowest, the jungle-belt, the bush-belt, and the belt of rock and tree.

The jungle is most densely interwoven with many tall shrubs or dwarf trees, which are yet more closely knit together by vast quantities of a climbing, straggling bamboo (*Guadua* [No. 359]), of a cyperaceous plant (*Cryptangium stellatum*, Bœckl. [No. 357], with rough, knife-edged leaves and tall, weak stems, which support themselves on, and at the same time densely clothe, the shrubs among which it grows *, and of a gigantic and handsome climbing fern (*Gleichenia pubescens*, H. B. K. [No. 343]). Among the shrubs also are two palms: one, in vast quantities, very stout and erect-stemmed, and large-leaved, *Geonoma Appuniana*, Spruce [No. 382]; the other, occurring only in a few scattered examples, a *Euterpe*, probably *E. edulis*, Mart., but, if so, in a most remarkably stunted and dwarfed form. It is worth noting here that, despite the reported specific abundance, by Schomburgk and Appun, of palms about Roraima, these are literally the only two plants of that Order which I saw on the mountain. Under the shrubs forming this jungle the ground was everywhere swathed with mosses, closely inter-mingled with innumerable ferns, especially filmy ferns; and this mossy covering reached up over the tree-stems and branches everywhere but where the sunlight fell. Under the shade of these shrubs, in the darkness and damp, grew various

---

* This is also a Kaieteur plant.

high-drawn terrestrial orchids, pallid plants with inconspicuous and pale flowers (*Steno-ptera viscosa*, Reichb. f. [No. 131]).

Undoubtedly the most striking feature of the vegetation of this jungle-belt was the curious abundance and variety of the Ferns. Of these, two seem to require special mention here. One is the *Gymnogramme* [No. 181] already mentioned as occurring on the rocks in the swamp; it was abundantly distributed from the swamp nearly to the top of the mountain. It will be further mentioned in connection with a closely allied species occurring on the top. The second fern to be distinguished represents a very remarkable new genus, on which Mr. Baker has dwelt at some length in his report on the plants of the expedition. The genus he has called *Eudoterosora* [No. 184]; the species he has been good enough to gratify me by naming after my friend the late William Hunter Campbell, LL.D., a man who, for very many reasons, but especially for his constant endeavours to forward the scientific interests of the colony, deserved so well of the people of Guiana. It is perhaps worthy of mention that this plant so closely resembles in outward appearance a form of an entirely different genus (*Polypodium bifurcatum*, L. [No. 184 ex parte]), that I collected and dried it in mistake for that plant. Were it possible to conceive that this resemblance could be of any benefit to the genus *Eudoterosora*, it might be supposed that its very close resemblance to *Polypodium bifurcatum* was an instance of 'mimicry.'

Above the jungle-belt comes the bush-belt. Here the shrubs, much fewer in number and so scattered over the ground as to leave wide intervening spaces, appeared to me generally of much the same species as in the lower belt. Here, however, as is not the case below, they are sufficiently distributed to be individually distinguishable. Among them the most prominent are a great number of species of *Psychotria* [Nos. 83, 115, 185, 232], and a very remarkable yellow-flowered *Melasma, M.? spathacenm*, Oliver, n. sp. [No. 210], of which Professor Oliver writes that the specimens supplied him are too imperfect to afford means of final determination whether this should not be regarded as the type of a new genus distinct from *Melasma*; and, in great abundance, a *Croton* (*C. surinamensi*, Muell. Arg., aff. [No. 235]). Here, too, as below, but as is not the case in the jungle-belt, occur a large number of plants of *Brocchinia cordylinoides*, still in its small Roraima, not in its larger Kaieteur form, as well as great quantities of the huge *Stegolepis guianensis*, Klotzsch. [No. 338], the *Iris*-like plants of which, being provided with a great abundance of slimy matter, made walking most difficult, in parts where they grew densely. The *Brocchinia*, too, grew in parts so densely that we had to walk, not on the ground, but on the crowns of the plants, which, as we crushed them with our feet, poured from the axils of their leaves the remarkably abundant water which they retain; and very cold water it was, over our already too cold feet. Nor must I omit to mention, though I propose afterward to sum up my observations on the *Brocchinia* and on the various species of *Utricularia*, that in this bush-belt a very few plants (I saw not more than three or four) of *Utricularia Humboldtii*, Schombk. [No. 43], of the dark Roraima form, were growing in the axils of the *Brocchinia*-leaves, as at the Kaieteur.

Two other very interesting plants appeared to us first in this bush-belt, though we afterwards found that they extended almost, if not quite, up to the top of the mountain. One, *Lisianthus*, *L. macrantho* aff. [No. 188], was a large succulent-leaved herb, almost shrub-like, with very large rich purple-crimson flowers centred with white, which would probably be a most valuable and gorgeous addition to our cultivated stove-plants. The other was the most delicately beautiful, the most fairy-like, and at the same time, for its size, the most showy plant I ever saw. It was a new *Utricularia*, which Professor Oliver, at my request, has kindly named also after William Hunter Campbell; *U. Campbelliana*, Oliv., n. sp. [No. 187], grew among the very dwarfest mosses clinging to the tree-trunks and boughs. The plant, that is the root and leaves, is so tiny that it was almost impossible to detect it when not in flower. The erect stem, an inch or more high, is hair-like; and on this is borne one (sometimes two) large and brilliant red flower, somewhat of the colour and size of the flowers of *Sophronitis grandiflora*.

One more feature of the bush-belt claims notice; the tree-ferns, occurring, indeed, in the lower jungle-belt, but there crushed out of all form and lost in the too densely packed struggle of plants, are here, in the greater and freer space, able to develop their true form and beauty, and so rise with stout erect stems to bear far overhead their regularly shaped majestic crowns of thickly growing fronds.

Next, of the rock and tree-belt all that need be said is that the same species as in the lower belt seem to occur, but that these are here, for some rather obscure reason, represented by larger and more developed individuals; that the Ferns, both the Tree-ferns and the more dwarf species, and one of the Palms, *Geonoma* [No. 382], become yet more abundant; and that the mossy universal covering which I have already dwelt on as occurring below, here becomes so immensely dense and all-pervading (the Mosses are so deep on rock and ground, and hang in such dense, long masses from all trees and branches) as to produce on the mind of one who penetrates into this remarkable spot, a wonderful and extraordinary effect of perfect and entire stillness, as though, everything being wrapped in so dense and so soft a covering, all sound and all possibility of sound were stilled, deadened, and annihilated.

Just where the rock and tree-belt meet the base of the cliff is a very narrow strip of quite distinct vegetation, so distinct, indeed, that we might almost regard it as a distinct belt, which we might call the bramble-belt. The ground there is covered by a dense thicket of bramble-bushes (*Rubus guianensis*, Focke [No. 106]), in general appearance altogether like English blackberry-bushes. Among this were large masses of the South-American form, appearing very similar to the English form, of the common Bracken, *Pteris aquilina*, L. There, too, were many little bushes of *Marcetia laxifolia*, very strongly suggestive of English heath, and there, also, was a flowering Laurustinus (*Viburnum glabratum*, H. B. K. [No. 220]), curiously like the familiar plant of our gardens. To me, after my long stay in the tropics, the whole scene suddenly seemed very home-like and pleasant. But the next minute, as I turned in another direction, the illusion was dispelled by the sight of great thickets of palms (*Geonoma Appuniana*) and a few singly standing and very stately tree-ferns.

Up from the bramble-belt, passing obliquely up the cliff face, ran the ledge by which we ascended to the top of Roraima. The lower part of the ledge, for perhaps two thirds of its length, is wide, much broken, and very uneven. This part is somewhat irregularly bush-covered. Then the continuity of the ledge is suddenly almost broken by a deep ravine, a part of the rock having been worn away by a stream which falls on to it from the cliff above. The ravine thus made is almost bare of vegetation. Above, the ledge slopes somewhat steeply, but evenly, from the point where it commences again to the top, and this part of it is covered by a dwarf vegetation never more than two or three feet high.

The shrubs on the part of the ledge below the ravine seem to be generally much the same as on the forest slope; but among these a few new ones appear. Among the latter were the very beautiful *Drimys granatensis*, Mutis [No. 242], with its very beautiful white flowers, like pendent wood-anemones, a new and beautiful *Microlicia* (*Microlicia bryanthoides*, Oliver, n. sp. [No. 239]), and several more species of *Psychotria* [Nos. 191, 291]. There, too, was an abundance of the *Lisianthus* [No. 188] already mentioned, and of *Utricularia Campbelliana*.

At the bottom of the ravine into which the stream falls the rocks are bare but for a large number of a pretty white-flowered *Myrtus* (*M. stenophylla*, Oliv., n. sp. [No. 324]), which, met with nowhere else, was growing abundantly in the spray of the falling water.

Beyond this ravine, on the upper part of the ledge, the true botanical paradise began. The main vegetation is formed of *Brocchinia cordylinoides*, Baker (in the axils of the leaves of which grows *Utricularia Humboldtii*). *Abolboda Sceptrum*, Oliv., and *Stegolepis guianensis*, Klotzsch [No. 338]. Among these were a great many plants entirely new to me and of most striking beauty. Many of these were shrubby, but of so diminutive a character as to be strictly alpine. Of these, by far the most beautiful was a wonderful heath-like plant, with dark green-leaved stems, stout and sturdy, but yet seeming almost overweighted by their great load of intensely vivid crimson star-like flowers. This plant [No. 308] Professor Oliver has identified as a *Ledothamnus*, possibly a variety of *L. guianensis*, Meissner, but of much more slender form than is attributed to that plant in Martius's Fl. Brasil. vii. 172.

Another shrublet, in character recalling the "Alpine rose" (*Rhododendron ferrugineum*), bore even more disproportionately large flowers, of an exquisite pink colour. It was a *Befaria*, approaching *B. resinosa*, Mutis [No. 310]. Other tiny shrubs were a white, feather-flowered *Weinmannia* (*W. glabra*, L. fil., var. [No. 244]), a myrtle (*M. n. sp. aff. myricoidi*, H. B. K. [No. 189]), yet another species of *Psychotria* (*P. imThurniana*, Oliver, n. sp. [No. 163]), a *Baccharis* (*B. Vitis-Idæa*, Oliver, n. sp. [No. 241]), and a *Vaccinium* (*V. floribundum*? H. B. K. [No. 329]). On most of these tiny shrubs was growing an appropriately tiny Misseltoe, *Phoradendron Roraimæ*, Oliver, n. sp. [No. 323], a miniature of an English plant. Among all these, many other interesting plants occurred. There grew, in far greater luxuriance and size than below, the pitcher-plant, *Heliamphora nutans*, Benth. [No. 258]; also great masses of two species of *Xyris*, *X. Fontanesiana*, Kunth [No. 257], and *X. wilsenioides*, Oliv., n. sp. [No. 240], the latter very striking and curious by reason of the *Wilsenia*-like habit of their dark green-leaved

2 s 2

stems, with pretty star-like yellow flowers. Lastly, I found a plant with a flower which, because of its form and colour, I at first sight mistook for a fritillary, like our "Snake's-head" (*F. meleagris*); but it was a new *Lisianthus*, which Professor Oliver has named *L. imThurnianus*, Oliv., n. sp. [No. 306]. There grew many small but pretty and bright-coloured orchids—two new species of *Epidendrum* (*E. montigenum*, Ridley, n. sp. [No. 322], and another [No. 304]); also a plant of a new genus of Cryptangieae named by Mr. Ridley *Ererardia* (*E. montana*, Ridley [No. 335]).

So the vegetation of the ledge continued to the top, and indeed actually extended over the top (woodcut, fig. 3).

Fig. 3.

View at the point of entrance of the plateau on the top of Roraima.

The general effect of the vegetation of Roraima, fitly rivalling in this respect the marvellously strange geological aspect of the place, is so strange as to be very difficult of precise description. It occupies more or less wide tracts, generally almost level, between the bare flat rocks and the groups of piled rocks which occupy the greater part of the plateau. In such places it forms a dense carpet of vegetation, which is generally but a few inches, never more than a couple of feet, in height, except where, from its general level, rise a few scattered individuals of the one shrub of any conspicuous height, *Bonnetia Roraimæ*, Oliv., n. sp. [No. 330]—and that was never more than from 30 to 40 inches in height—or the many and very remarkable flower-stems of *Abolboda Sceptrum*, Oliv. [No. 312], which, to my great delight, at that height still bore its beautiful blooms, the appearance of which I have already described. Through this carpet of vegetation ran many small streams; and even in other places much water everywhere saturated the turf. A very few small plants also grew in the crevices of the piled rocks, which otherwise were bare of vegetation.

The chief constituents of this turf-like vegetation were vast quantities of a new species of *Pæpalanthus* (*P. Roraimæ*, Oliv., n. sp. [No. 294]), and great masses of *Sphagnum*-like mosses. In the latter grew, in such abundance as to redden the ground, the pretty little Sundew (*Drosera communis*, A. St.-H. [No. 313]). Groups of very luxuriant Pitcher-plants (*Heliamphora*) were there also. Great quantities of tiny shrubs, of alpine character, interwove their branches with each other and with the mosses; among these were *Weinmannia guianensis*, Klotzsch [No. 327], *Marcetia juniperina*, DC. [No. 319], *Psychotria concinna*, Oliv., n. sp. *Baccharis* [No. 241], *Ledothamnus* [No. 308], *Befaria* [No. 310], *Vaccinium* [Nos. 326, 329], *Pernettya* [No. 333, ex parte], and *Gaultheria* [No. 332]. The small *Epidendra*, as on the ledge, were here too, as was also the tiny Misseltoe (*Phoradendron* [No. 323]) and the Fritillary-like *Lisianthus* [No. 306].

A beautiful *Tofieldia* (*T. Schomburgkiana*, Oliv., n. sp. [No. 297]) and the somewhat similar *Nietneria corymbosa*, Kl. & Sch. [No. 298], with large yellow flowers, were conspicuous.

In the crevices of the rocks the vegetation was different. There was a very beautiful *Utricularia* (*U. montana*? Jacq. [No. 293]), larger and deeper in colour, but slightly less graceful, than *U. Campbelliana*, and there were three species of fern. One of these latter was a very stunted form of *Lindsaya striata*, Dryand. [No. 301], which, in its ordinary form, is common in many parts of Guiana. The other two were absolutely new —one a *Hymenophyllum*, which Mr. Baker has named *H. dejectum*, Baker, n. sp., [No. 318]; the other a *Gymnogramma* (*G. cyclophylla*, Baker, n. sp. [No. 295], a second species of the same group of this genus to which belongs *G. elaphoglossoides*, Baker, n. sp., [Nos. 101, 215], found on the lower slopes of Roraima. Only one other species of this very distinct group is known, and that has been found in the Amazon valley.

I have now briefly noticed the most striking plants which we met with on Roraima; but, before closing this paper, there are one or two points which I wish, finally, to set down in order.

First, as to *Brocchinia cordylinoides*, Baker; this is only known to occur on the Kaieteur savannah and on Roraima, but in the latter place apparently only above a height of 5500 feet. There is a remarkable difference of vigour in the habit of the plant at these two places respectively. After seeing a large number of individuals of the plant at both places, it is obvious that at the Kaieteur it attains a much greater size and forms a much taller stem; and, if I may judge from the comparative abundance or scarcity of flower-stalks, it seems to flower much more freely at the Kaieteur than on Roraima. A possible explanation of some of these facts seems to be that the position and the circumstances that it finds on Roraima, are beneficial to the plant; that the most important of these circumstances of its existence is an atmosphere, like that of Roraima or of the Kaieteur, so saturated with moisture as to effect the constant replenishment of the large quantity of water retained in the leaf-axils of the plant; and that the plant having found its way to the Kaieteur (which, though much below the proper level, is atmospherically so peculiarly suited for it), it has taken root there and, in its new surroundings of higher temperature, has there developed a new vigour. Lastly, as regards this plant, I cannot refrain from once more alluding to its possible, even probable, distribution in the other widely scattered distinct areas already enumerated.

Closely connected with the *Brocchinia* is *Utricularia Humboldtii*. Like the *Brocchinia*, this plant grows both at the Kaieteur and on Roraima; but at the former station it apparently *always* grows floating in the water retained in the leaf-axils of the *Brocchinia*, while on Roraima it grows abundantly with its roots in the ground, and only very rarely in close association with the *Brocchinia*. The Roraima plant is, moreover, far more beautiful, its flowers are of a far more intense colour, than is the Kaieteur plant; this latter circumstance is possibly mostly due to the greater vigour which the plant displays when its roots are in the ground. I have already alluded to the occurrence of a very similar *Utricularia* on the Organ Mountains, associated with a huge Bromeliad, just as it is at the Kaieteur with the *Brocchinia*.

Next, the two other large-flowered species of *Utricularia* from Roraima claim notice, *U. Campbelliana* has already been described. It occurs abundantly, but apparently only on the forest-slope and for some distance from this up the cliff.

The other species, *U. montana*, Jacq., aff. [No. 293], appears to occur only in crevices in the rocks on the summit. *U. montana* has been previously recorded from the West Indies, Colombia, and Peru. The two species, though somewhat alike in general character, are, at a second glance, evidently very distinct. *U. Campbelliana* is altogether a more delicate plant; its leaves are much smaller, rounder, and its stems are shorter; its bladders are disk-shaped. The other species is altogether a stouter plant, with longer-stalked strap-shaped leaves and with spindle-shaped bladders.

To one other set of plants I should here like to call attention. These are represented from among the plants collected during the Roraima expedition by two species of *Epidendrum* (*E. Schomburgkii*, Lindley [No. 13], and *E. elongatum*, Jacq. [No. 42]). These seem to me to be plants, from the dry rocky ground of the interior of the country, which correspond more or less closely with three forms, in a fresh state evidently very distinct, but of which dried herbarium specimens have all been classed under the one name of *E. imatophyllum*, and all three of which occur on trees near the coast. Of these coast-forms, the most distinct is one of constantly bifloral character, which occurs low down on trees overhanging the brackish water at the estuaries of the rivers; another, occurring on the tops of bushes slightly higher up the rivers, is, in general facies and in colour, very similar to the typical *E. Schomburgkii*; and the third, occurring in similar positions, but more sparingly, more nearly approaches in facies *E. elongatum*, but is constantly of a peculiar scarlet colour. The two last-mentioned forms, unlike any of the others, are invariably associated with ants, either because these creatures prefer to make their nests in the roots of the plants, or because the seeds of the plants find their most suitable nidus, and germinate, in the ants' nests.

[Note.—The following determinations and descriptions of new plants were expressly drawn up for publication in the 'Transactions of the Linnean Society,' a confidential copy being given to Mr. E. F. im Thurn to help him in writing the foregoing Introduction. During the delay required to prepare the accompanying Plates, Mr. im Thurn has taken the unprecedented course of printing the whole of the unrevised draft, at Demerara, in 'Timehri, the Journal of the Royal Agricultural and Commercial Society of British Guiana,' vol. v. pp. 145–223 (Dec. 1886), thus forestalling the present publication.—Sec. L. S.]

II. *List of the Species of Plants collected, and Determinations of those that are new. By* Prof. OLIVER, *F.R.S., F.L.S.*

242. DRIMYS GRANATENSIS, Mutis. Ledge.

40. GUATTERIA.   In the absence of fruit, may be referred to *G. Ouregou*, Dun. Arapoo R.

258. HELIAMPHORA NUTANS, Benth. 5400 ft. and top.

96, 151. SAUVAGESIA ERECTA, L. forma. 5400 ft.

309. LEITGEBIA IMTHURNIANA, Oliv., sp. nov. (Plate XXXVII A. figs. 1–8); floribus distincte pedicellatis, coronæ squamulis oblongo-spathulatis antheris æquilongis v. longioribus.—Roraima : ledge and summit.

Caulis plus minus ramosus, pennæ corvinæ crassitie. Folia imbricata, coriacea, oblanceolata, acutiuscula, apicem versus utrinque 2–3-crenato-denticulata, glabra, oblique nervosa, ⅓ poll. longa ; stipulæ scariosæ, fimbriatæ. Flores ad apices ramulorum, ¼–⅔ poll. diam., pedicello ½ poll. longo, 2–3-bracteolato, bracteolis anguste linearibus, stipulatis, stipulis lineari-subulatis longe ciliatis. Sepala lineari-lanceolata, acuta, rigidiuscula, ⅓ poll. longa. Petala obovata, integra, ⅓ poll. longa. Corona basi filamentis coalita, squamulis 5 obtusis, coloratis. Ovarium glabrum, in stylum attenuatum.

Allied to *L. guianensis*, Eichl., but much more slender, with the flowers distinctly pedicellate, and the coronal squamæ equal to or overtopping the anthers.

26. POLYGALA HYGROPHILA, H. B. K. Arapoo R.

97. P. LONGICAULIS, H. B. K. 5400 ft.

252. P., an P. VARIABILIS, H. B. K. var. ? 5400 ft.

79. QUALEA SCHOMBURGKIANA, Warm. ? By Teroota.

337. MORONOBEA INTERMEDIA, Engl., sp. nov. ; ramulorum internodiis brevibus ; foliis crassis, valde coriaceis, concoloribus, obovato-oblongis, in petiolum brevem canaliculatum angustatis, nervis lateralibus numerosis, patentibus, subtus paullum prominulis; floribus breviter pedicellatis, sepalis 5 suborbicularibus, cinerascentibus ; petalis quam sepala circ. sexies longioribus ; staminum phalangibus 5-andris, superne tantum leviter spiraliter tortis, petala fere æquantibus ; ovario oblongo-ovoideo in stylum duplo breviorem stigmate 5-fido coronatum attenuato.

Roraima.

Omnino intermedia inter *Moronobea ripariam* et *Moronobea Jenmanni*, a priori nor: nisi foliis paullo majoribus et nervis minus prominulis, ab altera floribus duplo minoribus, ab utraque phalangibus androecei minus tortis diversa.—*Engler.*

72. MARCGRAAVIA CORIACEA, V. ?, vel UMBELLATA, L. (imperfect). Near house, 5400 ft.

11. BONNETIA SESSILIS, Benth. Between Ireng and Cotinga R.

Label misplaced or missing. B. PANICULATA, Spreng. ?

330. BONNETIA RORAIMÆ, Oliv., sp. nov. (Plate XXXVII. B. figs. 9–17); foliis coriaceis, parvis, oblanceolatis v. obovato-oblongis, obtusiusculis, apicem versus obscure denticulatis, eveniis, brevissime crassiuscule petiolatis; floribus ad apices ramulorum sessilibus bracteatis; sepalis late ellipticis, obtusis, breviter apiculatis, ciliolatis; petalis calyce longioribus cuneato-obovatis, truncatis v. leviter emarginatis; filamentis brevibus, basi in phalangibus 5 coalitis; antheris obovato-turbinatis, emarginatis; ovario in stylum crassiusculum apice 3-fidum angustato.

Summit of Roraima.

Folia conferta, imbricata, 4–7 lin. longa. Flores $\frac{1}{4}$–$\frac{1}{2}$ poll. diam.

A very distinct species, of which our material is rather imperfect.

8. MAHUREA EXISTIPULATA, Benth. Aroic Creek.
288. TERNSTRŒMIACEA? (inadequate). Path to upper savannah.
22. SIDA LINIFOLIA, Cav. Arapoo R.
130. BYRSONIMA CRASSIFOLIA, H. B. K., var.? Near house.
136. TETRAPTERIS? (no fruit). Near house.

255. TETRAPTERIS RHODOPTERON, Oliv., sp. nov.; ramulis appresse sericeis; foliis petiolatis, obovato- v. oblanceolato-ellipticis, breviter apiculatis, basi cuneatis, utrinque tomentello-pubescentibus, supra glabrescentibus; racemis folio brevioribus, sericeis; bracteis brevissimis, ovatis, bracteolis medio pedicelli insertis, obovatis v. late ellipticis, bractea majoribus; calyce 10-glanduloso, sericeo; samaræ alis lateralibus a basi divaricatis, coriaceis, nervosis, glabris, rubescentibus, obtusis, integris v. interdum inæqualiter dentatis.

Roraima.

Folia $2\frac{1}{2}$–3 poll. longa, $1\frac{1}{6}$–$1\frac{1}{2}$ poll. lata: petiolus $\frac{1}{4}$–$\frac{1}{2}$ poll. longus. Bracteolæ geminatæ, $\frac{1}{10}$–$\frac{1}{8}$ poll. longæ. Samara alis longioribus $\frac{1}{2}$ poll. longis.

211. RAVENIA RUELLIOIDES, Oliv., sp. nov. (Plate XXXVIII. A. figs. 1–6); ramulis appresse pubescentibus; foliis unifoliolatis, petiolatis, ovalibus, utrinque attenuatis v. basi obtusis, apice obtusiusculis, nervo medio utrinque cum petiolo appresse pubescente; pedunculis in axillis superioribus 2-vel 1-floris; sepalis 2 exterioribus majoribus, ovatis v. oblongo-ovatis; petalis longe coalitis, tubo corollæ calyce 4–5-plo longiore, leviter curvato; lobis ovatis lanceolatisve; antheris 2 fertilibus, basi appendiculatis.

Roraima, upper slope.

Folia $1\frac{1}{4}$–$2\frac{1}{2}$ poll. longa, 5–12 lin. lata; nervis subtus obliquis, prominulis; petiolo 2–3 lin. longo. Flores 1–$1\frac{1}{4}$ poll. longi; corolla sericea. Calyx sepalis exterioribus $\frac{1}{5}$–$\frac{1}{4}$ poll. longis. Antheræ appendicibus brevibus, reflexis, obtusis, obovatis v. truncatis.

Closely simulating some Acanthaceæ, with its opposite, simple (unifoliolate) leaves, and long curved corolla-tube, sheathed at the base by the unequal sepals. The reflexed, somewhat fleshy appendage at the base of the perfect anthers has not, I believe, been observed in the two other described species of the genus.

15. Fruiting specimen, leafless, of a *Pœcilandra*?, and flowering specimen of *Gomphia guyanensis* (*Ouratea*, Aubl.)? Arapoo R.

75. ILEX MACOUCOUA, Pers. forma ? 3500 ft.

107, 331. ILEX RETUSA, Kl. 5400 ft. and ledge.

35. CYRILLA ANTILLANA, Michx. Arapoo R.

334. CYRILLA ANTILLANA, var. BREVIFOLIA. Top.

21. RHYNCHOSIA SCHOMBURGKII, Benth. Arapoo R.

67. SWARTZIA, sp. nov. 5000 ft.

73. DIPTERYX RETICULATA, Benth.? (type is too imperfect to be quite sure). Kookenaam R.

71. CASSIA RORAIMÆ, Benth. Arapoo R.

39. DIMORPHANDRA MACROSTACHYA, Benth. Arapoo valley.

106. RUBUS GUYANENSIS, Focke (ex descr.). "*R. Schomburgkii*, Klotzsch." Base of Cliff.

244, 321. WEINMANNIA GLABRA, L.f., var.? near *W. humilis*, Engl., but with longer pedicels. Ledge and top.

327. WEINMANNIA GUIANENSIS, Klotzsch. Top.

313. DROSERA COMMUNIS, A. St.-Hil. var.? Top.

324. MYRTUS STENOPHYLLA, Oliv., sp. nov. (Plate XXXIX. A. figs. 1-9); ramosissima, ramulis ultimis gracilibus papilloso-scabridis, foliis patenti-recurvis anguste ovalibus v. lineari-oblongis acutiusculis basi in petiolum angustatis glabris, pedunculis folio brevioribus unifloris axillaribus recurvis apice bibracteolatis, bracteolis linearibus calycis tubo obovoideo obsolete puberulo longioribus, lobis calycis oblongo-lanceolatis obtusiusculis tubo subæqualibus petalis dimidio brevioribus, ovario 3-loculari, ovula in loculis plurima, bacca subglobosa, seminibus reniformibus. Fall on ledge of Roraima, 7500 ft.

Folia circ. ⅓ poll. longa, ⅔-¾ lin. lata; petiolus 1 lin. longus.

189. MYRTUS, sp. nov., aff. *M. myricoidi*, H. B. K. Top and upper slope.

74. MYRCIA (AULOMYRCIA) RORAIMÆ, Oliv., sp. nov. (Plate XXXVIII. B. figs. 7-13); ramulis teretibus pilosulo-puberulis glabrescentibus cineraceis, foliis pallidis obovato-ellipticis v. late oblanceolatis obtusis basi cuneatis subtus in nervo obsolete pilosulo, supra demum nitentibus, paniculis pedunculatis axillaribus et subterminalibus, pedunculis pauce pilosulis folio brevioribus v. subæquilongis, floribus breviter pedicellatis, pedicellis pubescentibus calycis tubo turbinato glabro sæpius brevioribus, lobis calycinis brevibus late rotundatis. Roraima, 3500 ft.

Folia 1-1½ poll. longa, ½-¾ poll. lata, vernatione supra parce pilosula; petiolus 1½ 2 lin. longus. Paniculæ cymosæ 1½-2 poll. longæ.

82. MYRCIA aff. *M. Kegeliana*, Berg. 3500 ft.

68. MARCETIA TAXIFOLIA, DC. (ex Tr.), an *M. cordigera*, DC.? Folia ovata basi cordata, marginibus late recurvis. 5400 ft.

174. MEISSNERIA MICROLICIOIDES, Naud., *M. cordifolia*, Benth., 5400 ft.

239. MICROLICIA BRYANTHOIDES, Oliv., sp. nov. (Plate XXXIX. B. figs. 10–18); fruticulosa ut videtur fastigiatim ramosa, glabra, ramulis ultimis foliiferis acute tetragonis internodiis folio 3–6-plo brevioribus, foliis patulis lineari- vel oblongo-ovalibus obtusiusculis brevissime petiolatis, floribus solitariis breviter pedicellatis ad apices ramulorum 5-meris, lobis calycinis ovato-lanceolatis tubo fere æquilongis persistentibus, antheris majoribus connectivo producto subæquilongis.

Roraima, ledge 6500 ft.

Folia ¼–⅓ poll. longa, ¹⁄₅ poll. lata. Flores ½–⅔ poll. diam. Capsula calyce persistente vestita ⅜ poll. longa, lobis calycis (temp. fruct.) erectis deltoideo-subulatis rigidis.

59. PTEROLEPIS LASIOPHYLLA, Tr.

20. PLEROMA TIBOUCHINUM, Tr. (*Tibouchina aspera*, Aubl.). Arapoo R.

319. MARCETIA JUNIPERINA, DC. Top.

89. CENTRONIA CRASSIRAMIS, Tr. 5750 ft.

216, 305. MONOCHÆTUM BONPLANDII?, Naud. Upper slope and top.

277. OXYMERIS aff. *O. glandaliferæ*, Tr. (Facies *Miconiæ pauperulæ*, Naud. ?) Path to upper savannah.

Closely resembles the above *Miconia*, but our specimen is not good.

256. MICONIA FOTHERGILLA, Naud. House.

223. MICONIA, sp. (inadequate). Path.

30, 70. MICONIA DECUSSATA, Don. Arapoo R.

222. MERIANIA? aff. *M. sclerophyllæ*, Tr. (Imperfect.) Forest slope, 6000 ft.

2. CUPHEA GRACILIS, H. B. K., var. MEDIA.

4. PASSIFLORA FŒTIDA, L., var. Konkarmo.

84. PASSIFLORA, sp., e sect. *Murucuiæ* (ut videtur). Folia petiolata, petiolis pollicaribus apice utroque latere glandula majuscula circulari prædita, laminis 4½–5 poll. long., 2½ poll. lat., glabris subtus glaucescentibus subcoriaceis late ovato-oblongis acutis basi rotundatis, raro arcuatim nervosis. . . . . . Pedunculi . . . . . foliis subæquilongi apice racemosi. . . . . Alabastra cylindrato-oblonga acutiuscula. Floris tubus elongatus, obconicus. Sepala petalaque, ut videtur, brevia oblonga obtusa vel rotundata. Corona faucialis e ligulis petaloideis brevibus constans . . . Gynandrophorum gracile . . . . cæt. desunt.—*M. T. Masters*.

Roraima.

110. PASSIFLORA, sp., e sect. *Astrophea*? Fruticosa cirrosa. Folia breve petiolata, petiolis. . . . . sub ½ poll. long., laminis 2¼ poll. long., 1½ poll. lat., coriaceis glabris raro arcuatim venosis oblongis basi apiceque rotundatis. . . . Cirri simplices. . . . Bracteæ. . . . Alabastra oblonga obtusa. Floris tubus brevis tubulato-campanulatus basi haud intrusus. Sepala 5–6 lin. longa oblonga obtusa navicularia extus tomentosa intus maculis linearibus purpureis verrucisque albidis notatis. Petala sepalis conformia parum breviora tenuiora, membranacea, albida maculis purpureis minimis

crebris obsita. Corona faucialis biserialis, series extima e ligulis petalis æquilongis petaloideis, purpureo-maculatis, dolabriformibus, apice obliquis et in acumen
longiusculum tortum prolatis, series intima e filis numerosis præcedentibus dimidio
brevioribus, capitatellatis. Corona mediana e tubo versus medium assurgens basi
membranacea, apice in fila brevia divisa. Corona infra mediana e tubo versus
basin emergens annularis, subcarnosa margine deflexa. Tubi facies interna, inter
coronas, processubus parvis membranaceis ut videtur dense obsita. . . . cæt. desunt.
Gynandrophorum basi ut videtur quinquangulum, angulis anguste alatis, supra
medium tumidum ibique puberulum. Antheræ oblongæ obtusæ flavidæ. Ovarium
ut videtur oblongum angulatum longitudinaliter costatum puberulum. Stigmata
majuscula reniformia.—*M. T. Masters.*
Roraima.

141. BEGONIA TOVARENSIS, Klotzsch, var. ? ; fructibus breviter alatis. House.

—

ARALIACEÆ. By M. E. MARCHAL.

CREPINELLA, nov. gen. Flores hermaphroditi. Calycis margo brevis obsolete 4-dentatus.
Petala 4 valvata. Stamina tot quot petala, sub disco epigyno explanato superne in
stylum sulcatum abeunte inserta, filamentis brevibus et antheris ovatis. Ovarium
1-loculare, 1-ovulatum, ovulo pedulo. Fructus ignotus.

Frutex (?) glaber. Folia digitata. Flores in umbellas compositas terminales digesti.
Bracteæ parvæ squamiformes. Pedicelli sub flore continui.

Notwithstanding the absence of fruit, the genus *Crepinella* is very different from other
Araliaceæ with 1-celled, 1-ovuled ovary, differing from *Eremopanax*, Baillon, *Cuphocarpus*,
Decne. & Naud., and *Mastixia*, Blume, in its digitate leaves and umbellate tetramerous
flowers.

Dedicated to Mons. Crépin, Director of the Botanic Gardens, Brussels.

162. CREPINELLA GRACILIS, March., n. sp. (Plate XL. figs. 1-6) : foliis 5-natis, petiolo
sulcato basi abrupte dilatato, foliolis breviter petiolulatis, ovato-ellipticis, apice
obtusis vel marginatis, basi acutiusculis, margine integerrimis sive revolutis, perga-
maceis, costa infra prominente, umbellulis longiuscule pedunculatis, 8-12-floris,
pedunculo gracili profunde sulcato superne incrassato ; floribus minutis pedicello basi
bracteolato 4-plo brevioribus, calycis tubo obconico, 8-sulcato, corolla hemisphærica
acutiuscula sulcata, petalis ellipticis, apice leviter incrassatis incurvis, nervia extus
impressa notatis, stylo gracili latitudinem disci vix æquante, fructu. . . . .
Roraima.
Rami supremi graciles. Petiolus communis circ. 5 cm. longus. Petioluli 6-10 mill.
longi. Foliola 4-5 cm. longa atque 3 cm. lata. Pedicelli 5-7 mill. longi.

128. SCIADOPHYLLUM CORIACEUM, March., nov. sp. (Plate XLI. figs. 1-8) ; inflorescentiis
foliisque subtus tomento adpresso subferrugineo demum hinc inde deterso vestitis,

foliis digitatis, 5-7-natis, foliolis ellipticis, apice rotundatis v. sæpius leviter emarginatis basi acutiusculis margine integerrimis anguste revolutis crassiusculis coriaceis,
supra denudatis, reticulo nervorum densiusculo infra valde prominente, floribus in
umbellas duas compositas superpositasque digestis, umbellulis numerosis, 9-12-floris,
pedunculo compresso elongato superne dilatato, radiis liliformibus basi bracteolatis,
calycis limbo minute 5-dentato, corolla hemisphærica acutiuscula, petalis apice
cohærentibus demum a basi secedentibus, staminum filamentis brevibus, stylis in
unum sulcatum 5-fidum latitudinem disci epigyni vix æquantem concretis fructu. . . .
Roraima.

Allied to *Sciadophyllum japurense*, Mart. et Zucc., but differing in leaves, inflorescence,
and style.

Arbor. Rami supremi 2 cm. crassi. Petiolus communis 20 cm. longus. Petioli 2-4 cm.
longi. Foliola 11-13 cm. longa atque 4-5 cm. lata. Pedicelli 5-8 mill. longi.

---

220. VIBURNUM GLABRATUM, H. B. K. Base of cliff.

134. COCCOCYPSELUM CANESCENS, Willd., var. House.

6. KOTCHUBEA (*Synisoon Schomburgkianum*, Baill.). Aroie Creek.

69. DECLIEUXIA CHIOCOCCOIDES, H. B. K. House.

29. SIPANEA PRATENSIS, Aubl. Arapoo R.

135. CEPHAËLIS AXILLARIS?, Sw. House; upper slope.

83. PSYCHOTRIA INUNDATA, Benth. 3500 ft. Upper slope.

115, 232. PSYCHOTRIA CRASSA, Benth.? House. Upper slope.

185. PSYCHOTRIA, sp. (=Schomhk. 1018 B and Appun. 1103). Upper slope.

163, 320. PSYCHOTRIA IMTHURNIANA, Oliv., sp. nov. (Plate XLII. A. figs. 1-7.) Glaberrima ; ramulis gracilibus internodiis rectis subteretibus, foliis subsessilibus anguste vel
lineari-lanceolatis acuminatis basi obtusissimis subcordatisve, costa prominula,
nervis secundariis utrinque circ. 10-15 incurvis prominulis nervum marginalem attingentibus cum venulis intermediis, stipulis basi connatis deltoideo-subulatis brevibus,
cymis terminalibus pedunculatis 9-15-floris laxiusculis bracteis obsoletis, calycis
limbo 4-dentato dentibus deltoideis, corollæ tubo cylindrico limbo 2-plo longiore.
Roraima, upper slope and ledge, 7000 ft.

Folia tenuiter coriacea flavescentia, $1\frac{3}{4}$-$2\frac{1}{4}$ poll. longa, $\frac{1}{4}$-$\frac{1}{3}$ poll. lata. Flores 2-$2\frac{1}{2}$ lin.
longi ; corollæ limbus 2-$2\frac{1}{2}$ lin. diam., lobis ovatis obtusis, tubo intus piloso. Ovarium
biloculare.

191, 214. PSYCHOTRIA, sp. (Imperfect.) Upper slope and path.

291. PSYCHOTRIA? sp. Path to upper savannah.

PSYCHOTRIA CONCINNA, Oliv., sp. nov. (Plate XLII. B. figs. 8-15.) Glaberrima,
ramulis gracilibus atro-purpureis, foliis petiolatis parvis coriaceis ovalibus acutis v.
acutiusculis, supra costa subprominula nervis lateralibus obsoletis, subtus costa prominente nervis secundariis utroque latere 7-10 prominulis patentim curvatis nervum

marginalem attingentibus, stipulis liberis (utrinque geminatis) e basi crassiuscula erectis subulatis rigidiusculis, floribus in cymis paucifloris parvis breviter pedunculatis terminalibus dispositis, pedicellis brevissimis, calycis lobis minutis ovatis, corollæ tubo recto gracili glabro intus medium versus pilosulo superne leviter dilatato, lobis brevibus ovatis.

Roraima, ledge 6500 ft. and summit.

Folia 7-12 lin. longa, ¼-⅜ poll. lata; petiolus 1-1½ lin. longus. Cymæ 5-8-floræ. Corolla 6-7 lin. longa (lobi 1 lin.).

66. PALICOUREA RIPARIA ?, Benth., forma angustifolia.
85. PALICOUREA RIGIDA, Kunth.
90. RELBUNIUM (=Schombk. 646, 984 β). 5400 ft.
23. EUPATORIUM AMYGDALINUM, DC. Arapoo R.
No label. EUPATORIUM, sp. ? (not identified).
95. EUPATORIUM CONYZOIDES, Vahl, var. 5400 ft.
91. MIKANIA PANNOSA, Baker. 5400 ft.
16. PECTIS ELONGATA, H. B. K. Wai-ireng R.

241, 325. BACCHARIS VITIS-IDÆA, Oliv., sp. nov. (Plate XLIII. A. figs. 1-8); ramulis ultimis puberulis, foliis crebris tenuiter coriaceis oblanceolatis obtusis apice 1-3-5-mucronatis in petiolum basi cuneatim angustatis glabris, capitulis campanulato-hemisphæricis 15-20-floris in corymbis terminalibus sæpius sessilibus dispositis, involucri bracteis pauciseriatis, interioribus (in cap. ♀) scariosis anguste lineari-oblongis deciduis, pappo albido.

Roraima, ledge 7300 ft. and summit.

Folia ½-1 poll. longa, 3-4½ lin. lata. Capitula ¼-⅛ poll. diam.; bracteis exterioribus ovatis v. ovato-lanceolatis plus minus scariosis margine apicem versus sæpe denticulatis v. minute fimbriatis (in invol. ♂ ut videtur obtusioribus). Achænia lineam longa angulata glabrata; pappus achænio longior, setis circ. 30 minute barbellatis.

Resembles some forms of *B. ligustrina*, DC.

328. BACCHARIS aff. *B. cassiniæfoliæ*, DC., an var. ?
63. ACHYROCLINE FLACCIDA, DC. 4000 ft.
250. GNAPHALIUM SPICATUM, Lam. 5400 ft.
86. VERBESINA GUIANENSIS, Baker. 5400 ft.

27. CALEA TERNIFOLIA, Oliv., sp. nov. (Plate XLIII. B. figs. 9-16.) Suffrutex scaber, foliis ternatis ellipticis v. ovato- v. obovato-lanceolatis breviter petiolatis late acutatis utrinque apicem versus 1-3-dentatis supra scabris subtus præcipue in costa nervisque setulosis, capitulis circ. 30-floris homogamis pedunculatis ad apices ramulorum umbellatim dispositis, involucri squamis exterioribus herbaceis ovatis v. ovato-oblongis capitula brevioribus, squamis interioribus rigidiusculis late oblongis obtusis striatis, paleis concavis obtusis superne leviter dilatatis, ovariis parce setulosis paleis pappi acuminato-subulatis brevioribus.

Arapoo River.

Folia rigida ¾-1⅓ poll. longa, 5-8 lin. lata ; petiolus ad 1 lin. longus. Umbellæ 3-5-cephalæ, pedunculis hispidulis capitulis sæpe paullo longioribus. Capitula late campanulata ⅓ poll. longa atque lata.

247. ERECHTHITES HIERACIIFOLIA, Raf. 5400 ft.
　10. STIFFTIA CONDENSATA, Baker. Near Wuctipoo M.
314, 316. CENTROPOGON LÆVIGATUS, A. DC., var. ? Ledge 5400 ft.
　77. C. SURINAMENSIS, Presl ? 3500 ft.
　56. PSAMMISIA ? sp. (inadequate). 5400 ft.

　49. PSAMMISIA, with glabrous smooth purple-brown stem, ovate-oblong, shortly apiculate quintuplinerved leaves of 4 to 6 in., and contracted umbelliform racemes of flowers 1 in. in length on pedicels of ⅓-¾ in. This is probably Schomburgk's nos. 670, 97 b, of which corollas are wanting in our example. Whether it be Klotzsch's *P. guya-nensis* I cannot say.
Roraima, upper slope.
　Under the same no. is apparently another *Psammisia* in early bud, with more broadly elliptical leaves and acute calyx-segments.

109. NOTOPORA SCHOMBURGKII, Hook. f. 5400 ft.
243. SOPHOCLESIA aff. *S. subscandenti* (ovario glabro). Ledge 7300 ft.
329. (333 ?). VACCINIUM, an *V. floribundum*, H. B. K. ? (*V. polystachyum*, Benth.). Top and ledge.
326 365. VACCINIUM, an *V. floribundum*, H. B. K., var. ? Top.

308. LEDOTHAMNUS GUYANENSIS, Meissner in Mart. Fl. Bras. vii. 172. (Plate XLIV. A. figs. 1-6.) 172. Var. MINOR ; foliis minoribus imbricatis acutis ciliolatis, floribus sessilibus v. subsessilibus, filamentis anthera 3-5-plo longioribus.
Roraima, upper part of ledge and summit.
　Possibly a distinct species, but, as our Schomburgk specimens are more advanced and scarcely in a comparable state, it is better left as above for the present. The leaves are only about 2½ lines long (in the type 4 lines), minutely setulose-ciliolate. Flowers 1 to 1¼ in. in diameter, of vivid crimson. In our type the flowers are on pedicels, of ¼ to 1 in., but these may perhaps elongate after flowering.

Label missing. BEFARIA GUIANENSIS, Klotzsch.
310. BEFARIA aff. *B. resinosæ*, Mutis (sepalis obtusioribus). (2 forms.) Top.
With no. 333. PERNETTYA, near *P. parvifolia*, Benth., and allies (in fruit).
103. GAULTHERIA CORDIFOLIA, H. B. K. 5400 ft.
332. GAULTHERIA aff. *G. vestitæ*, Benth. (pedicellis longioribus). Top.
137. LUCUMA RIGIDA, Mart. & Eichl. 5400 ft.
108. GRAMMADENIA LINEATA, Benth. 5400 ft.
　36. DITASSA TAXIFOLIA, Decne. Arapoo R.

155. VINCETOXICUM (ORTHOSIA) HIRTELLUM, Oliv., sp. nov.; volubile, caule gracili pilis brevibus subpatentibus hirto, foliis ovali-oblongis rigidiusculo apiculatis, marginibus revolutis, supra hirtellis in sicco rugulosis, subtus praecipue in costa pilis patentibus hirtis, cymis sessilibus v. brevissime pedunculatis pauci- v. pluri-floris foliis brevioribus, floribus subsessilibus v. pedicello calyce vix longiore, corollae lobis angustis intus hirsutis, coronae segmentis 5 basi in annulo brevissimo continuo insertis lineari-lanceolatis gynostegium fere aequantibus, stigmate obtuso.

Roraima.

Folia $\frac{2}{3}-\frac{3}{4}$ poll. longa ; petiolus $\frac{1}{12}$ poll. longus v. brevior. Flores $\frac{1}{8}$ poll. longi Very much resembles in general facies *Ditassa pauciflora*.

147. NEPHRADENIA LINEARIS, Benth. ?
113. CURTIA (*Schnebleria tenuifolia*, Don). 5400 ft.
47. LISIANTHUS AMOENUS, Miq. 5400 ft.

306. LISIANTHUS IMTHURNIANUS, Oliv., sp. nov. Gracilis, glaberrimus, caule inferne folioso teretiusculo internodiis folio brevioribus utrinque lineis elevatis duabus notatis, foliis coriaceis obovatis ellipticisve obtusis v. obtusiusculis margine anguste revolutis triplinerviis, pedunculo elongato cymis 3-2-floris, floribus longe pedunculatis, calyce ($\frac{1}{4}-\frac{1}{3}$ poll. longo) 5-fido, lobis ovato-lanceolatis acutiusculis, corollae (2-poll.) tubo leviter dilatato, limbi lobis oblongo-ovatis acutis, filamentis elongatis gracilibus glabris inclusis, antheris oblongo-ellipsoideis inappendiculatis.

Roraima, ledge and summit.

Caulis 1-pedalis erectus v. basi decumbens. Folia $\frac{2}{3}-\frac{3}{4}$ poll. longa, basi in petiolum angustata, $\frac{1}{4}-\frac{1}{2}$ poll. lata. Pedunculus communis 3-6 poll. longus ; bracteae superiores lineares v. ovales. Discus hypogynus.

In our specimens the limb of the corolla looks as though it might remain straight or even slightly incurved in flower.

188. LISIANTHUS aff. *L. macrantho*, sed calycis lobis acuminatis corollae tubum aequantibus. Upper slope.
3. HELIOTROPIUM aff. *H. fruticoso*, conf. *H. strictissimum*=Schombk. 185, 283, and 573. Konkarmo.
24. SOLANUM, an *S. Convolvulus*, Sendtn. ? (inadequate). Arapoo R.

210. MELASMA ? SPATHACEUM, Oliv., sp. nov.; scabrum, foliis suboppositis v. inferioribus alternis brevissime petiolatis ovato-ellipticis basi rotundatis v. leviter cordatis dentatis supra scabris, floribus pedunculatis in axillis superioribus pedunculis folio subaequilongis apice bibracteolatis, bracteolis linearibus v. oblanceolatis basi angustatis, calyce alabastro acuminato florifero antice fisso spathaceo, corolla exserta leviter incurva tubo superne leviter dilatato, limbi brevis lobis subaequalibus, lobo postico truncato emarginato, lateralibus obtusissimis, antico obovato-rotundato bifido.

Roraima, upper slope.

Ramuli retrorsum hispiduli. Folia (exsicc. nigrescentia) $\frac{3}{4}$-1$\frac{1}{4}$ poll. longa, 4-7 lin. lata. Calyx 5-nervius, alabastro oblongo-ellipsoideus apice acuminatus, parce, præcipue in nervis, scabridus, 10-12 lin. longus. Corolla 1$\frac{1}{4}$ poll. longa. Stamina inclusa didynama; filamenta glabra; antheræ sagittatæ glabræ dorsifixæ, loculis æqualibus basi apiculatis. Ovarium glabrum.

I have had too imperfect material to determine finally if this plant should be left in *Melasma*, or regarded as the type of a new genus. There are no ripe fruits, and I should like to be more confident about the form of the corolla-lobes and their æstivation.

129. BEYRICHIA OCYMOIDES, Cham.   Circ. 5400 ft.
 43. UTRICULARIA HUMBOLDTII, Schombk.   5400 ft.

187. UTRICULARIA (§ ORCHIDIOIDES) CAMPBELLIANUM, Oliv., sp. nov. (Plate XLIV. B. figs. 7-11); scapo gracili (1$\frac{1}{2}$-2$\frac{1}{2}$-pollicari) unifloro sæpius squamis linearibus v. lineari-lanceolatis remotis bracteiformibus instructo, foliis tenuibus obovatis obtusis basi in petiolum angustatis, bracteis ternis ovatis v. oblongo-ellipticis pedicello brevioribus v. æquilongis, calycis lobis ovato-cordatis obtusis, corollæ labio superiore brevi calycem vix superante, labio inferiore amplo rotundato integro, calcari gracili cylindrico acutato incurvo labium corollæ æquante.
Roraima (*Schomburgk*), upper slope.
Folia cum petiolo $\frac{3}{4}$ poll. longa, lamina $\frac{1}{6}$-$\frac{1}{4}$ poll. lata. Calyx lobis 4-5 lin. longis latisque. Corolla labio inferiore 1 poll. lato.

293. UTRICULARIA aff. *U. montanæ*, Jacq. (*U. uniflora*, Ruiz & Pav.).   Top.
 78. UTRICULARIA, an *tenuifolia*, Benj. ?   3500 ft.
287. GESNERACEA ?   In fruit only.   Path to upper savannah.

 64. TABEBUIA RORAIMÆ, Oliv., sp. nov. (Plate XLV. figs. 1, 2); ramulis ultimis puberulo- vel scabrido-lepidotis, foliis trifoliolatis foliolis oblongo-ellipticis obtusis sæpe mucronulatis, lateralibus breviter petiolulatis, supra glabrata subtus cano-lepidotis nervis conspicuis depresso-areolatis, racemis terminalibus pauci- v. plurifloris, bracteis lineari-spathulatis scaberulis, pedicellis erectis bibracteolatis calyce infundibuliformi lepidoto-puberulo, lobis breviter ovato-rotundatis, corollæ tubo calyce triplo longiore infundibuliformi, limbi lobis patulis late rotundatis.
Roraima, 5000 ft.
Folia petiolata; petiolus (in ramulis floriferis) 1-1$\frac{1}{2}$ poll. longus; foliola 2-3$\frac{1}{4}$ poll. longa, 10-16 lin. lata; petiolulus centr. $\frac{1}{4}$-$\frac{1}{2}$ poll. longus. Flores 3$\frac{1}{4}$-4 poll. longi, limbo 2$\frac{1}{2}$-3 poll. lato.

 14. APHELANDRA PULCHERRIMA ?, Kunth, v. A. TETRAGONA, Nees.   Ireng R.
 81. JUSTICIA, sp.,=Appun, 1387 (in part.).   Kookenaam valley.
 62. LIPPIA SCHOMBURGKIANA, Schau.
  1. STACHYTARPHETA MUTABILIS, Vahl.   Konkarmo.
 38. HYPTIS ARBOREA, Benth.   Arapoo R.

98, 249. HYPTIS LANTANÆFOLIA, Poit. 5400 ft.
111. COCCOLOBA SCHOMBURGKII, Meiss. 5400 ft.
139. PEPEROMIA, not identified; material scarcely adequate. 5400 ft.
140, 196. PEPEROMIA, an *P. tenella*, Dietr.? 5400 ft., and upper slope.
224. PEPEROMIA REFLEXA, Dietr. Upper slope.
219, 236. HEDYOSMUM BRASILIENSE, Mart. ? Upper slope.

323. PHORADENDRON RORAIMÆ, Oliv., sp. nov. Flavescens, ramulis teretibus infra nodos interdum compressis crassitie pennæ corvinæ parce hirtellis, foliis lineari-oblongis v. anguste ovalibus acutiusculis, floribus monoicis, spicis 1-articulatis 5–7-floris, baccis ellipsoideis lævibus? carnosis.

Roraima, ledge and summit.

Folia carnosula moderate coriacea parce pilosula v. glabrata basi in petiolum brevem angustata, 5–9 lin. longa, 1–2 lin. lata; internodia ½–1 poll. longa. Spicæ axillares solitariæ apiculatæ 1–2 lin. longæ; vagina bracteali leviter bidentata v. subtruncata lateraliter compressa.

Mr. im Thurn's no. 276 (Roraima, path to upper savannah) may be a glabrate form of this plant with rather broader obtuse obscurely mucronulate leaves.

142. PHYLLANTHUS PYCNOPHYLLUS, Muell. Arg. Circ. 5400 ft.
235. CROTON, aff. *C. surinamensi*, Muell. Arg. Forest belt.
76. SPONIA MICRANTHA, Sw. 3500 ft.
58. BURMANNIA BICOLOR, Mart. 4000 ft.
121. DICTYOSTEGIA OROBANCHOIDES, Miers. Upper slope.

ORCHIDEÆ. By H. N. RIDLEY, Esq., M.A., F.L.S.

280. PLEUROTHALLIS STENOPETALA, Lindl. Upper slope, Roraima.
183. STELIS GRANDIFLORA, Lindl. Upper slope, Roraima.
285. STELIS TRISTYLA, Lindl. Upper slope, Roraima.
127. LEPANTHES (inadequate). 5400 ft. (our house).
275. OCTOMERIA? sp. Upper slope.
289. MICROSTYLIS UMBELLULATA?, Sw.
279. MASDEVALLIA PICTURATA, Reichb. f. Upper slope.
286. MASDEVALLIA BREVIS, Reichb. f. Upper slope.
57. BULBOPHYLLUM GERAENSE, Reichb. f. (Our house, 5400 ft.)
290. ELLEANTHUS FURFURACEUS, Reichb. f. Upper slope.
274. EPIDENDRUM TIGRINUM, Lindl. Upper slope.
13. EPIDENDRUM SCHOMBURGKII, Lindl. Treng River.
42. EPIDENDRUM ELONGATUM, Jacq. (Our house, 5400 ft.)

296. EPIDENDRUM ALSUM, Ridley, n. sp. (§ Euepidendra planifolia paniculata.) Caulis

validus, ¼ unciam crassus, ramosa. Folia coriacea brevia ovata obtusa, 1¼ ad ¾ unciam longa, ¾ lata, vaginis rugosis vix uncialibus. Panicula abrupte deflexa, ramis duobus flexuosis 1 ad 2½ uncias longis. Flores parvi carnosi, 8 in ramo, dissiti. Bracteæ ovatæ cucullatæ subobtusæ. Sepala lanceolata carinata. Petala angusta lanceolata quam sepala dimidio breviora, et paullo tenuiora. Labellum cymbiforme, ovatum, cordatum, carnosum. Columna brevis.

Top of Roraima.   The affinity of this plant is with *E. frigidum*, Linden.

299. EPIDENDRUM IMTHURNII, Ridley, n. sp.   (Plate XLVI. A. figs. 1–6.) Caulis gracilis teres parum ramosus ultra 7-uncialis. Folia angusta lineari-lanceolata coriacea carinata, unciam longa, ⅛ unciam lata, vaginis rugosis. Racemi 2 vel 3, deflexi, vix unciales, sex-flori. Flores parvi, tenues. Bracteæ ovatæ, pedicelli ⅔ æquantes. Pedicelli ½-unciales. Sepala lanceolata oblonga obtusa curva, circiter ½ unciam longa. Petala linearia angusta uninervia. Labellum ovatum cordatum cymbiforme, basi angustatum. Columna gracilis paullo recurva. Anthera pileata subconica obtusa. Capsula fusiformis.

Top of Roraima.

322. EPIDENDRUM MONTIGENA, Ridley, n. sp. Caulis teres gracilis, ultra semipedalis. Folia elliptica lanceolata mucronata carinata, unciam longa, ¾ lata, vaginis ¾-uncialibus rugosis. Racemi deflexi multiflori, haud ramosi, circiter 3 uncias longi. Flores parvi, tenues. Bracteæ ovatæ subacutæ patentes. Sepala lanceolata, ovata falcata, ¼ unciam longa. Petala angustiora lanceolata. Labellum cymbiforme, late cordatum, carnosum. Ledge and top.

51. EPIDENDRUM DURUM, Lindl.   Our house.

360. EPIDENDRUM VIOLASCENS, Ridley, n. sp. (Plate XLVI. B. figs. 7–10.) Caulis semipedalis gracilis foliis distichis tectus. Folia brevia lanceolata crassiuscula recurva, ¼ unciam longa, vaginis superiorum violaceis. Panicula erecta gracilis 5-uncialis, ramis paucis tenuibus. Flores pauci perparvi. Bracteæ lanceolatæ breves recurvæ. Sepalum posticum lanceolatum obtusum trinerve, lateralia basi connata, et ad basin labello adnata, lanceolata obliqua, apicibus excurvis, trinervia. Petala linearia angusta uninervia. Labellum rotundatum subreniforme, marginibus serrulatis; costæ tres elevatæ, versus apices attenuatæ. Columna crassiuscula.

Top of Roraima.

304. EPIDENDRUM, sp.   Ledge, 7500 ft.

80. CATTLEYA LAWRENCEANA, Reichb. f.   From the locality given, I believe this to be *C. pumila*, Schomb., Reise Brit. Guian. p. 1068 (non Hooker). There is a picture of it among Schomburgk's drawings preserved in the British Museum. Roraima.

55. CYRTOPODIUM PARVIFLORUM, Lindl.   Roraima, 4000 ft.

61. KOELLENSTEINIA KELLNERIANA, Reichb. f.   Roraima, 4000 ft.

50. ZYGOPETALUM BURKEI, Reichb. f.   Our house.

360. ZYGOPETALUM VENUSTUM, Ridley, n. sp. (Plate XLVII. figs. 1–6.) Planta cæspitosa, pseudobulbis nullis. Folia bina, evoluta, lanceolata acuta, basi attenuata, subcoriacea, costis tribus elevatis in dorso, 7 ad 8 uncias longa, ⅚ lata. Scapus lateralis erectus, 13 uncias longus, vaginis 2–3, apicibus obtusis, amplexis, paullo ampliatis remotis. Racemus laxus, 10-florus. Flores mediocres, unciam longi et lati. Bracteæ pedicellis multo breviores, cylindricæ, ovatæ, acutæ, inferiores vaginantes. Pedicelli ½ unciam longi. Sepala ovata, lanceolata, subacuta patula. Petala subsimilia, obtusiora et angustiora. Labellum integrum, mentum plicatum, lamina rhomboidea, obtusa, lata. Columna brevis crassiuscula, alis magnis obtusis falcatulis, apicibus curvis. Anthera subconica. Stigma semilunare.

Kookenaam River, 3000 ft.

There is a figure of what seems to be the same species in the drawings made by Schomburgk, preserved in the British Museum. It was obtained at Takootoo, and is represented as having white flowers, with the base of the lip and the mentum yellow and a few faint purple stains towards the apex of the lip, and purple streaks on the face of the column. The fruit is deflexed, oblong in shape. In the absence of a distinct pseudobulb, this plant differs from the rest of the genus, but the flowers are exactly those of *Zygopetalum*.

114. ONCIDIUM NIGRATUM, Lindl. 5400 ft. (our house).

12. ONCIDIUM ORTHOSTATES, Ridley, n. sp. (Pluritubereulata Homœantha expansa.) Pseudobulbus oblongus, 2 uncias longus. Folium lanceolatum oblongum, 3 uncias longum, 1 unciam latum. Scapus elatus validulus rigidus ultra bipedalis. Bracteæ lanceolatæ deflexæ breves ¼-unciales. Flores mediocres, iis *O. cæsii* æquantes. Pedicelli ½ unciam longi. Sepala lanceolata subacuta. Petala subsimilia viridia brunneo maculata (ex sicco). Labelli lobi laterales spathulati obtusi, medius basi angustatus rotundatus reniformis emarginatus, cuspide minuto. Callus, carina lamellas duas breves gerens. Columna brevis stelidiis obtusis magnis dolabriformibus tenuibus. Pedicellus polliniorum elongatus ligulatus, discus oblongus quadratus, margine exteriore eroso.

Treng River ; also 23, Savannah, *W. H. Campbell* in Herb. Kew.

19. SOBRALIA STENOPHYLLA, Lindl. Spelinioola, Arapoo River.
273. SOBRALIA (inadequate). Upper slope, Roraima.
115. POGONIA PARVIFLORA, Reichb. f. 5400 ft. (our house).

342. SPIRANTHES BIFIDA, Ridley, n. sp. Tubera elongata clavata. Folia ovata petiolata acuta tenuia parva, lamina semiunciam longa, ¼ unciam lata, petiolus vix semiuncialis. Caulis debilis parce pubescens, ferme 10-uncialis ; vaginis circiter 9, laxis lanceolatis acuminatis dissitis ½ unciam longis. Racemus densus spiralis, unciam longus. Bracteæ flores superantes, lanceolatæ acuminatæ. Sepala, petala et labellum subsimilia, lanceolata angusta obtusa, marginibus involutis, apicibus bifidis, minute

papillosa. Petala quam sepala angustiora. Columna brevis. Anthera erecta obtuse acuta. Ovarium breve minute pubescens.

Our house, Roraima.

131. STENOPTERA VISCOSA, Reichb. f. (Our house, 5400 ft.)

173. STENOPTERA ADNATA, Ridley, n. sp. (Plate XLVIII. A. figs. 1–6.) Tubera plura lanata elongata. Folia tenuia membranacea lanceolata acuta 3 uncias longa, ½ unciam lata. Caulis validulus 17-uncialis superne pubescens, vaginis pluribus dissitis lanceolatis acuminatis usque ad basin fissis, longissima 1½-uncialis. Racemus multiflorus densus pubescens. Flores parvi resupinati. Bracteæ lanceolatæ acutæ ⅗-unciales floribus æquantes. Ovarium breve crassiusculum pubescens. Galea (sepalum posticum petalis adnatum) ovata cucullata obtusa, marginibus fimbriatis. Sepala lateralia oblonga ovata acuta. Labellum ovatum lanceolatum, lobis lateralibus tenuibus erectis vix distinctis, medio linguiformi carnoso, obtuso, supra canaliculato, basi subtus pubescenti. Columna elongata gracilis apice clavata, parte inferiore pubescente.

Upper slope.

9. PELEXIA APHYLLA, Ridley, n. sp. (Plate XLVIII. B. figs. 7–11.) Tubera desunt. Folia radicalia nulla, caulina lanceolata acuminata 6 dissita, superiora latiora. Caulis 8-uncialis pubescens præsertim versus basin. Flores pauci, mediocres, albi. Sepalum posticum petalis adnatum, galeam efformans, lanceolatam acuminatam cucullatam, petala quam sepalum breviora. Sepala lateralia lanceolata linearia porrecta marginibus involutis. Labellum cuneatum spathulatum obtusum minute pubescens, submarginatum lobulo obscuro in medio; calcar ad ovarium arcte adnatum. Columna brevissima, rostellum prolongatum oblongum obtusum canaliculatum porrectum. Anthera lanceolata obtusa vix biloculata. Pollinia pyriformia bicrura; discus ovalis rotundatus.

Waetipoo Mountain; also Serra de Piedade, Minas Geraes, Brazil, *Gardner* (no. 5193, "Flowers white," in Herb. Brit. Mus.).

46. HABENARIA PARVIFLORA, Lindl. (Our house, 5400 ft.) Roraima 251, at 5000 ft.

367. HABENARIA MORITZII, Ridley, n. sp. Caulis ½ ad pedalis foliatus. Folia erecta lanceolata acuta dissita, maxima 2 uncias longa, ¼ lata. Racemus laxus circiter 15-florus. Bracteæ lanceolatæ acuminatæ. Flores parvi. Sepalum posticum erectum, lateralia deflexa, ovata, lanceolata, mucronata. Petala bifida, lacinia postica erecta anguste linearis lanceolata, quam sepalum posticum paullo brevior, antica anguste linearis obtusa recurva. Labellum trilobum, lobi laterales filiformes quam medius longiores et angustiores. Calcar filiforme clavatum ¼ unciam longum. Columna majuscula. Anthera obtusa, apices breves recti. Lobi stigmatici crassiusculi obtusi breves.

At 4000 ft., Roraima; also in Venezuela, *Moritz* 630 b.

53. SELENIPEDIUM LINDLEYANUM, Reichb. f. (Our house, 5400 ft.) Roraima.

31. SELENIPEDIUM KLOTZSCHEANUM, Reichb. f. Colunga River.

315 or 311 (2 labels). TILLANDSIA STRICTA, var. ?
316. TILLANDSIA, sp. ? Inadequate.
45. PUYA (probably new). (Inadequate.)
366. CIPURA PALUDOSA, Aubl.
28. SISYRINCHIUM ALATUM, Hook.
298. NIETNERIA CORYMBOSA, Klotzsch & Schomb. Top.

} J. G. Baker.

297. TOFIELDIA SCHOMBURGKIANA, Oliv., sp. nov. (Plate XLIX. A. figs. 1–6); foliis elongato-linearibus longe acuminatis minutissime ciliolatis longitudinaliter striatis basi distiche vaginantibus, scapo erecto tereti glabro foliis longioribus, floribus strictis racemosis pedicello erecto subæquilongis, calyculi bracteolis ovatis acutis perianthio 6-plo brevioribus, segmentis perianthii erectis oblongis acutis valide 5–7-striatis.

Roraima, 6000 ft., *Schomburgk*; summit, *E. F. im Thurn*.

Folia 3–12 poll. longa, ½–¼ poll. lata. Scapus ½–2 ped. longus, 5–9 (3–∞)-florus. Flores flavido-virentes semipollicares; perianthii segmenta temp. florif. acutata persistentia rigida. Bracteæ ovato-lanceolatæ appressæ.

Nearly allied to *T. falcata*, Pers. (*T. frigida*, H. B. K.), from which it differs in its strict inflorescence and longer pedicels and flowers.

Schomburgk describes the leaves as margined with red.

257. XYRIS FONTANESIANA, Kunth. 5400 ft.

62. XYRIS SETIGERA, Oliv., sp. nov. (Plate L. A. figs. 1–8.) Subacaulis, foliis linearibus setoso-acuminatis marginibus minutissime setuloso-scabridis, scapo foliis 4–5-plo longiore stricto gracillimo subtereti glabro, capitulo ovoideo paucifloro bracteis coriaceis obtusis ovatis v. ovato-ellipticis, staminodiis ad faucem corollæ insertis bipartitis penicillatis, antheris filamento libero longioribus.

Roraima, 4000 ft., *E. F. im Thurn*.

Folia 1–2 poll. longa, ¼–⅛ poll. lata. Scapi 5–7 poll. longi, 1 v. 2 ex una radice; vagina carinata angusta foliis paullo longior. Bracteæ interiores cymbiformes oblongo-ellipticæ obtusæ v. emarginatæ, ⅓ poll. longæ. Sepala lateralia linearia complicata anguste carinata, carina obsolete denticulata.

240. XYRIS WITSENIOIDES, Oliv., sp. nov. (Pl. L. B. figs. 9–15.) Caulescens, caule decumbente sub scapo sæpius dichotomo, foliis rigidis distiche arcte imbricatis linearibus longitudinaliter striatis glabris ad apicem acutissimum gradatim angustatis, basi vaginante scariosa spadicea, scapo gracili foliis 3–5-plo longiore, capitulis paucifloris, bracteis glabris obtusis v. interioribus majoribus emarginatis, sepalis lateralibus incurvis rigidis carinatis carina scabriuscula, staminodiis flabellatim dilatatis longe penicillato-plumosis, ovario apice rostrato, rostro persistente.

Roraima, ledge 7300 ft., *E. F. im Thurn*.

Folia 2½ poll. longa, 1 lin. lata, leviter falcatim incurva. Scapus in dichotomiis solitarius compressiusculus v. subangulatus, 6–9 poll. longus; vagina foliis brevior. Capitula ½ poll. longa, bracteis haud arcte imbricatis.

Singular in the *Witsenia*-like habit of its stout stems; in our specimens 3–4 inches (ranging to 6–8 inches, *E. F. im Thurn*) in length, lateral branches being given off immediately under the solitary scapes.

312. ADOLBODA SCEPTRUM, Oliv., sp. nov.; foliis lineari-lanceolatis acutis rigidis laete viridibus leviter glaucescentibus, scapo crassitie pennae anserinae, floribus capitalis, capitulis floriferis 4–5 poll. diam., bracteis ovatis acutis rigidis sepalis ½–⅔ brevioribus, sepalis ovato-lanceolatis subaequilongis lateralibus carinatis, petalis limbo ovato flabellatim venoso, ovario ovoideo, stylo longo basi appendicibus 3 crassiusculis arcte uncinatis ovario aequilongis circumdato, ovula plurima.

Roraima, summit, *E. F. im Thurn*.

Folia 6–7 poll. longa. Scapus . . . . . Bracteae ovatae v. interiores ovato-lanceolatae, ¾–1½ poll. longae. Sepala 1½–1¾ poll. longa. Petala 2–2½ poll. longa, inferne in tubum leviter curvatum coalita. Stamina petalis breviora; filamenta anguste linearia; antherae lineares. Ovarium cartilagineum, ¼ poll. longum; stylus 1¾ poll. longus.

The leaves I have not seen, Mr. im Thurn having kindly supplied me with a note of their size and form. He describes the foliage as "Yucca-like." Our specimen consists of a well-developed capitulum and 8–9 inches of its scape. The flowers hardly admit of being satisfactorily analyzed. They are very much larger than in other species seen by me, and the tube of the united petals much wider. The singular uncinate appendages are inserted with the style upon the ovary, not, as in some species, at a distinct interval above it. There is a figure of this remarkable plant in the Schomburgk collection of drawings at the British Museum.

338. STEGOLEPIS GUIANENSIS, Klotzsch. 6000 ft.

34. ERIOCAULON HUMBOLDTII, Kunth? (= specimen from Roraima, *Schomburgk*). Arapoo R.

33. PAEPALANTHUS SCHOMBURGKII, Klotzsch. Arapoo R.

60. PAEPALANTHUS FLAVESCENS, Koern. (*eriocephalus*, Klotzsch). 4000 ft.

294. PAEPALANTHUS RORAIMAE, Oliv., sp. nov. (Plate XLIX. B. figs. 7–14.) Acaulis, foliis dense rosulatis brevibus rigidis linearibus obtusiusculis basi latioribus leviter falcatis rectisve, basi arcte imbricata lanuginosa excepta glabra, longitudinaliter striata, scapo solitario vaginato, vagina foliis subduplo longiore spathacea v. bifida glabra, involucri bracteis lineari-lanceolatis glabratis v. parce pilosis, fuliginosis, bracteis disci flores stipantibus oblanceolatis v. obovato-cuneatis cymbiformibus.

Roraima, summit, *E. F. im Thurn*.

Folia ¾–1 poll. longa. Scapus glabrescens v. apicem versus obsolete puberulus 3½–4½ poll. longus. Capitula hemisphaerica ½ poll. diam. Flores breviter pedicellati. Perianthium segmentis exterioribus liberis obovatis concavis apicem versus coloratis interioribus staminigeris subaequilongis. Ovarium triquetrum.

264. ANTHURIUM RORAIMENSE, N. E. Brown, sp. nov.; cataphyllis magnis lanceolatis, petiolis teretibus elongatis, lamina cordata subacuminata, lobis posticis semioblongis

quam antico subtriplo brevioribus sinu parabolico sejunctis, nervis primariis 13, venis primariis costa utrinque 6–7, omnibus supra et subtus prominentibus; pedunculo valido tereti; spatha oblongo-lanceolata, filiformi-acuminata; spadice stipitato spatha subæquante valido.

Hab. Roraima, British Guiana, *E. F. im Thurn.*

Cataphylla minora 3 poll. longa, majora 7–8 poll. longa, 1–1¼ poll. lata. Petiolus 2 ped. longus. Lamina 20 poll. longa, 12 poll. lata, pergamentacea, reticulato-venosa, nervi intramarginali margine valde approximato. Spatha 5½ poll. longa, 1¾ poll. lata. Spadix (cum stipite ½ poll. longa) 5 poll. longus, ½ poll. crassus. Flores 1 lin. diam., stylo conico brevissime exserto.—*N. E. Brown.*

382. Geonoma Appuniana, Spr.
358. Euterpe. 5400 ft.

CYPERACEÆ. By H. N. Ridley, Esq., M.A., F.L.S.

259. Fimbristylis hispidula, Kunth. (Our house, 5400 ft.) Roraima.
245. Rhynchospora glauca, Vahl. (Our house, 5400 ft.)
253. Rhynchospora capillacea, Torrey. (Our house, 5400 ft.)
Rhynchospora leptostachya, Bœckl. (Our house, 5400 ft.)
248. Scleria hirtella, Swartz.
209. Scleria bracteata, Cavanilles.

357. Cryptangium stellatum, Bœckeler, ♂. (Plate LI. figs. 1–6.) Upper slope, Roraima.

The male plant of this species does not seem to have been hitherto met with or described; I therefore add a description of it.

Panicula longissima, ramis gracilibus. Spiculæ plures, binæ, castaneæ, ¼ unciam longæ. Bractea lanceolata, trinervis, longe mucronata, mucrone ciliato. Glumæ vacuæ 8, floriferæ 2. Stamina tria, apiculis longis acuminatis, dimidio antheræ æquantibus.

Everardia, nov. gen. *Cryptangiearum.*

Herba perennis, caule valido descendente lignoso. Folia conferta rigida recurva. Culmus paniculatus validus lateralis, ex axilla folii inferioris oriens. Panicula laxa, rami plurimi inferiores masculi, supremi feminei. Spiculæ masculæ plurifloræ, glumis vacuis 3, floriferis 6. Stamina plura. Spiculæ femineæ parvæ, glumis vacuis 4, florifera 1. Stylus brevis, stigma bifidum lobis brevibus planis lanceolatis. Ovarium triangulatum breviter pedicellatum, cupula nulla. Setæ hypogynæ copiosæ tortæ.

335. Everardia montana, Ridley, n. sp. (Plate LII. figs. 1–8.) Caulis brevis, vaginis latis decompositis superne tectus. Folia lineari-lanceolata acuta acuminata carinata recurva, marginibus albo-ciliatis, longissima 7 uncias longa, ¼ unciam lata. Culmus 14 uncias longus, validus, compressus, anceps, pro maxima parte paniculata, efoliata, vaginis paucis brunneis fissis compressis, sæpius lamina parva lanceolata obtusa

rigida. Spiculæ masculæ singulæ, copiosæ, ¾ unciam longæ, castaneæ, inferiores pedunculatæ. Glumæ 3 vacuæ, staminiferæ 6, lanceolatæ aristatæ, marginibus parce ciliatis, arista brevis crassiuscula. Stamina in flore circiter 6. Anthera acuminata filamento æqualis, ½ unciam longa, apiculus brevissimus, trichomatum fasciculo terminali brevi. Spiculæ feminere parvæ angustæ. Glumæ vacuæ 4, suprema fertilis, exteriores cartilagineæ lanceolatæ brevi-aristatæ, castaneæ, interiores scariosæ, carina violacea. Stylus stigmati æqualis, teres, crassiusculus brevis. Stigma breviter bifidum lobis lanceolatis obtusis planis, violaceis. Ovarium ellipticum oblongum obtuse triquetrum breviter pedicellatum, pedicello subtereti. Setæ hypogynæ, copiosæ, tortæ. Pistillum ¼-unciale; caryopsis fere ⅛ unciam longa.

Ledge, Roraima.

This genus is most nearly allied to *Lagenocarpus*, but differs entirely from that genus, and from the rest of the *Cryptangieæ*, in the lateral inflorescence, the bifid stigma, with short flat lobes, the absence of any cupule, and the presence of a large number of hypogynous bristles.

262. PASPALUM STELLATUM, Flügge, var. ?
261. PANICUM NERVOSUM, Lam. ? 5400 ft.
254. ARUNDINELLA BRASILIENSIS, Raddi. 5400 ft.
154. ECHINOLÆNA SCABRA, H. B. K. 5400 ft.
246. SACCHARUM (§ ERIOCHRYSIS) CAYENNENSIS, Beauv. 5400 ft.
260. ISCHEMUM LATIFOLIUM, Kunth. 5400 ft.
359. ? GUADUA (barren). 5400 ft.
18. ? CHUSQUEA (barren). Arapoo R.
302. GRAM. DUB. (barren). Top.

FERNS. By J. G. BAKER, F.R.S., F.L.S.

The following is a complete list of the Ferns collected. The numbers are Mr. im Thurn's collecting-numbers. Those enclosed within brackets indicate the position of the new species in the sequence followed in our 'Synopsis Filicum.' In determining the species I have had the kind help of Mr. Jenman, the government botanist of the colony, who has paid special attention to Ferns ever since he has lived in Demerara.

343. GLEICHENIA PUBESCENS, H. B. K., var. (G. LONGIPINNATA, Hook.). Upper slopes of the mountain.

92. CYATHEA VESTITA, Mart. In the neighbourhood of the encampment.

270. ALSOPHILA BIPINNATIFIDA, Baker. With a slender caudex 6 or 7 feet in length, in the neighbourhood of the encampment.

87 (16*). ALSOPHILA MACROSORA, Baker, n. sp.; stipitibus basi paleis linearibus brunneis imbricatis dense vestitis, frondibus amplis deltoideis tripinnatifidis crassiusculis

praeter venas primarias faciei superioris glabris, pinnis oblongo-lanceolatis, pinnulis lanceolatis inferioribus distincte petiolatis basi truncatis ad costam alatam pinnatifidis, segmentis tertiariis oblongis crenulatis, venis simplicibus erecto-patentibus 5–6-jugis, soris magnis globosis superficialibus intramarginalibus, receptaculis dense paraphysatis.

Basal paleae extending 4–5 inches up the stipe, glossy, moderately firm in texture, the largest ½ in. long. Stipe a foot long, brownish, deeply grooved down the face. Lower pinnae 15–18 in. long, 8–9 in. broad. Lower pinnules 4 in. long ⅞ in. broad, with a petiole ⅛ in. long, which is articulated at the base. Tertiary segments ⅛ in. broad.

Allied to the Bahian *A. praecincta*, from which it differs by its more coriaceous texture, crowded sori, and densely paraphysate receptacle.

37. ALSOPHILA VILLOSA, Presl.

318 (16*). HYMENOPHYLLUM DEJECTUM, n. sp.; stipitibus productis paleis pallidis ascendentibus lanceolatis praeditis, frondibus oblongo-lanceolatis tripinnatifidis erectis glabris, pinnis lanceolatis confertis decurvatis pinnulis, superioribus simplicibus inferioribus profunde pinnatifidis, segmentis ultimis linearibus integris uninervatis, soris breviter pedicellatis ad basin segmentorum ultimorum impositis, involucro campanulato valvis argute serratis.

Rootstock not seen. Stipes 2–3 in. long, clothed with minute inconspicuous pale membranous paleae, as is also the rhachis. Lamina 4–5 in. long, ¾–1 in. broad. Pinnae decurved, not more than ½–¾ in. long. Final segments 1/12–⅛ in. long, not more than ⅛ line broad. Involucre ⅛ line broad.

A very distinct novelty. Allied to *H. demissum* and *H. javanicum*.

118, 199, 374. HYMENOPHYLLUM POLYANTHOS, Sw. Upper slope of the mountain.
207, 302, 370, 372, 373. HYMENOPHYLLUM MICROCARPUM, Hook. Upper slope of the mountain. This is evidently not more than a variety of *H. polyanthos*.
205. HYMENOPHYLLUM CRISPUM, H. B. K. Upper slope of the mountain.
203, 375. HYMENOPHYLLUM LINEARE, Sw. Upper slope of the mountain; and 200, var. ANTILLENSE, Jenman.
292. HYMENOPHYLLUM FUCOIDES, Sw. Upper slopes of the mountain.
271. TRICHOMANES MACILENTUM, Van den Bosch. Upper slopes of the mountain. Will have, I think, to be regarded as not more than a variety of *T. Bancroftii*.
198, 201, 319. TRICHOMANES PYXIDIFERUM, L. Upper slopes of the mountain. 319 represents the variety *T. cucifolium*, C. Müll.
99, 347. TRICHOMANES CRISPUM, Sw. The higher number from the upper slopes of the mountain, the lower from the neighbourhood of the encampment.
119. TRICHOMANES RIGIDUM, Sw. Neighbourhood of the encampment.
120. DAVALLIA IMRAYANA, Hook. Upper slopes of the mountain.
344. LINDSAYANA GUIANENSIS, Dryand. Upper slopes of the mountain.

149, 150, 301. LINDSAYA STRICTA, Dryand. The two lower numbers gathered near the encampment, the other on the mountain-top.

161, 303. HYPOLEPIS REPENS, Presl. Base of the cliff. 194, 195 are young forms of *Hypolepis*, most likely the same species.

144. PTERIS LOMARIACEA, Kunze. Neighbourhood of the encampment.

160. PTERIS INCISA, Thunb. Base of the cliff.

156. LOMARIA PLUMIERI, Desv. Upper slopes of the mountain.

88, 167. LOMARIA PROCERA, Spreng. Upper slopes of the mountain and in the neighbourhood of the encampment.

48. LOMARIA BORYANA, Willd. Neighbourhood of the encampment.

157, 369. ASPLENIUM LUNULATUM, Sw., var. (A. ERECTUM, Bory). Base of the cliff.

171. ASPLENIUM RHIZOPHORUM, L., var. (A. FLABELLATUM, Kunze). Upper slopes of the mountain.

143. ASPLENIUM FURCATUM, Thunb. Neighbourhood of the encampment.

272. ASPIDIUM CAPENSE, Willd. Path to the upper savannah.

275 (4*). NEPHRODIUM (§ LASTREA) BRACHYPODUM, n. sp.; caudice erecto, stipitibus brevissimis cæspitosis pilosis, frondibus parvis lanceolatis firmulis subglabris simpliciter pinnatis e medio ad basin et apicem sensim attenuatis, rhachide piloso paleis paucis patulis lanceolatis prædito, pinnis sessilibus lanceolatis basi utrinque auriculatis centralibus profunde serratis reliquis integris infimis deltoideis, venis superioribus pinnarum simplicibus erecto-patentibus, inferioribus furcatis vel parce pinnatis, soris superficialibus medialibus, involucro membranaceo subpersistente.

Frond 5–6 in. long, an inch broad, narrowed very gradually from the middle to both ends. Lower pinnæ not more than $\frac{1}{8}$ in. long. Stipes not above half an inch long. Central pinnæ $\frac{1}{4}$ in. broad above the dilated base.

Upper slopes of the mountain.

May be an involucrate form of the well-known West-Indian *Polypodium hastæfolium*, Sw., which it resembles very closely in size, shape, texture, and venation.

94, 380. NEPHRODIUM CONTERMINUM, Desv. Upper slopes of the mountain and neighbourhood of the encampment.

269. NEPHRODIUM LEPRIEURII, Hook. Neighbourhood of the encampment.

126, 169, 225. NEPHRODIUM DENTICULATUM, Hook. Upper slopes of the mountain and neighbourhood of the encampment.

354. NEPHRODIUM AMPLISSIMUM, Hook. Upper slopes of the mountain.

102, 339. NEPHROLEPIS CORDIFOLIA, Presl. Neighbourhood of the encampment.

356 (13*). POLYPODIUM (§ PHEGOPTERIS) DEMERARANUM, n. sp.; caudice erecto, stipite producto pubescente basi paleis paucis lanceolatis brunneis membranaceis prædito, frondibus oblongo-lanceolatis bipinnatifidis præsertim ad venas pilosis, pinnis sessilibus lanceolatis ad costam alatam pinnatifidis inferioribus reductis infimis remotis perparvis, pinnulis oblongo-lanceolatis integris obtusis, venulis simplicibus 8–9-jugis pilosis, soris superficialibus parvis supramedialibus.

Stipes 6–8 in. long below the much-dwarfed lowest pair of pinnæ, grey and pubescent, as is the rhachis. Largest basal paleæ half an inch long. Lamina 1½–2 ft. long, 7–8 in. broad at the middle. Largest pinnæ 4–4½ in. long, about an inch broad. Pinnules above ⅛ in. broad.

Closely allied to the Himalayan *P. auriculatum*, Wall., in size, texture, and cutting, but quite different in the position of the sori. Found on the upper slopes of the mountain. Gathered previously by Appun, 1138.

168 (15*). POLYPODIUM (§ PHEGOPTERIS) RORAIMENSE, n. sp.; caudice erecto, stipite producto glabro stramineo, frondibus oblongo-lanceolatis bipinnatis præter costas faciei superioris glabris, pinnis sessilibus lanceolatis simpliciter pinnatis inferioribus reductis infimis remotis perparvis, pinnulis oblongo-lanceolatis subintegris obtusis, venulis 7–8-jugis ascendentibus simplicibus, soris globosis superficialibus supramedialibus.

Stipes 3–4 in. long below the dwarfed lowest pinnæ. Lamina 1½ ft. long, 8–9 in. broad at the middle. Largest pinnæ 4–4½ in. long, about an inch broad. Pinnules ⅛ in. broad.

Closely allied to the preceding and to the West-Indian *P. Germanianum* and *ctenoides*. Gathered upon the upper slopes of the mountain.

177, 182, 282, 307, 345, 352, 376. POLYPODIUM MARGINELLUM, Sw. Upper slopes of the mountain. in the crevices of rocks.

184 (ex parte). POLYPODIUM TRIFURCATUM, L. Upper slopes of the mountain, mixed with *Enterosora Campbellii*.

166, 350, 368, 377. POLYPODIUM FURCATUM, Mett. Summit and upper slopes of the mountain.

133. POLYPODIUM SERRULATUM, Mett. The type in the neighbourhood of the encampment, and no. 351. var. (*Niphopteris Jamesoni*, Hook.), on the upper slopes of the mountain.

178. POLYPODIUM TRICHOMANOIDES, Sw. Upper slopes of the mountain.

348. POLYPODIUM TRUNCICOLA, Klotzsch. Upper slopes of the mountain. New to Guiana.

181. POLYPODIUM MONILIFORME, Lag., var. (P. SAXICOLUM, Baker). Upper slopes of the mountain.

179. POLYPODIUM TOVARENSE, Klotzsch. Upper slopes of the mountain.

186 (159*). POLYPODIUM (§ EUPOLYPODIUM) KALBREYERI. n. sp.; rhizomate breviter repente paleis parvis patulis linearibus brunneis vestito, stipitibus contiguis elongatis erectisatro-brunneis, frondibus deltoideis simpliciter pinnatis coriaceis glabris, rhachide nudo castaneo, pinnis linearibus adnatis contiguis integris superioribus sensim minoribus, venis immersis occultis furcatis, soris globosis superficialibus latitudinem totam pinnarum inter costam et marginem occupantibus.

Stipes 8–10 in. long, naked or furnished towards the base with minute, squarrose, soft, hair-like paleæ. Rhachis castaneous, like the stipe. Lamina 5–6 in. long, 3–3½ in. broad

2 x 2

292 PROF. OLIVER ON NEW PLANTS FROM RORAIMA.

at the base. Pinnæ about 20 on a side below the caudate apex of the frond, ⅙ in. broad
at the base, narrowed gradually to an acute point. Sori a line in diameter, 12–16-jugate
on the lower pinnæ.

Nearest the Andine *P. melanopus*, Hook. & Grev., from which it differs by its stiffly
erect stipes, frond broadest at the base, and obscure immersed veins. Found on the
upper slopes of the mountain, and gathered previously by Kalbreyer on the mountains
of the province of Ocana, in New Granada, at an elevation of 6500 ft.

186* (159*). POLYPODIUM KOOKENAMÆ, Jenman MSS., n. sp.; rhizomate valido breviter repente vel suberecto paleis subulatis castaneis ciliatis dense vestito, stipitibus
castaneis elongatis parce ciliatis, frondibus oblongo-lanceolatis subcoriaceis glabris
simpliciter subpinnatis, rhachide primario anguste alato, pinnis lanceolatis acutis integris basi confluentibus, costis immersis, venis furcatis, soris medialibus obscure
immersis.

Stipes 6–9 in. long. Lamina 6–8 in. long, 2 in. broad, truncate at the base, dark green
above, pale beneath. Pinnæ 16–20 on a side below the subentire acuminate apex of the
frond, the largest an inch long, ⅜–¼ in. broad. Primary rhachis purpuraceous on both
sides of the frond. Sori terminal on the anterior fork of each vein.

This I have not seen, and insert entirely on Mr. Jenman's authority. I have merely
altered the form of the description which he has sent, so as to make it uniform with the
others. It did duty for no. 186 in set C of the distribution. Mr. Jenman says it is
intermediate between *P. Kalbreyeri* and the Jamaican *P. brunneo-ciride*.

180, 379. POLYPODIUM TAXIFOLIUM, Linn. Upper slopes of the mountain.
104. POLYPODIUM PECTINATUM, Linn. In the neighbourhood of the encampment.
124. POLYPODIUM CULTRATUM, Willd. In the neighbourhood of the encampment.
217. POLYPODIUM XANTHOTRICHIUM, Klotzsch (*P. ellipticosorum*, Fée). Upper slopes
of the mountain. Appears to be distinct specifically from *P. cultratum* by its
uniformly elliptical sori.
281. POLYPODIUM RIGESCENS, Bory. Upper slopes of the mountain.
176. POLYPODIUM FIRMUM, Klotzsch. Upper slopes of the mountain.
378. POLYPODIUM SUBSESSILE, Baker. Upper slopes of the mountain.
190. POLYPODIUM CAPILLARE, Desv. Upper slopes of the mountain.

125 (212*). POLYPODIUM (§ EUPOLYPODIUM) MELANOTRICHUM, n. sp.; caudice erecto
paleis subulatis crispatis vestito, stipite brevissimo gracillimo, frondibus oblongo-
lanceolatis parvis flaccidis membranaceis glabris bipinnatifidis, pinnis lanceolatis
adnatis profunde pectinato-pinnatifidis inferioribus sensim minoribus, segmentis
deltoideis acutis, venis brevibus simplicibus erecto-patentibus, soris globosis superficialibus costularibus ad apicem venarum impositis.

Stipes and rhachis black, thread-like, glabrous. Lamina 3–4 in. long, an inch broad at
the middle. Central pinnæ half an inch long, ⅛ in. broad, with 6–8 pairs of deltoid
segments with a single sorus in the centre of each.

Allied to the Brazilian *P. achilleæfolium*, Kaulf., but quite different in texture, in the shape of the segments, and by its very short simple veins. Found in the neighbourhood of the encampment.

172. POLYPODIUM (§ GONIOPHLEBIUM) LORICEUM, Linn. Base of the great cliff.

340. POLYPODIUM (§ PHLEBODIUM) AUREUM, Linn., var. (P. AREOLATUM, H. B. K.). In the neighbourhood of the encampment.

208. POLYPODIUM (§ CAMPYLONEURON) ANGUSTIFOLIUM, Sw., var. (P. AMPHOSTEMON, Kunze). In the neighbourhood of the encampment.

295 (14*). GYMNOGRAMME (§ PTEROZONIUM) CYCLOPHYLLA, n. sp. (Plate LIII. figs. 1, 2) ; caudice erecto, stipitibus cæspitosis elongatis erectis basi primum paleis minutis lineari-subulatis patulis præditis, frondibus parvis nitidis rigide coriaceis apice rotundatis margine recurvato basi cuneatis margine plano, venis flabellatis immersis, soris oblongis ad venarum apicem solum productis cito confluentibus zonam angustam intramarginalem formantibus.

Stipes wiry, 5–6 in. long. Lamina only about an inch long and broad. Found on the summit of the mountain.

101, 215 (14*). GYMNOGRAMME (§ PTEROZONIUM) ELAPHOGLOSSOIDES, n. sp. (Plate LIV. figs. 1–5) ; caudice valido lignoso paleis parvis subulatis nigro-castaneis dense vestito, stipitibus elongatis erectis nudis castaneis, frondibus simplicibus integris rigide coriaceis nudis elliptico-lanceolatis acutis vel obtusis conspicue costatis basi cordatis, venis confertis patulis parallelis simplicibus vel furcatis intra marginem evanescentibus, soris linearibus cito confluentibus frondis faciem totam inferiorem præter zonam angustam marginalem occupantibus.

Stipes wiry, sometimes above half a foot long. Fronds 6–8 in. long, fertile 1–2 inches, sterile sometimes 3 inches broad. Sori occupying the whole under surface except a marginal border. Not more than ½–¹⁄₁₂ in. broad. Found both upon the upper slopes of the mountain and in the neighbourhood of the encampment.

These two interesting novelties both fall under the genus *Pterozonium* of Fée, figured on tab. 16 of his ‘Genera Filicum.’ The only species known previously is the very rare *Gymnogramme reniformis*, Mart., figured Icon. Crypt. Bras. t. 26, and also in Hooker's ‘Second Century of Ferns,’ t. 9, and on tab. 49 of the Fern volume of ‘Flora Brasiliensis.’ The two new species are very distinct, both from one another and *G. reniformis*. In *G. cyclophylla* the sori form a narrow band just within the margin ; in *G. reniformis* a broad semicircle, a distinct space within the margin, whilst in *G. elaphoglossoides* they cover the whole surface except a narrow border.

164. GYMNOGRAMME SCHOMBURGKIANA, Kunze. Upper slopes of the mountain.

197. GYMNOGRAMME HIRTA, Desv. Upper slopes of the mountain. New to Guiana.

159. GYMNOGRAMME FLEXUOSA, Desv. Upper slopes of the mountain. Also new to Guiana.

ENTEROSORA, nov. gen.

Sori oblongi vel oblongo-cylindrici exindusiati ad venas decurrentes, intra frondis laminam orti, demum ad frondis faciem inferiorem rimis angustis obliquis imperfecte obvii. Venæ pinnatæ, venulis paucis ascendentibus prope frondis marginem anastomosantibus et areolas steriles hexagonas soro unico centrali includentes formantibus.

Most resembles *Gymnogramme*, from which it differs mainly by having the sori immersed in the centre of the frond, and only appearing very partially on its lower surface even in a mature stage.

184 (ex parte). ENTEROSORA CAMPBELLII, Baker.   (Plate LV. figs. 1–5.)

The only species : upper slopes of the mountain, with *Polypodium trifurcatum*. Rootstock cylindrical, suberect, densely clothed with small brown membranous lanceolate paleæ. Stipes slender, brown, erect, wiry, 4–5 in. long, with a few very inconspicuous spreading fibrillose paleæ downwards. Lamina oblanceolate, simple, subcoriaceous, glabrous, 6–8 in. long, under an inch broad, obtuse, narrowed gradually to the base, conspicuously repand on the margin, with broad rounded lobes. Veins very distinct when the frond is held up to the light, arranged in pinnate groups, one opposite each lobe, the sterile veinlets forming unequal hexagonal areolæ, with a single vein bearing a sorus in the centre of each. Sori ⅛–¼ in. long, 4–6 to each of the central pinnated groups, erecto-patent as regards the whole lamina, seen partially at last on the lower surface by slits that seem as if they were made with a knife through the epidermis.

Frond in shape and texture much resembling that of *Polypodium trifurcatum*, from which it differs by its long stipes and totally different veining, in addition to the entirely dissimilar shape and position of its sori. In naming it after the late W. H. Campbell, Esq., I am carrying out the wish of Mr. im Thurn.

170. VITTARIA LINEATA, Sw.   Upper slopes of the mountain.

212, 218. VITTARIA STIPULATA, Kunze.   Upper slopes of the mountain.   New to Guiana.

229, 231. ACROSTICHUM LATIFOLIUM, Sw.   Upper slopes of the mountains.   Two different varieties, both rigid in texture, narrowed very gradually from the middle to the base, and 229 dotted over the under surface with minute subpeltate brown paleæ.

233, 238. ACROSTICHUM LINGUA, Raddi.

267. ACROSTICHUM STENOPTERIS, Klotzsch.   In the neighbourhood of the encampment. New to Guiana.

266. ACROSTICHUM DECORATUM, Kunze.   In the neighbourhood of the encampment.

278. ACROSTICHUM AUBERTII, Desv., var. CRINITUM, nov. var.   Recedes from the Brazilian and Colombian type of the species towards *A. villosum* by its much more crinite lamina both in the sterile and fertile frond, and by the stipes being densely clothed with squarrose subulate brown paleæ, as in the Venezuelan *A. Reichenbachii*, Moritz.   Path to the upper slope.   The species is new to Guiana.

237 (45*). ACROSTICHUM (§ ELAPHOGLOSSUM) LEPTOPHLEBIUM, n. sp.; rhizomate repente cylindrico lignoso paleis parvis membranaceis lanceolatis brunneis crispatis dense vestito, stipite elongato stramineo subnudo, fronde sterili lanceolato membranaceo glabro paleis paucis lanceolatis ad marginem et faciem inferiorem prædito, venis laxis perspicuis erecto-patentibus simplicibus vel furcatis intra marginem terminantibus, fronde sterili multo minore, stipite longiore.

Sterile lamina a foot or more long, 18-20 lines broad, cuneate at the base, with a slender fragile stipe 4-5 inches long. Fertile lamina 4-5 inches long, an inch broad, with a stipe about a foot long. Found upon the upper slopes of the mountain.

93. ACROSTICHUM MUSCOSUM, Sw., var. A. ENGELJI, Karst. In the neighbourhood of the encampment.

213. ACROSTICHUM SQUAMOSUM, Sw. Upper slopes of the mountain.

41. ACROSTICHUM (§ RHIPIDOPTERIS) PELTATUM, Sw. In the neighbourhood of the encampment.

100. SCHIZÆA DICHOTOMA, Sw. In the neighbourhood of the encampment. New to Guiana.

85. SCHIZÆA ELEGANS, Sw. In the neighbourhood of the encampment.

263. ANEMIA TOMENTOSA, Sw. In the neighbourhood of the encampment.

146. LYCOPODIUM ALOPECUROIDES, L. In the neighbourhood of the encampment.

192. LYCOPODIUM LINIFOLIUM, L., var. SARMENTOSUM RUBESCENS, Spring. Upper slopes of the mountain.

230. LYCOPODIUM SUBULATUM, Desv. Base of the cliff.

226 (159*). SELAGINELLA (§ STACHYGYNANDRUM) VERNICOSA, n. sp. (Plate LVI. A. figs. 1-7); caule basi decumbente superne recto laxe pinnato, ramulis paucis brevibus ascendentibus, foliis heteromorphis distichis crassis firmis nitide viridibus, planæ inferioris confertis erecto-patentibus ovatis obtusis margine ubique denticulatis planæ superioris duplo brevioribus ascendentibus ovatis obtusis valde imbricatis, spicis tetragonis brevissimis, bracteis conformibus magnis ovatis acutis.

This belongs to the *Atrovirides* group in the neighbourhood of *S. Martensii*. The main stems are about half a foot long, the leafy branches an eighth of an inch broad, and the leaves of the lower plane a line long. The type (A. figs. 1-7) as described was found at the base of the cliff, and a variety (No. 351) (B. fig. 8, var. *oligoclada*), with much fewer more elongated branches, near the encampment.

122 (186*). SELAGINELLA (§ STACHYGYNANDRUM) RORAIMENSIS, n. sp. (Plate LVI. C. figs. 9-14); caule erecto 3-4-pinnato, ramis laxe dispositis ascendentibus ramulis brevibus, foliis heteromorphis distichis membranaceis, planæ inferioris laxis oblongolanceolatis acutis valde inæquilateralibus basi superiore producto late rotundato, planæ superioris ovatis ascendentibus cuspidatis, spicis tetragonis, bracteis conformibus ovatis acutis valde imbricatis acute carinatis sporangiis duplo longioribus.

Belongs to the *Radiatæ* group in the neighbourhood of *S. radiata* and *confusa*. The main stems are 4 or 5 inches long, the leafy branches ½ in. broad, and the leaves of the lower plane a line long. Found in the neighbourhood of the encampment.

(271*.) SELAGINELLA (§ HETEROSTACHYS) RHODOSTACHYA, n. sp. ; caule decumbente, ramis alternis deltoideis flabellato-bipinnatis, foliis heteromorphis distichis membranaceis, planæ inferioris laxe dispositis erecto-patentibus ovatis obtusis paulo inæquilateralibus, planæ superioris consimilibus duplo minoribus valde ascendentibus, spicis brevissimis platystachyoideis, bracteis dimorphis ovatis acutis membranaceis.

Belongs to the group *Proniflorœ* in the neighbourhood of *S. consimilis* and *Otonis*. The stems are half a foot in length, and the leafy branches ⅛ in. broad. This was contained in the collection without any number.

MUSCI. By Mr. W. MITTEN, A.L.S.

HOOKERIA (§ OMALIADELPHUS) CRISPA, C. Müll. Bot. Zeit. 1855, p. 768. Perfectly fruited, near encampment, no. 123.

HYPOPTERYGIUM TAMARISCI, Brid. ; *Hypnum Tamarisci*, Sw. ; Hedw. Musc. Frond. t. 51. Without fruit. Near encampment, no. 265.

POLYTRICHUM ARISTIFLORUM, Mitt. Journ. Linn. Soc., Bot. vol. xii. p. 620. A few barren stems, near encampment, no. 116.

Creeping over the roots of this are a few stems of *Jungermannia perfoliata*, Swartz, or of one of the closely allied South-American species of the little group to which Mr. Spruce has applied the name *Syzygiella* in the 'Journal of Botany,' 1876, intending it to include *Jungermannia perfoliata*, *J. contigua*, and *J. concreta*, Gottsche, *J. plagiochiloides* and *J. pectiniformis*, Spruce, also *J. macrocalyx*, Mont.; to these must be added *J. geminifolia*, Mitt., Journ. Linn. Soc., Bot. vol. vii. p. 164, from tropical Africa, and the *J. subintegerrima*, Reinw. Bl. et Nees, Hep. Jav. in the 'Synopsis Hepaticorum,' placed in *Plagiochila* (p. 55). To this species belong *P. caricgata*, Lindenb., *P. variabilis*, Lacoste, and also *P. securifolia*, Lindenb. Sp. Hep. t. x., all of which have the leaf-angles united on both sides of the stem, even when they are not opposite, a characteristic which is not mentioned in their original descriptions, nor depicted in their figures, nor in that of the *J. macrocalyx* as found in the 'Synopsis.' The perianth in *J. subintegerrima* agrees with that found in the species allied to *J. colorata*, and, as in their case, is subtended by shortened and dentate involucral leaves. Exactly similar instances of conjugation of the leaf-angles are found in *Plagiochila*, some of which do not otherwise resemble each other.

PLAGIOCHILA ADIANTOIDES, Lindenb. Male stems only, upper slope, no. 283.

ANEURA BIPINNATA, Nees (*Jungermannia*, Sw.). Specimens taken from large tufts, upper slopes, nos. 204, 284.

In these specimens the stems are 4-5 cm. high, including the side branches 1 cm. wide, the ultimate ramuli with a limb of about two rows of more pellucid cells ; in *A. fucoides*, Hook. Musc. Exot. t. 85, this limb is very much wider ; in *A. Poeppigiana* it is nearly or quite obsolete. Besides these there are several other remarkable South-American species : *A. alata*, Gottsche, from Chili, a very large species ; *A. prehensilis*, Hook. f. et Tayl. Fl. Ant. t. 160. fig. 9 (under *Jungermannia*), originally from Hermite Island, since collected by Cunningham, with stems nearly six inches high, and always with its pruinose look when dry ; *A. polyclada*, Mitt., gathered in Otway Harbour, Patagonia, during the visit of the 'Challenger' Expedition, a small species about an inch and a half high (frons dorso planus lævis, ramis valde approximatis bipinnatis, ventre ramulis curvulis crispulis telam spongiosam formantibus, margine ubique limbo e cellularum 3–4 lato pellucidiore distincto) ; *A. polyptera*, Mitt., from Magellan, collected in Cockle Cove by Dr. Coppinger, H.M.S. 'Alert' (frons 10 cm. alt., 2 cm. lat., ramis approximatis tripinnatis ubique lamina 5–6 cell. lata, limbatus dorso planus lævis ventre præcipue in ramis ramulisque lamellis angustis longitudinalibus vestitus) ; and *A. denticulata*, Mitt., from the Andes of Bogota, gathered amongst mosses by Weir (frons 5–6 cm. altus cum ramulis 1 cm. latus, ramis remotiusculis bipinnatis ubique limbo pellucidiore cell. 4 lato margine denticulis divaricatis angustis subciliatus). All these species show that in South America there is a development of larger forms than are yet known elsewhere.

BLEPHAROZIA RORAIMÆ. Folia erecto-patentia imbricata, cochleariformi-concava integerrima e lobulato obtusa ; involucralia conformia, perianthia (abortiva) cylindracea abrupta obtusissima, ore parvo rotundo.

From the top of Roraima, one stem only.

Entire plant of a dark red-brown colour, about 4 cm. high ; it is divided below into two, one branch being again forked, the leaves are imbricated in bifarious order and are repeatedly in interrupted series ; each innovation arises from towards one side of the dorsal base of the perianth with small leaves, which increase rapidly in size upwards, the largest being the involucral, here the greatest diameter is about 4 mm. : the perianths are also about 4 mm. long, and of these as many as four are observable on the undivided stem, and as each innovation arises from the same position, they stand at the side of the stem rather towards the ventral side ; in all particulars they closely resemble the abortive perianths seen on *B. sphagnoides* and other species ; the young innovation also closely agrees with that of the male amenta of that species ; but there is no trace of the lobule, which is not, as has been supposed, distinct from the leaf in *B. cochleariformis*, but is seen, from being an almost closed sac in some species, to be opened out in *B. evoluta*.

DESCRIPTION OF THE PLATES.

PLATE XXXVII.

Figs. 1–8. (A.) *Leitgebia Imthurniana*, Oliver, sp. n. 1, plant in flower; 2, leaf; 3, pedicel and calyx ; 4, bract ; 5, corona ; 6, two stamens and segment of corona ; 7, pistil ; 8, transverse section of ovary.

Figs. 9–17. (B.) *Bonnetia Roraimæ*, Oliver, sp. n. 9, plant in flower ; 10, leaf ; 11, flower ; 12, calyx ; 13, petal ; 14, phalange of stamens ; 15, a back and front view of stamen ; 16, pistil ; 17, transverse section of ovary.

Figs. 1 and 9 reduced sketches, fig. 8 nat. size ; all the other figures enlarged.

Plate XXXVIII.

Figs. 1–6. (A.) *Rareuia ruellioides*, Oliver, sp. n. 1, portion of plant in flower; 2, calyx and pistil; 3, corolla, laid open ; 4, anther, back and front ; 5, pistil; 6, vertical section of ovary and disk. All enlarged.

Figs. 7–13. (B.) *Myrcia* (§ *Aulomyrcia*) *Roraimæ*, Oliver, sp. n. 7, plant ; 8, bud ; 9, expanded flower ; 10, calyx, the petals and stamens removed ; 11, stamen, back and front; 12, longitudinal section of ovary and calyx-tube ; 13, transverse section of ovary.

Plate XXXIX.

Figs. 1–9. (A.) *Myrtus stenophylla*, Oliver, sp. n. 1, plant in flower and fruit; 2 & 3, leaf, above and below ; 4, expanded flower ; 5, calyx and bracteoles ; 6, stamen, front and back view ; 7, transverse section of ovary ; 8, fruit ; 9, seed. All enlarged.

Figs. 10–18. (B.) *Microlicia bryanthoides*, Oliver, sp. n. 10, plant in flower and fruit ; 11, leaves ; 12, bud ; 13, expanded flower ; 14, longer, 15, shorter stamens ; 16, apex of ovary and style ; 17, fruit ; 18, seed. All enlarged.

Plate XL.

Figs. 1–6. *Crepinella gracilis*, March., sp. n. 1, plant in flower ; 2, bud ; 3, expanded flower ; 4, stamen, front and back view ; 5, calyx-tube and ovary ; 6, longitudinal section of ovary. All enlarged.

Plate XLI.

Figs. 1–8. *Sciadophyllum coriaceum*, March., sp. n. 1, plant in flower; 2, bud ; 3, coherent petals ; 4, petal apart; 5, anther, back and front; 6, ovary ; 7, transverse section of ovary ; 8, young fruit. All enlarged.

Plate XLII.

Figs. 1–7. (A.) *Psychotria Imthurniana*, Oliver, sp. n. 1, plant in flower ; 2, stipules ; 3, expanded flower ; 4, corolla, laid open ; 5, stamen, back and front; 6, ovary and style ; 7, longitudinal section of ovary.

Figs. 8–15. (B.) *Psychotria concinna*, Oliver, sp. n. 8, plant in flower ; 9, stipules ; 10, flower ; 11, corolla, laid open ; 12, anther, back and front; 13, ovary and style ; 14, epigynous disk ; 15, longitudinal section of ovary. All enlarged.

Plate XLIII.

Figs. 1–8. (A.) *Baccharis Vitis-Idæa*, Oliver, sp. n. 1, male plant, and 2, female plant ; 3, male capitulum ; 4, floret ; 5, seta of pappus ; 6, stamens ; 7, style ; 8, female floret. All enlarged.

Figs. 9–16. (B.) *Calea ternifolia*, Oliver, sp. n. 9, plant in flower; 10 & 11, scales of involucre ; 12, palea of receptacle ; 13, floret ; 14, seta of pappus ; 15, anthers ; 16, style. All enlarged.

Plate XLIV.

Figs. 1–6. (A.) *Ledothamnus guyanensis*, Meissn. 1, plant in flower ; 2 & 3, leaves ; 4, sepal ; 5, stamens, front and back view : 6, pistil. All enlarged.

Figs. 7–11. (B.) *Utricularia* (§ *Orchidioides*) *Campbelliana*, Oliver, sp. n. 7, different views of plant in flower , 8, ampullæ; 9, calyx-lobe ; 10, lower lip of corolla and spur ?; 11, stamens. All enlarged.

PLATE XLV.

Figs. 1 & 2. *Tabebuia Roraimæ*, Oliver, sp. n. 1, plant in flower; 2, stamens. All enlarged.

PLATE XLVI.

Figs. 1-6. (A.) *Epidendrum Imthurnii*, Ridley, sp. n. 1, plant in flower; 2, flower; 3, labellum and column, front view; 4, ditto, side view; 5, anther-case; 6, pollinia. All enlarged.

Figs. 7-10. (B.) *Epidendrum violascens*, Ridley, sp. n. 7, plant in flower; 8, expanded flower; 9, same, posterior sepal and lateral petal attached; 10, fruiting specimen. Figs. 7 and 10 about nat. size, 8 and 9 are enlarged.

PLATE XLVII.

Figs. 1-6. *Zygopetalum venustum*, Ridley, sp. n. 1, plant in flower; 2, labellum and column; 3, labellum, side view; 4, column; 5, anther-case; 6, pollinium. All enlarged.

PLATE XLVIII.

Figs. 1-6. (A.) *Stenoptera adnata*, Ridley, sp. n. 1, plant in flower; 2, flower; 3, labellum; 4, column; 5, same, side view; 6, pollen. All enlarged.

Figs. 7-11. (B.) *Pelexia aphylla*, Ridley, sp. n. 7, plant in flower; 8, expanded flower; 9, longitudinal section of perianth-tube, with labellum; 10, column; 11, pollen. All enlarged.

PLATE XLIX.

Figs. 1-6. (A.) *Tofieldia Schomburgkiana*, Oliver, sp. n. 1, plant in flower; 2, fragment of leaf, showing ciliolate margin; 3, flower; 4, stamen; 5, pistil; 6, transverse section of ovary. All enlarged.

Figs. 7-14. (B.) *Pæpalanthus Roraimæ*, Oliver, sp. n. 7, plant; 8, outer smaller, and inner larger involucral bracts; 9, staminate flower and bracteole; 10, same, expanded; 11, inner perianth-segment and adnate stamen; 12, stamen, back and front view; 13, pistillate flower; 14, pistil. All enlarged.

PLATE L.

Figs. 1-8. (A.) *Xyris setigera*, Oliver, sp. n. 1, plant in flower; 2, fragment of leaf, showing setose margin; 3, involucral bract; 4, flower; 5, perianth, laid open; 6, stamen; 7, penicillate staminodia; 8, style-branches. All enlarged.

Figs. 9-15. (B.) *Xyris witsenioides*, Oliver, sp. n. 9, plant in flower; 10 & 11, involucral scales; 12, perianth, laid open; 13, 13 a, anthers, back and front; 14, staminode; 15, pistil. All enlarged.

PLATE LI.

Figs. 1-6. *Cryptangium stellatum*, Bœckl. 1, plant; 2, branchlet of inflorescence; 3, spikelet; 4 & 5, outer and inner glumes; 6, anther. All enlarged.

PLATE LII.

Figs. 1-8. *Everardia montana*, Ridley, sp. n. 1, plant; 2, branchlet of inflorescence; 3, male spikelet; 4, florets; 5, glume; 6, stamens; 7, female spikelet; 8, pistil and hypogynous setæ. Fig. 1 about nat. size, all others enlarged.

PLATE LIII.

Figs. 1, 2. *Gymnogramme* (§ *Pterozonium*) *cyclophylla*, Baker, sp. n. 1, plant; 2, portion of frond, enlarged.

PLATE LIV.

Figs. 1–5. *Gymnogramme* (§ *Pterozonium*) *elaphoglossoides*, Baker, sp. n. 1, upper, 2, lower surface of frond; 3, palea; 4, portion of frond, showing venation and position of sori; 5, rootstock. Figs. 3 and 4 enlarged.

PLATE LV.

Figs. 1–5. *Enterosora Campbellii*, Baker, gen. nov. 1, plant; 2, palea; 3, portion of frond, showing venation and sori; 4, horizontal section of a frond; 5, portion of same, much enlarged.

PLATE LVI.

Figs. 1–7. (A.) *Selaginella* (§ *Stachygynandrum*) *vernicosa*, Baker, sp. n. 1, plant; 2, fertile branch; 3, front view of portion of stem, and 4, back view of same; 5, stipule (or smaller leaf); 6, bract; 7, capsule.
Fig. 8. (B.) *Selaginella* (§ *Stachygynandrum*) *vernicosa*, var. *oligoclada*.
Figs. 9–14. (C.) *Selaginella* (§ *Stachygynandrum*) *roraimensis*, Baker, sp. n. 9, plant; 10, fertile branch; 11, back of stem; 12, leaf; 13, stipule; 14, bract with capsule.
Figs. 1, 8, and 9 of natural size, all the others enlarged.

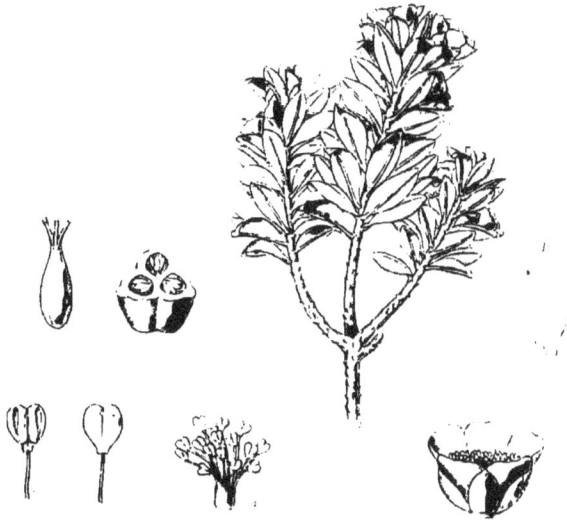

1
3   2   4   5   6

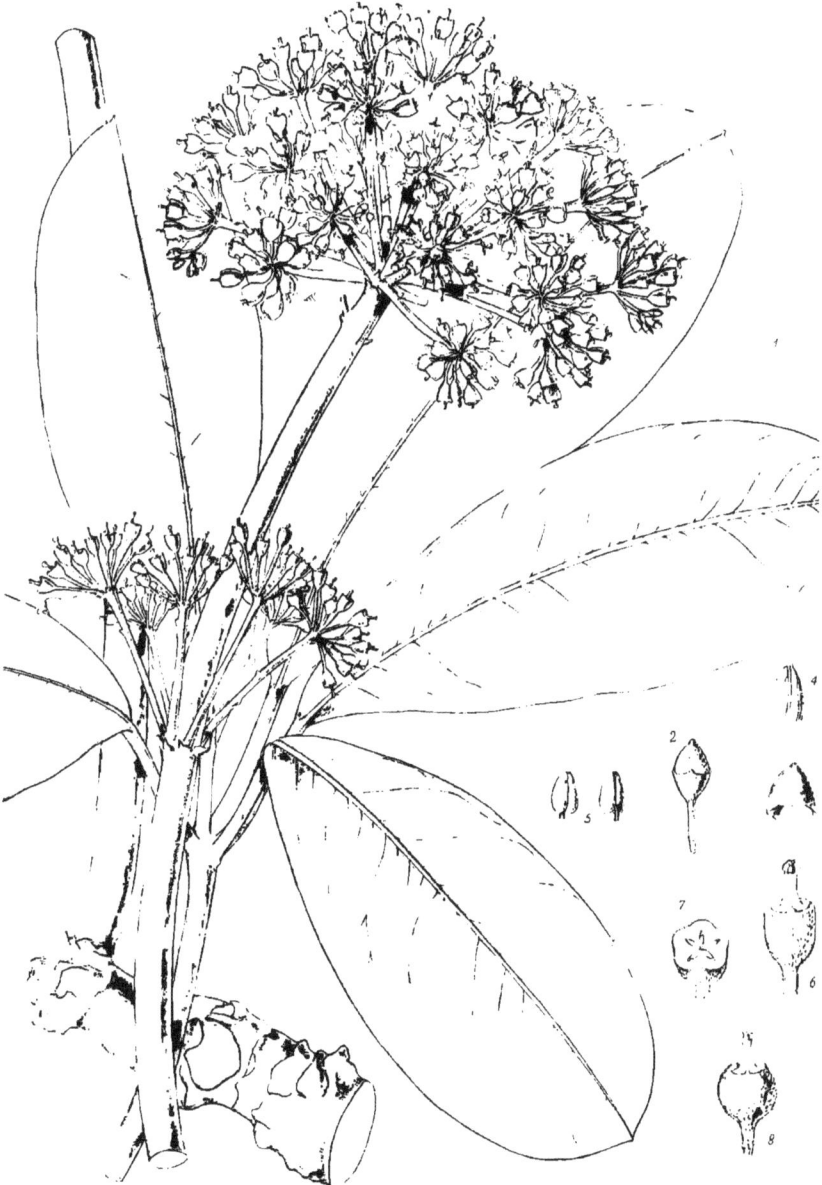

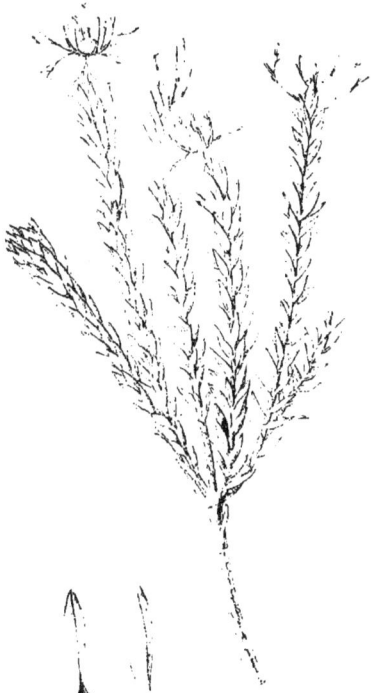

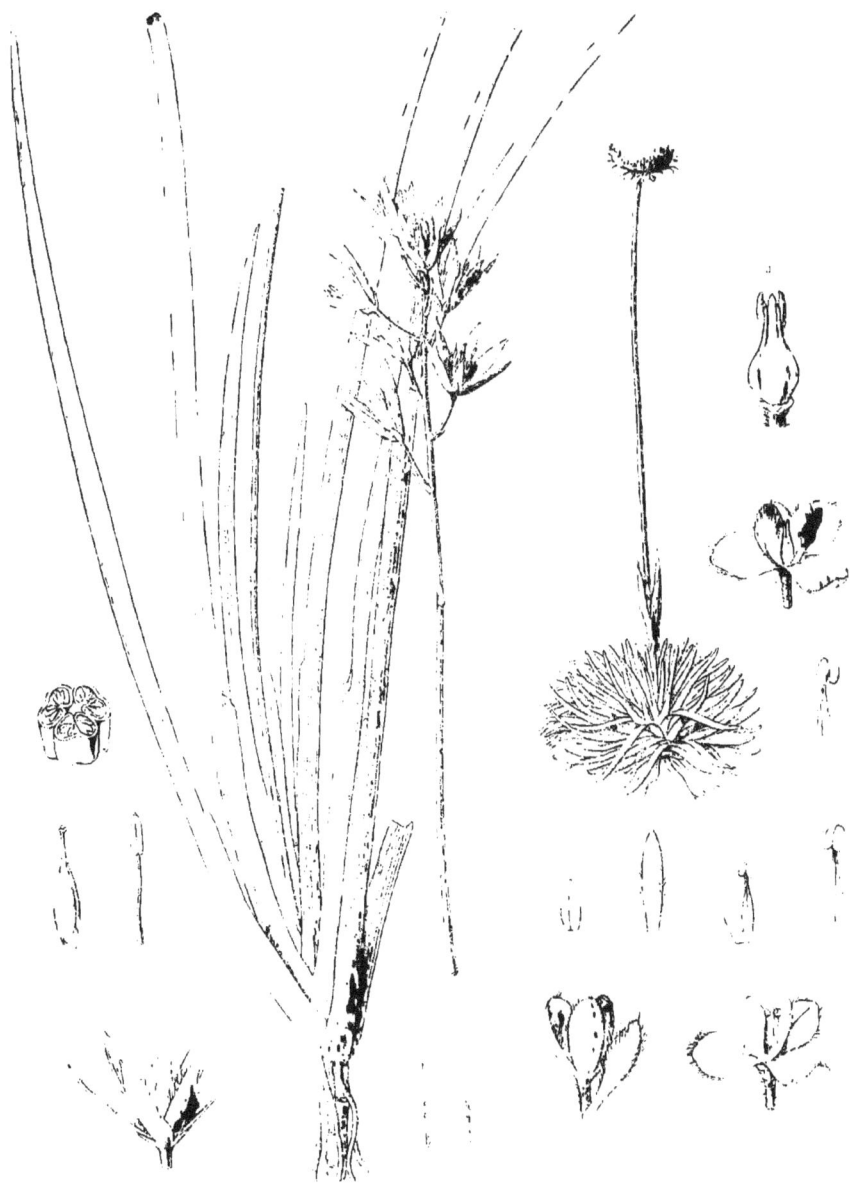

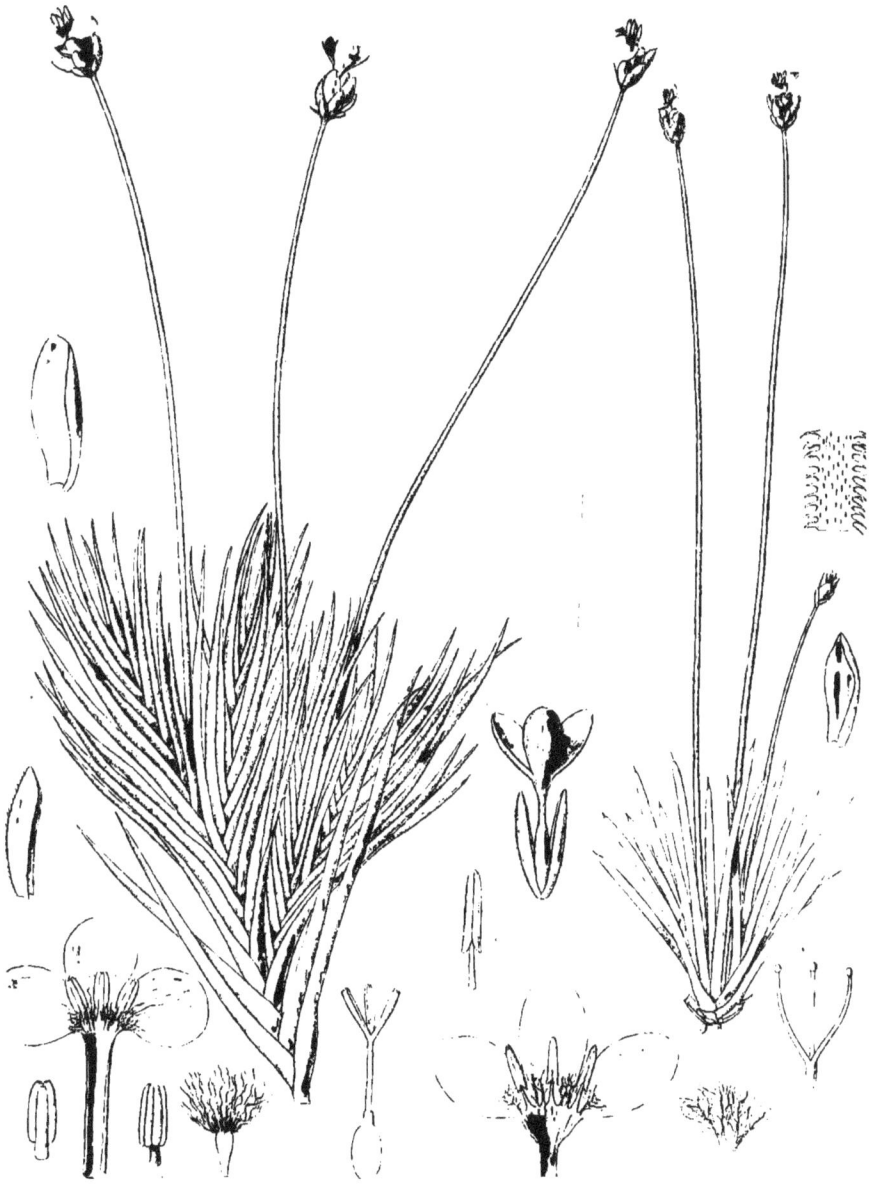

2

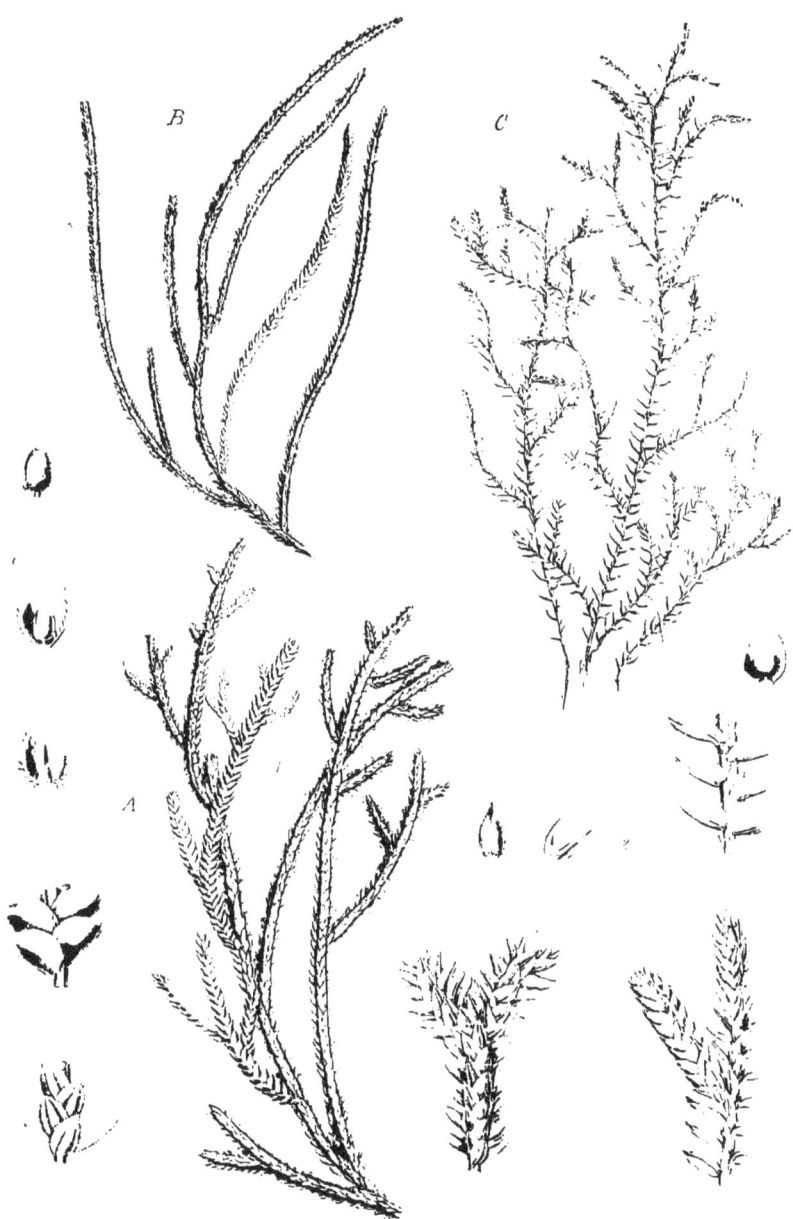

LINNEAN SOCIETY OF LONDON.

MEMORANDA CONCERNING PUBLICATIONS.

JOURNALS.—The first VIII. volumes contain papers both on Botany and Zoology, and each volume is divided into *Four* parts at 3s. each, or 12s. per vol. From Vol. IX. the Zoological and Botanical sections have been published separately, and each consists of Eight numbers at 2s., or 16s. per vol. From Vol. XIV. Zoology, and Vol. XVII. Botany, each separate number is 3s. to the public and 2s. 3d. to Fellows, or the volume 24s. to the public, and 18s. to Fellows.

TRANSACTIONS.—The First Series of the Transactions, containing both Botanical and Zoological contributions, has been completed in 30 Vols., and a few entire sets are still for sale. Only certain single volumes, or parts to complete sets, may be obtained at the original prices. The price of the Index to Vols. 1–25 is 8s. to the public, and 6s. to Fellows; to Vols. 26–30, 4s. to the public, and 3s. to Fellows.

The Second Series of the Transactions is divided into Zoological and Botanical sections. The prices of the various parts which have been published of these are as undermentioned :—

Volume.	When Published.	Price to the Public.	Price to Fellows.	Volume.	When Published.	Price to the Public.	Price to Fellows.
		£ s. d.	£ s. d.			£ s. d.	£ s. d.
SECOND SERIES.—ZOOLOGY.				**SECOND SERIES.—ZOOLOGY** (*continued*).			
I. Part I.	1875.	1 4 0	0 18 0	III. Part 1.	1884.	1 14 0	1 5 6
Part II.	1875.	0 6 0	0 4 6	Part II.	1884.	1 12 0	1 4 0
Part III.	1876.	1 8 0	1 1 0	Part III.	1885.	1 10 0	1 2 6
Part IV.	1877.	0 16 0	0 12 0	Part IV.	1885.	0 8 0	0 6 0
Part V.	1877.	0 18 0	0 13 6	IV. Part I.	1886.	1 4 0	0 18 0
Part VI.	1877.	1 2 0	0 16 6	**SECOND SERIES.—BOTANY.**			
Part VII.	1878.	1 16 0	1 7 0	I. Part I.	1875.	0 8 0	0 6 0
Part VIII.	1879.	1 0 0	0 15 0	Part II.	1875.	0 16 0	0 12 0
II. Part I.	1879.	1 4 0	0 18 0	Part III.	1876.	0 12 0	0 9 0
Part II.	1881.	0 15 0	0 11 6	Part IV.	1876.	0 10 0	0 7 6
Part III.	1882.	1 8 0	1 1 0	Part V.	1878.	1 4 0	0 18 0
Part IV.	1882.	0 7 6	0 5 6	Part VI.	1879.	1 6 0	0 19 6
Part V.	1882.	0 3 0	0 2 3	Part VII.	1880.	1 4 0	0 18 0
Part VI.	1883.	1 0 0	0 15 0	Part VIII.	1880.	1 1 0	0 16 0
Part VII.	1883.	0 5 0	0 3 9	Part IX.	1880.	1 0 0	0 15 0
Part VIII.	1883.	0 3 0	0 2 3	II. Part I.	1881.	0 12 0	0 9 0
Part IX.	1883.	0 3 0	0 2 3	Part II.	1882.	0 5 0	0 3 9
Part X.	1884.	0 4 6	0 3 6	Part III.	1883.	0 10 0	0 7 6
Part XI.	1884.	0 10 0	0 7 6	Part IV.	1883.	0 3 0	0 2 3
Part XII.	1885.	0 6 0	0 4 6	Part V.	1883.	0 3 0	0 2 3
Part XIII.	1884.	0 6 0	0 4 6	Part VI.	1884.	0 13 6	0 10 0
Part XIV.	1885.	0 6 0	0 4 6	Part VII.	1884.	0 9 6	0 7 0
Part XV.	1885.	0 4 6	0 3 6	Part VIII.	1884.	0 10 0	0 7 6
Part XVI.	1885.	0 5 0	0 3 9	Part IX.	1886.	0 7 0	0 5 0
Part XVII.	1886.	0 3 0	0 2 3	Part X.	1887.	0 3 4	0 2 6
				Part XI.	1886.	0 6 0	0 4 6
				Part XII.	1886.	0 8 0	0 6 0
				Part XIII.	1887.	1 7 0	1 0 0

2nd Ser. BOTANY.]   [VOL. VI. PART 1.

THE

TRANSACTIONS

OF

THE LINNEAN SOCIETY OF LONDON.

REPORT ON TWO BOTANICAL COLLECTIONS MADE BY MESSRS. F. V. McCONNELL AND J. J. QUELCH AT MOUNT RORAIMA IN BRITISH GUIANA.

BY

N. E. BROWN, A.L.S., & others.

(*Communicated by* Sir W. Thiselton-Dyer, K.C.M.G., F.R.S.)

LONDON:

PRINTED FOR THE LINNEAN SOCIETY

BY TAYLOR AND FRANCIS, RED LION COURT, FLEET STREET.

SOLD AT THE SOCIETY'S APARTMENTS, BURLINGTON-HOUSE, PICCADILLY, W.,

AND BY LONGMANS, GREEN, AND CO., PATERNOSTER-ROW.

January 1901.

TRANSACTIONS

THE LINNEAN SOCIETY.

I. *Report on two Botanical Collections made by* Messrs. F. V. McConnell *and* J. J. Quelch *at Mount Roraima in British Guiana. By* N. E. Brown, *A.L.S., and others.* (*Communicated by Sir* William Thiselton-Dyer, *K.C.M.G., F.R.S., F.L.S., Director of the Royal Botanic Gardens, Kew.*)

(Plates I.-XIV.)

Read 15th March, 1900.

CONTENTS.

INTRODUCTION.

By I. H. Burkill, M.A., F.L.S.

In the autumn of 1894 Messrs. F. V. McConnell and J. J. Quelch first visited Roraima : they were there again in the autumn of 1898, and on both occasions not only encamped higher on the slopes of the mountain than any previous traveller, but they spent nights on the summit in order that the time given to collecting its flora and fauna should be uninterrupted. The collections of plants were transmitted to Kew, and both are enumerated in this paper.

In 1894 the journey to Roraima commenced (October 16) at Kwaimatta, a village on the open savannah to the south-east in latitude 3° 50′ N. The Ireng was crossed at the Karona Falls, the Kotinga at Sokoking, a ford not named on the older maps, but situated a little to the south of the meeting of the Kotinga and Karakanang streams. Thence the way led into the Arabapu Valley (November 3), on the north and west sides of which rise the slopes of Roraima. The return journey was commenced on November 11, and the route taken crossed the Kotinga nearer its source at Orinidoni (apparently the "Orinidouk" of the old maps), and the Ireng again at the Karona Falls.

In 1898 the journey was commenced (August 20) on the lower Mazaruni River. The great bend of this river, where the Peaiman Falls occur, was avoided by a porterage from the Kurubung Creek to the upper Mazaruni, which was again left by the Kako River; the Kako was paddled up until a point was reached about twenty miles north-east of Roraima, and thence, leaving the canoes, a track through dense forest was taken until, in the second week of October, the south-eastern face of the mountain was reached. Roraima was left again at the end of October, and the way retraced to the lower Mazaruni.

Three days in 1894, nine in 1898, were spent in making collections upon the broken plateau which forms the summit of Roraima.

VISITORS TO RORAIMA.

	Year.	Month.	Height reached.	Route to Roraima.	Return Journey.
R. H. Schomburgk	1838	Nov.	Base of Mountain.	From S. over Hamirida Mtns.	Retraced steps.
R. H. and Richard Schomburgk.	1842	End Oct. to Dec. 5. End Oct. to Nov. 22.	Base of cliff on S. side.	ditto.	At first S., then to W. of Roraima. Retraced steps.
Karl Appun	1864	End Jan. to end Feb.	Base of cliff on E. and S. sides.	From N. over Merume Mtns.	Towards S.E. to Pirara.
C. B. Brown and J. G. Sawkins.	1869	Early Feb.	Upper slopes.	From S.E.	
J. W. Boddam-Whetham and M. McTurk.	1878	March.	ditto.	From N. over Merume Mtns.	Retraced steps.
D. Burke	1881		ditto.		
Siedel	1884	Feb. to Apr. and Nov.	ditto.	From N.	
E. F. im Thurn and H. I. Perkins.	1884	Nov. to Dec.	Summit from the S. side.	From R. Potaro to Ireng, then to Roraima from S.E.	Retraced steps.
E. Kromer	1886	Nov.	ditto.		
Dressel	1887	Oct.	ditto.	From N. over Merume Mtns.	
F. V. McConnell and J. J. Quelch.	1894	Nov.	ditto.	From S.E.	To S.E. by a somewhat parallel track.
F. V. McConnell and J. J. Quelch.	1898	Oct.	ditto.	From N. over Merume Mtns.	Retraced steps.

Appearance and Structure of Roraima, and its Geographical Relations to the Mountain-systems of South America.—Im Thurn and Perkins, who made the first ascent on December 18, 1884, reached the top under unfavourable conditions: they had ascended that day from their base-camp at 5400 feet, and only reached the summit in the afternoon, when clouds almost invariably envelop it; they had no means of remaining there, and were forced to return after a very short stay of three hours. Perkins speaks of these clouds as impenetrable (Proc. Roy. Geogr. Soc. vii. 1885, p. 532) [*]; at all events they limited the range of exploration, and the report was made that "the vegetation on the summit is extremely scanty and insignificant, there being no trees, only small bushes from three to six feet in height, growing at long intervals." It has been reserved for McConnell and Quelch to ascertain that there exist in favoured places trees which attain a height of no less than forty feet.

Of the ascents of Dressel and Kromer I can glean no more than is in a brief notice in 'Timehri,' 1887, p. 330. Neither can have remained on the summit for more than a few hours.

The features of this summit are:—Blackened elevated ridges, irregularly terraced and rugged; winding gullies which drain away the superabundant rain through shallow pools; patches of sand in their shelter with isolated small bushes; clumps of vegetation lodged in the most protected spots; piles of wind-cut rocks without a sign of plant-life, rising into pinnacles; no soil; the keen northerly wind, and mists which gather at least after noon on almost every day in the whole year. The highest pinnacle rises to 8740 feet; the deepest gully may be 400 feet below it.

The known sides of the mountain which face north-east and south-east, produce rocky savannah up to 5000 or 5400 feet, the rocks so numerous that Appun likens the country to a grave-yard; then forest to 7100 feet, dense below but stunted and more open above; and from this altitude rise the precipitous cliffs, which give to the whole the appearance of a vast fortress with a tree-clad glacis slope.

These precipices were deemed impossible of ascent by the travellers they had baffled until Whitely indicated, and im Thurn showed practicable, the one known ledge leading to the summit.

The rock is a quartzose sandstone interbedded with diorite. The topmost and thickest bed of diorite comes to the surface where the dense forest is; the lower beds make a series of terraces down the lower slopes. These beds lie perfectly horizontal without folding or other sign of any great disturbance. Diorite lends itself to the formation of a soil [†], the sandstone does not.

Such sandstones as constitute Roraima have a very wide extension in South America; they pass eastward into Surinam; Duida is made of them; they form the bed-rock of the llanos of Venezuela, and appear in the Caripe mountains to the east of Caracas; in Brazil the area occupied by them is immense.

[*] *Cf.* im Thurn in 'Timehri,' 1885, p. 41.
[†] The Indians prepare their provision-grounds on the diorite (see Brown & Sawkins, Reports, p. 17), and those living under the south-eastern face of Roraima have placed them far up the sister-mountain of Kukenaam, where the diorite comes to the surface (Quelch, in 'Timehri,' 1895, p. 164).

All this sandstone area belongs to the oldest land of South America: against the edge of it the Andes were heaped up—newer land which grew to its present form in the tertiary period, and formed a link of high ground round the head of the then existing Amazon valley.

It is significant to us that the chief mountain-systems of South America outside the Andes reach very similar heights and similarly stand more or less parallel to the nearest coast, whence the trade-winds bring an abundance of rain. These mountain-systems are three: (1) the Coast Andes of Venezuela, of direct eruptive origin, but continued eastward from Caracas in the lesser sandstone mountains of Caripe; (2) the Parime mountains with Roraima at the eastern end and Duida at the western end; and (3) the mountains of South Brazil formed of schists tipped at a high angle.

Heights * north of the Equator.

Coast Andes.		Parime Mountains.	
Niaguata	9125 feet.	Roraima	8740 feet.
Silla of Caracas	8741 ,,	Duida	8278 ,,
Tamaya	8052 ,,	[Peaks near Duida estimated at 10,000 feet.]	

Heights * in South Brazil.

Itatiaia	8999 feet.	Itambe	5960 feet.
Organ Mountains	6609 ,, and more.	Serra da Piedada	5874 ,,
Serra da Caraça	6441 ,,	Itacolumi	5760 ,,

Unlike in geological structure the three systems are unlike as well in their relation to the Andes. The Casiquiare, by uniting the Orinoco and Amazon, encircles the Parime mountains, and the undulating country of little elevation to the west of it effectually separates this system from the Andes; the plains of Matto Grosso, &c., wherein rise within a few miles of each other the Paraguay and Madeira, to flow the one north, the other south, separate the Brazilian mountains and the Andes; but the Venezuelan coast-range is most intimately bound to the Andes proper through the Cordillera of Merida.

Spanish settlers in the New World soon came to recognize a belt on the mountains of the tropics suited to their needs and for the growth of their food-plants. They called it the temperate land—" tierra templada,"—and the range of its mean annual temperature may be set down as 15°–20° C. (59 –77° F.). Above the " tierra templada " is the " tierra fria," below it the " tierra caliente."

The limits of these belts depend on exposure. In the Venezuelan mountains, according to Sievers (' Venezuela,' p. 26), the " tierra fria " extends from about 7200 feet upwards; among the Great Andes it sometimes commences as high as 10,000 feet; on Roraima

---

* The heights of the Coast Andes are taken from Sievers's ' Venezuela' (Hamburg, 1888), pp. 277, 278; those of Duida and neighbouring peaks from Sir Robert Schomburgk's narrative in Proc. Roy. Geogr. Soc. x. 1840, p. 245; and those of the Brazilian mountains, Itambe excepted, from Liais, 'Climats, Géologie, Faune et Géographie botanique du Brésil' (Paris, 1872), pp. 45–49. Most astounding are the erroneous statements published regarding the altitudes of the Brazilian mountains; for instance, the Serra dos Pyrenaos, estimated previously to reach 9760 feet, proves to be no more than 4543 feet (Cruls, ' Relatorio da Commisão exploradora,' Rio, 1894, p. 26).

it descends presumedly into the forest-belt or to the base of the cliffs *. Roraima bears the most eastern patch of " tierra fria " upon the northern side of the Amazon.

Some hundreds of feet above the commencement of the " tierra fria " is the limit of trees. There are reasons for believing that both the Coast Andes and Roraima just reach this limit ; they do not distinctly rise above it.

The Flora.—Passing on to a consideration of the nature of the flora of Roraima I have given in the table on pp. 8-16 as complete a list as is now possible of the species found on the mountain above 5000 feet, and we have in it :

239 Spermatophyta, of which 121 (50·6 per cent.) are endemic.
88 Pteridophyta, of which 16 (18·2 per cent.) are endemic.
63 Bryophyta, of which 15 (23·8 per cent.) are endemic.
11 Thallophyta, of which 3 (27·3 per cent.) are endemic.

The proportion of endemic Spermatophyta may seem large, but does not exceed that on record for some of the mountains of Mexico. Of far greater interest is the number of endemic genera. The law that mountains by their isolation and extension, as well as by their latitude, produce endemic genera, is illustrated by their number in the ranges of Cis-equatorial South America ; thus, there are eleven among the Spermatophyta on Roraima, and only two on the Coast Andes, which are comparatively small and not isolated ; but I am aware of no fewer than thirty-six in the extensive Andes of Colombia, including with them the Cordillera of Merida.

The endemic genera of Roraima are enumerated on p. 7. They belong to as many orders. One of them—*Heliamphora*—has no kindred in South America, but belongs, like *Cyrilla*, to a North-American group ; all the rest have more or less close allies in genera of the South-American continent. *Ledothamnus*, however, deserves further remark because it is one of the very few Ericaceæ with ericoid leaves which exist in the New World.

* This belief is based chiefly upon the nature of the flora. With regard to temperature the following may be added :—Hann (' Handbuch der Climatologie,' Stuttgart, 1883, p. 152), after quoting Boussingault's estimate for the Andes of the tropics that ·57° C. in mean annual temperature is lost for every 100 metres ascended, and Humboldt's for Mexico and Colombia of ·53° C. for every 100 metres, adds : " as a general rule for the tropics one may allow ·58° C. for the amount of heat lost in every 100 metres ascended." This is equivalent to ·4° F. for every 100 feet. As the mean annual temperature of Demerara is 81 , we obtain for Roraima these figures :—65° F. at 4000 feet, 60° at 5400, 53 at 7100, 47° at 8600, and 46 at 8710 feet. The following are all the recorded observations of which I am aware :—

	Night.	6 8 A.M.	Midday and afternoon.
Summit, Quelch in 1894	47° F.	49·52° F.	61·5 F.
„ „ im Thurn		....	51° (in mist).
About 7000 ft., Appun	50°		
About 6400 ft., Quelch	50		
About 5400 ft., R. Schomburgk	52°		
„ „ „ im Thurn	48°		
At the base, R. Schomburgk	58 and below	62°	{ 87° (shade).
			{ 100° (sun).
„ „ „	58·5		
„ „ Brown	....	59°	
„ „ Boddam-Whetham	below 60		
„ „ Quelch	54°		

The endemic genera of the Coast Andes are *Enosmia* and *Caracasia*. *Enosmia*, Humb. & Bonpl., belongs to the Rubiaceæ, and was found by Humboldt and Bonpland in the mountains of Caripe ; it is a little obscure and needs re-examination. *Caracasia*, Szyszy. (*Fargasia*, Ernst) is a genus of the Marcgraviæ, with two species found near Caracas ; it is nearly related to the genus *Ruyschia*, found in the West Indies and from Guiana to Peru.

Following the list of endemic genera on p. 7 are three lists to be considered together. All are of genera represented in the tierra fria of the Andes : the first contains seven found on Roraima, throughout the Andes to Chili, and in South Brazil ; the second contains fourteen found on Roraima and in the Northern Andes, but reaching neither Chili nor the mountains of South Brazil ; the third list contains thirteen found in the Andes, which have passed along the Coast Andes to Niaguata or the Silla of Caracas*, but have not yet been found on Roraima.

These lists illustrate two points :—in the first place, they indicate how the Coast Andes belong essentially to the Andes proper,—and the community of genera extends to species in *Cinchona*, *Acæna*, *Cardamine*, and *Berberis* ; in the second place, that Roraima and the mountains of South Brazil only have in common among woody plants montane genera so widely Andine as to pass from Colombia to Chili. One is then led to suspect that the mountains near Rio de Janeiro obtained their Andine shrubby genera from the south-west, and that in their case the plains of Matto Grosso have been a very similar barrier to immigration as the wooded hills on the west of the Casiquiare have been to the Parime mountains.

Six more genera are named in a last list ; they are common to Roraima and to the mountains of South Brazil, without reaching Chili ; but they all descend to low levels in the Province of Alto Amazonas, and obviously are not montane in a restricted sense.

Other genera which cannot be regarded as truly montane, contribute montane forms to the flora of Roraima. The most notable of these is *Abolboda*, of which genus *A. Sceptrum* is by far the largest species.

Saxofredericia regalis is, like *Abolboda Sceptrum*, the largest of its genus. *Lisianthus Elizabethæ* and another species collected under this name by Appun are among the largest-flowered of these gentians ; and *Utricularia Humboldtii* so impressed Sir Robert Schomburgk by its showy blossoms as to cause him to name the place where he first saw it (the El Dorado Swamp), after the treasure-city Raleigh and others sought in Guiana.

im Thurn has suggested a resemblance between the floras of Roraima and the Brazilian mountains (Trans. Linn. Soc., ser. II. Bot. ii. (1887), p. 257), but the similarities he notes are much more due to similarities of climate than to any evidently intimate relationship between them in times past.

A very rough estimate of the number of genera of Spermatophyta in the flora of British Guiana places the total at 1070. The orders most strongly represented are :—Leguminosæ 86, Orchidaceæ 66, Rubiaceæ 54, Compositæ 44, Gramineæ 43, Euphorbiaceæ 31, and Melastomaceæ 28. On Roraima above 5000 feet, the order

---

* Ernst in Journ. Bot. x. 1872, p. 261 ; in Bull. Soc. Bot. France, xxii. Rev. Bibl. p. 239 ; in ' Idea general de la Flora de Venezuela ' in ' Estudios sobre la Flora y Fauna de Venezuela ' (Caracas, 1877), pp. 212-235 ; and elsewhere.

Endemic Genera (2 occur on the Kaieteur Savannah).

Heliamphora (Sarraceniaceæ).
Leitgebia (Violaceæ).
Blepharandra (Malpighiaceæ).
Crepinella (Araliaceæ).
Chalepophyllum (Rubiaceæ).
Quelchia (Compositæ).

Notopora (Vacciniaceæ).
Ledothamnus (Ericaceæ).
Connellia (Bromeliaceæ).
Nietneria (Liliaceæ).
Everardia (Cyperaceæ).
[Enterosora (Filices)].

Genus found at either end of the Parime Mountains.
Stegolepis (Rapateaceæ).

Genera of the Andes (as regards S. America) extending from the North to Chile, also to Roraima and the Mountains of South Brazil.

Drimys (Magnoliaceæ)
? Monnina (Polygalaceæ).
Weinmannia (Saxifrageæ).
Relbunium (Rubiaceæ).

Gaultheria (Ericaceæ).
Pernettya (Ericaceæ).
Puya (Bromeliaceæ).

Genera of the Northern Andes (as regards S. America), not overpassing Bolivia southwards, reaching Roraima, but not South Brazil.

Chætolepis (Melastomaceæ).
Centronia (Melastomaceæ).
Monochætum (Melastomaceæ).
Viburnum (Caprifoliaceæ).
Psammisia (Vacciniaceæ).
Cavendishia (Vacciniaceæ).
Vaccinium (Vacciniaceæ).

Sophoclesia (Vacciniaceæ).
Sphyrospermum (Vacciniaceæ).
Befaria (Ericaceæ).
Grammadenia (Myrsinaceæ).
Scaphosepalum (Orchidaceæ).
Lepanthes (Orchidaceæ).
Tofieldia (Liliaceæ).

Genera extending from the Andes along the Coast Andes of Venezuela to the Neighbourhood of Caracas, but not yet found on the Parime Mountains.

Berberis (Berberidaceæ).
Cardamine (Cruciferæ).
Arenaria (Caryophyllaceæ).
Adesmia (Leguminosæ).
Acæna (Rosaceæ).
Potentilla (Rosaceæ).
Escallonia (Saxifragaceæ).

Sedum (Crassulaceæ).
Cinchona (Rubiaceæ).
Galium (Rubiaceæ).
Espeletia (Compositæ).
Gaylussacia (Vacciniaceæ).
Muehlenbergia (Gramineæ).

Genera found on Roraima and the Mountains of South Brazil, avoiding the Chilian Andes, but occurring at low levels in Alto Amazonas, &c.

Remijia (Rubiaceæ).
Ladenbergia (Rubiaceæ).
Stifftia (Compositæ).

Hedyosmum (Chloranthaceæ).
Masdevallia (Orchidaceæ).
Stenoptera (Orchidaceæ).

of the Orchidaceæ comes first, Melastomaceæ second, Compositæ third, and Rubiaceæ and Gramineæ bracketed fourth.

It is unfortunate that all the plants collected on the upper parts of Roraima have been gathered in the last three months of the year. February brings to Roraima a few bare trees (Appun, 'Unten den Tropen,' ii. p. 226): March brings copious Gesnerads into flower, at least at the foot of the mountain (Boddam-Whetham, 'Roraima'); and April is a month producing more flowers than November (Siedel *fide* im Thurn in Trans. Linn. Soc., ser. II. ii. p. 250); but I am unable to record anything collected above 5000 feet during these months.

In conclusion, my thanks for help are due to Messrs. McConnell, Quelch, and C. B. Clarke, to my colleagues, and also to Professor T. McKenny Hughes and Dr. William Pollard.

The Flora of Roraima above 5000 feet, as now known, with the Geographical Distribution of each Species.

		N. Brazil.	S. Brazil, Paraguay.	Columbia to Bolivia.	Venezuela and Trinidad.	W. Indies.	Central America.	Elsewhere in America.	Old World.
MAGNOLIACEÆ.									
Drimys granatensis, Mutis	Ledge.			*	*	*		*	S.
SARRACENIACEÆ.									
Heliamphora nutans, Benth.	to Summit.								
VIOLACEÆ.									
Sauvagesia erecta, Linn.	to Ledge.	*	*	*	*	*	*	*	*
Leitgebia lutheraiana, Oliver......	Ledge & Summit.								
POLYGALEÆ.									
Polygala glochidiata, H. B. & K.....	to 5400 ft.	*	*	*	*	*	*		
„ *hygrophila*, H. B. & K.....	to 5400 ft.	*	*	*	*				
„ *longicaulis*, H. B. & K.....	to 5400 ft.	*	*	*	*	*			
„ *variabilis?*, H. B. & K.....	to 5400 ft.	*	*	..	*				
Moninia cacumina, N. E. Br.	Summit.								
GUTTIFERÆ.									
Marumbea intermedia, Engl.	at 5400 ft.								
Clusia palmicida, Rich.	to 6000 ft.	*			*				
TERNSTRŒMIACEÆ.									
Marcgravia sp.....	at 5400 ft.								
Bonnetia Roraimæ, Oliver	Summit.								
Archytaa multiflora, Benth.	to 6000 ft.								
MALVACEÆ.									
Sida linifolia, Benth.	to 5400 ft.	*	*	*	*	*	*		Africa.
MALPIGHIACEÆ.									
Byrsonima crassifolia, H. B. & K. ..	to 5400 ft.	*	*	*	*	*	*		
Heteropteris oleifolia, Griseb.......	to Upper slopes.								
Tetrapteris rhodopteron, Oliver	to 5400 ft.								
„ sp.	to 5400 ft.								
RUTACEÆ.									
Ravenia rutlioides, Oliver	Upper slope.								
ILICACEÆ.									
Ilex retusa, Klotzsch	to Summit.								
„ *apicidens*, N. E. Br.	Summit.								
„ *vacciniifolia*, Klotzsch	to 6000 ft.								

		N. Brazil	S. Brazil, Paraguay	Colombia to Bolivia	Venezuela and Trinidad	W. Indies	Central America	Elsewhere in America	Old World
CYRILLACEÆ.									
Cyrilla brevifolia, N. E. Br.........	Summit.								
LEGUMINOSÆ.									
Swartzia sp.....................	at 5000 ft.								
Cassia insignis, N. E. Br.	to Upper slopes.								
,, polystachya, Benth........	to Upper slopes.								
Pithecolobium ferrugineum, Benth. ...	to Upper slopes.								
ROSACEÆ.									
Rubus guianensis, Focke	to 7100 ft.								
,, urticæfolius, Poir...........	to 7100 ft.	*	*	*				*	
SAXIFRAGACEÆ.									
Weinmannia guyanensis, Klotzsch ..	to Summit.								
,, elliptica, H. B. & K. ..	to 6000 ft.				*				
,, jayuroides, H. B. & K.	Summit.				*				
DROSERACEÆ.									
Drosera communis, St. Hil.	to Summit.	*	*	*	*	*	*		
MYRTACEÆ.									
Myrtus myrcioides, H. B. & K.	to Summit.				*		*		
,, roraimensis, N. E. Br.......	Summit.								
,, stenophylla, Oliver	Ledge.								
MELASTOMACEÆ.									
Microlicia bryanthoides, Oliver	to Summit.								
Cambessedesia Roraimæ, Rich. Schomb.	to 6000 ft.								
Siphanthera microliciaides, Cogn. ..	to 5400 ft.								
Macairea aspera, N. E. Br.	Upper slopes.								
Tibouchina fraterna, N. E. Br.	Upper slopes.								
,, lasiophylla, Cogn.	to 5400 ft.								
,, aspera, Aubl.	to 5400 ft.	*	*	*					
Chætolepis anisandra, Naud.	to Ledge.								
Marcetia taxifolia, DC.	to 7100 ft.	*	*						
,, juniperina, DC.	Summit.			*	*				
Monochætum Bonplandii, Naud.	to Summit.			*	*				
Meriania sp.	at 6000 ft.								
Centronia crassicaulis, Triana	at 5750 ft.								
Miconia tinifolia, Naud.	to Summit.				*				
,, holosericea, DC.	Upper slopes.	*	*	*	*				
,, fothergilla, Naud.	to 5400 ft.	*	*	*	*	*	*		
Tococa aristata, Benth.	to 6000 ft.	*	*	*	*				
,, guyanensis, Aubl...........	to 6000 ft.	*	*	*	*				
,, nitens, Triana	to 6000 ft.	*		*	*				
Clidemia capitata, Benth.	to 6000 ft.				*				*
PASSIFLORACEÆ.									
Passiflora, 2 (possibly 3) species....	about 5400 ft.								
BEGONIACEÆ.									
Begonia tovarensis, Klotzsch	at 5400 ft.			*	*				
ARALIACEÆ.									
Didymopanax rugosum, N. E. Br. ..	Summit.								
Sciadophyllum coriaceum, March. ...	to 5400 ft.								
,, umbellatum, N. E. Br.	Upper slopes.								
Crepinella gracilis, March.	Summit.								
CAPRIFOLIACEÆ.									
Viburnum glabratum, H. B. & K. ..	to 7100 ft.			*	*		*		
RUBIACEÆ.									
Remijia Roraimæ, K. Schum.	to 6000 ft.	*							
,, tenuiflora, Benth.	to 6000 ft.	*							
,, densiflora, Benth.	to 6000 ft.								
Ladenbergia Lambertiana, Klotzsch	to 6000 ft.	*							
Chalepophyllum speciosum, N. E. Br.	Summit.								

		N. Brazil	S. Brazil, Paraguay	Colombia, Bolivia	Venezuela and Trinidad	W. Indies	Central America	Elsewhere in America	Old World
RUBIACEÆ (*cont.*).									
Sipanea pratensis, Aubl.	to 5400 ft.								
Coccocypselum canescens, Willd.	to 5400 ft.	*	*	*	*	*			
Retiniphyllum laxiflorum, N. E. Br.	Upper slopes.	*	*	*	*	..			
Psychotria concinna, Oliver	to Summit.								
„ *crassa*, Benth.	to 6000 ft.	*		..		*			
„ *inundata*, Benth.	to 6000 ft.	*	*						
„ *Imthurniana*, Oliver	to Ledge.								
„ 2 spp.	to 6000 ft.								
Declieuxia chiococcoides, H. B. & K.	to 5400 ft.								
Cephaëlis axillaris, Sw.	to 5400 ft.	*	*	*	*				
Relbunium sp.	to 5400 ft.	..			*	..	*		
COMPOSITÆ.									
Vernonia thretiæfolia, Benth.	to 6000 ft.	*							
„ *remotiflora*, Rich.	to 6000 ft.	*							
Eupatorium conyzoides, Vahl	to 5400 ft.	*	*	*	*	*	*	N. & S.	
„ *rorainense*, N. E. Br.	Summit.								
„ *fuscum*, N. E. Br.	Summit.								
Mikania pinnosa, Baker	at 5400 ft.								
Baccharis Vitis-idæa, Oliver	to Summit.								
„ sp., near *B. cassinæ-folia*	Summit.								
Heterothalamus densus, N. E. Br.	Summit.								
Gnaphalium purpureum, Linn.	to 5400 ft.	*	*	*	*	*	*	N. & S.	*
Verbesina guianensis, Baker	to 5400 ft.								
Pectis elongata, H. B. & K.	to 5400 ft.	*	*	*	*	*	..		
Quelchia conferta, N. E. Br.	Summit.								
Erechtites hieraciifolia, Rafin.	to 5400 ft.	*	*	*	*	*	*	N. & S.	Introd.
Stifftia condensata, Baker	to Summit.								
„ *Connellii*, N. E. Br.	Summit.								
LOBELIACEÆ.									
Centropogon laevigatus, A. DC.	to Ledge.	*							
„ *surinamensis*, Presl	to 5400 ft.				*	*	*	*	
VACCINIACEÆ.									
Psammisia guianensis, Klotzsch	at 6000 ft.								
„ *formosa*, Klotzsch	at 6000 ft.								
„ *coriacea*, N. E. Br.	Summit.								
„ 2 spp.	to 5400 ft.								
Notopora Schomburgkii, Hook. f.	to 5100 ft.								
Cavendishia sp. (*Thibaudia antuss.* Klotzsch)	at 6000 ft.								
Vaccinium puberulum, Klotzsch	to 6000 ft.								
„ *rorainense*, N. E. Br.	Summit.								
Sphyrospermum Rorainae, Klotzsch	to 6000 ft.+								
Sophoclesia sp.	Ledge.								
ERICACEÆ.									
Pernettya marginata, N. E. Br.	Summit.								
Gaultheria setulosa, N. E. Br.	Summit.								
„ *cordifolia*, H. B. & K. (*G. Rorainae*, Klotzsch)	to 5400 ft.			*	*		*		
L. dothamnus sessiliflorus, N. E. Br.	to Summit.								
Befaria guianensis, Klotzsch	to Ledge.								
„ *Imthurnii*, N. E. Br.	Summit.								
„ *Schomburgkii*, Klotzsch	to 6000 ft.								
MYRSINACEÆ.									
Myrsine sp.	to 6000 ft.								
Cybianthus sp.	at 6000 ft.								

+ If synonymous with *Hughsia guianensis*, Klotzsch & Rich. Schomb.

	N. Brazil	S. Brazil, Paraguay	Colombia to Bolivia	Venezuela and Trinidad	W. Indies	Central America	Elsewhere in America	Old World
MYRSINACEÆ (*cont.*).								
Cyrillopsidenia lineata, Benth. ...... to 5100 ft.								
Ardisia Quelchii, N. E. Br. .... Summit.								
SAPOTACEÆ.								
Chrysophyllum emarginatum,								
Klotzsch † .... at 6000 ft.				*				
Lucuma rigida, Mart. & Eichl. ... at 5100 ft.								
APOCYNACEÆ.								
Mandevilla angustifolia (*Echites an-*								
gustifolia, Benth.) .. to 6000 ft.								
„ *glabra*, N. E. Br. .... Upper slopes.								
ASCLEPIADACEÆ.								
Nephradenia linearis?, Benth. ..... to 5100 ft.	*				*			
LOGANIACEÆ.								
Antonia ovata, Pohl .... to Upper slopes.	*		*					
GENTIANACEÆ.								
Curtia tenuiflora (*Schuebleria tenui-*								
flora, G. Don) .... to 5100 ft.	*	*		*			*	
Lisianthus uliginosus, Miq. .... to Upper slopes.	*	*						
„ *Elisabethæ*, Grisebach ..... to Ledge.								
„ *Imthurnianus*, Oliver .. Summit.								
„ *Quelchii*, N. E. Br. .... Summit.								
SCROPHULARIACEÆ.								
Melasma? spathaceum, Oliver .... Upper slopes.								
Beyrichia scutellarioides, Benth. .... to Upper slopes.	*	*						
LENTIBULARIACEÆ.								
Utricularia Humboldtii, Rob.								
Schomb. .... to Ledge.								
Utricularia nervosa?, Web. .... Upper slopes.	*			*				
„ *Campbelliana*, Oliver .. to Upper slopes.								
„ *alpina*, Jacq. (*U. mon-*								
tana, Jacq.) .... to Upper slopes.						*		
„ *Quelchii*, N. E. Br. .... Summit.								
„ *coruiaensis*, N. E. Br. .. Summit.								
Genlisea coruiaensis, N. E. Br. .... Summit.								
BIGNONIACEÆ.								
Tabebuia Roraimae, Oliver .... to Upper slopes.								
VERBENACEÆ.								
Lippia Schomburgkiana, Schauer .. to Upper slopes.	*							
LABIATÆ.								
Hyptis lantanæfolia, Poit. .... to 5400 ft.	*	*	*		*	*	*	*
POLYGONACEÆ.								
Coccoloba Schomburgkii, Meissn. .... to 5100 ft.								
PIPERACEÆ.								
Peperomia reflexa, A. Dietr. ...... to Upper slopes.	*	*		*	*	*	x	*
„ *tenella?*, A. Dietr. .... to Upper slopes.	..	*			*	*	*	
„ sp. .... at 5100 ft.								
CHLORANTHACEÆ.								
Hedyosmum brasiliense?, Mart. Upper slopes.				..	*			
PROTEACEÆ.								
Roupala Schomburgkii, Klotzsch at 6000 ft.								
LORANTHACEÆ.								
Loranthus sp. .... to 6000 ft.								
Phoradendron Roraimæ, Oliver .... Ledge & Summit.								
EUPHORBIACEÆ.								
Phyllanthus pycnophyllus, Muell.-								
Arg. .... at 5100 ft.								

† Apparently *C. auratum*, Miq.

		N. Brazil.	S. Brazil. Paraguay.	Colombia to Bolivia.	Venezuela and Trinidad.	W. Indies.	Central America.	Elsewhere in America.	Old World.
EUPHORBIACEÆ (cont.).									
Phyllanthus sp.									
Croton lobatus, Linn.	at 6000 ft.	*	*	*	*	*	*		Africa.
„ sp.	Upper slopes.								
BURMANNIACEÆ.									
Burmannia bicolor, Mart.	to Upper slopes.	*	*	*	*	*			Africa.
Dictyostegia orobanchoides, Miers	to Upper slopes.	*	*	*	*	*			
ORCHIDACEÆ.									
Pleurothallis stenopetala, Lindl.	to Upper slopes.			*			*		
„ roraimensis, Rolfe	Summit.								
Stelis grandiflora, Lindl.	Upper slopes.			*					
„ tristyla, Lindl.	Upper slopes.			*					
Lepanthes sp.	at 5400 ft.								
Masdevallia picturata, Reichb. f.	to Upper slopes.					*	*	*	
Scaphosepalum breve, Rolfe	to Upper slopes.								
Octomeria parviflora, Rolfe	Summit.								
„ Connellii, Rolfe	Summit.								
„ sp.	Upper slope.								
Bulbophyllum sp. (B. geraïnse, Ridley,									
vix Reichb. f.)	to 5400 ft.								
„ roraimense, Rolfe	Summit.								
Elleanthus furfuraceus, Reichb. f.	Upper slopes.					*	*		
Epidendrum elongatum, Jacq.	to Summit.	*	*	*	*	*			
„ alsum, Ridley	Summit.								
„ Imthurnii, Ridley	Summit.								
„ tigrinum, Lindl.	to Upper slopes.					*	*		
„ durum, Lindl.	to 5400 ft.					*			
„ montigenum, Ridley	Summit.								
„ violascens, Ridley	Summit.								
Cattleya Lawrenceana, Reichb. f.	to 6000 ft.								
Zygopetalum Burkei, Reichb. f.	to Upper slopes.								
Eriopsis Schomburgkii, Reichb. f.	to Upper slopes.	*							
Houlletia roraimensis, Rolfe	to Upper slopes.								
Catasetum discolor, Lindl.	to Upper slopes.	*	*						
Maxillaria Quelchii, Rolfe	Summit.								
Oncidium nigratum, Lindl.	to 4500 ft.	*	*						
Sobralia Liliastrum, Lindl.	to 6000 ft.	*	*						
„ sp.	Upper slope.	*	*						
Epistephium lucidum, Cogn.	to Upper slopes.	*	*						
Stenoptera viscosa, Reichb. f.	to Upper slopes.					*	*		
„ elauta, Ridley	Upper slopes.								
Spiranthes bifida, Ridley	to 5400 ft.								
Pogonia parviflora, Lindl.	to Upper slopes.			*					S.
„ rosea, Hemsl.	to Upper slopes.	*				*			
„ tenuis, Reichb. f.	Summit.	*		*	*	*			
Habenaria roraimensis, Rolfe	Summit.								
„ parviflora, Lindl.	to 5400 ft.	*	*	*	*				S.
„ Moritzii, Ridley	to Upper slopes.			*		*	*		
Selenipedium Lindleyanum, Reichb. f.	to 5400 ft.								
BROMELIACEÆ.									
Brocchinia cordylinoides, Baker	to Ledge.								
Puya floccosa, Morren	at 6000 ft.								
Connellia Augusta, N. E. Br.	to Summit.			*	*				
„ Quelchii, N. E. Br.	Summit.								
Tillandsia rhodocincta, Baker	Summit.								

	N. Brazil.	S. Brazil, Paraguay.	Colombia to Bolivia.	Venezuela and Trinidad.	W. Indies.	Central America.	Elsewhere in America.	Old World.
LILIACEÆ.								
Nietneria corymbosa, Klotzsch & Rich. Schomb. .... to Summit.								
Tofieldia Schomburgkiana, Oliver .. to Summit.								
XYRIDACEÆ.								
Xyris setigera, Oliver .... to Ledge.	*							
„ *Seubertii*, Nills.† .... Upper slopes (? Ledge).								
„ *witserioides*, Oliver .... to 7300 ft.								
„ *concinna*, N. E. Br. .... Summit.								
Abolboda Sceptrum, Oliver .... to Summit.								
RAPATEACEÆ.								
Saxofridericia regalis, Rob. Schomb. to 5600 ft.								
Stegolepis guianensis, Klotzsch .... to Summit.								
PALMÆ.								
Euterpe sp. .... at 5400 ft.								
Geonoma Appuniana, Spruce ...... to Upper slopes.								
ARACEÆ.								
Anthurium roraimense, N. E. Br. .. at 5400 ft.								
ERIOCAULACEÆ.								
Paepalanthus Schomburgkii, Klotzsch to 5400 ft.								
„ *flavescens*, Koern. .... to Upper slopes.	*	*	*	*				
„ *Roraimae*, Oliver .... to Summit.								
„ *fraternus*, N. E. Br. .. Summit.								
CYPERACEÆ.								
Fimbristylis exilis, Roem. & Schult... to 5400 ft.	*	..	..	*	*	*	..	Africa.
Rhynchospora stenophylla, Britton‡. at 5400 ft.	..	..	..	*	*	*	N.	
„ *tenuis*, Britton ...... to 5400 ft.	*	*	..	.	*	*	S.	
Lagenocarpus stellatus, C. B. Clarke (*Cryptangium stellatum*, Boeckl.) . Upper slopes.								
Everardia montana, Ridley .... to Summit.								
„ *angusta*, N. E. Br. ...... Summit.								
Scleria hirtella, Sw. .... to 5400 ft.	*	*	*	*	*	..	*	N. Africa.
„ *bracteata*, Cav. .... to 5400 ft.	*	*	*	*	..	*	..	*
GRAMINEÆ.								
Saccharum cayennense, Beauv....... to 5400 ft.	*	*	*	*	*	*	S.	
Ischaemum latifolium, Kunth ...... to 5400 ft.	*	*	*	*	*	*		
Arundinella brasiliensis, Raddi .... to 5400 ft.	*	*	*	*	*	*	S.	*
Paspalum stellatum, Fluegge ...... to 5400 ft.	*	*	*	*				
Panicum cligulatum, N. E. Br. .... Summit.								
„ *nervosum?*, Lam. .... to 5400 ft.	*		..		*			
Echinolaena hirta, Desv. .... to Upper slopes.	*	*						
Arundo roraimensis, N. E. Br. .... Summit.								
Arundinaria deflexa, N. E. Br. .... Summit.								
Chusquea linearis, N. E. Br. ...... Summit.								
Guadua sp. .... to Upper slopes.								
Total of SPERMATOPHYTA	67	55	53	60	30	33	11	10

† *X. Fontanesiana*, Oliver in Trans. Linn. Soc., ser. II. Bot. ii. (1887), p. 285, appears to be *X. Seubertii.* It is not *X. Fontanesiana*, Kunth.

‡ *R. capillacea*, Oliver *l. c.* p. 287, not of Torrey (*teste* C. B. Clarke).

	N. Brazil	S. Brazil, Paraguay.	Colombia to Bolivia.	Venezuela and Trinidad.	W. Indies.	Central America.	Elsewhere in America.	Old World.
SELAGINELLACEÆ.								
Selaginella vernicosa, Baker ...... to Summit.								
,, *voraimensis,* Baker .... at 5400 ft.	*							
LYCOPODIACEÆ.								
Lycopodium alopecuroides, Linn..... to Upper slopes.	*	*	*	*	..		N. & S.	
,, *carolinianum,* Linn. .. to Upper slopes.	*	*	*	*	*		N.	
,, *contiguum,* Klotzsch .. to Summit.	*							*
,, *linifolium,* Linn....... to Upper slopes.	*	*	..	*	*			
,, *subulatum,* Desv. .... to 7200 ft.	..	*	*	*	*			Pacific.
FILICES.								
Gleichenia pubescens, H. B. & K. ... to Upper slopes.	*	*	*	*	*	*	S.	
Cyathea vestita, Mart............. to 5400 ft.	*	*	*					
Alsophila bipinnatifida, Baker .... 5400 ft.	*	*						
,, *macrosora,* Baker ...... at 5400 ft.	*	*						
Dicksonia coniifolia, Hook........ to Summit.	*	*	*	*	*			
Hymenophyllum crispum, H. B. & K. to Summit.	*	*	*	*	*			
,, *dejectum,* Baker .. 5000 ft. to Summit.	*							
,, *polyanthos,* Sw. ... to Summit.	*	*	*	*	*	*	S.	*
,, *fucoides,* Sw. ..... to Upper slopes.	*	*	*	*	*	*	S.	
,, *microcarpum,* Hook. Upper slopes.	*	*	*	*	*			
,, *sericeum,* Sw. ..... to Summit.	*	*	*	*	*	*		
,, *lineare,* Sw. ...... to Summit.	*	*	*	*	*	*		Africa.
Trichomanes elegans, Rudge ...... to Upper slopes.	*	..	*	*	*	..		
,, *voraimense,* Jenman .. Summit.	*							
,, *nuccileatum,* V. d. Bosch to Upper slopes.	*	*	*	*				
,, *rigidum,* Sw......... to 5400 ft.	*	*	*	*	*			*
,, *pyxidiferum,* Linn. ... to Upper slopes.	*	*	*	*	*			*
Davallia Luvaraguana, Hook......... to Upper slopes.	*	*	*	*	*			
Lindsaya guianensis, Dryand...... to Upper slopes.	*	*	*					
,, *stricta,* Dryand. .... to Summit.	*	*	*	*	*			
Hypolepis repens, Presl .... to 7200 ft.	*	*	*	*	*	*	N. & S.	
Pteris aquilina, Linn............. to Summit.	*	*	*	*	*	*	S.	*
,, *incisa,* Thunb. .... to 7200 ft.	*	*	*	*	*	*	S.	*
,, *lomariacea,* Kunze .... to 5400 ft.	*	*	*	*	*			
Lomaria Plumieri, Desv.... to Upper slopes.	*	*	*	*	*			Africa.
,, *Boryana,* Willd. .... to Summit.	*	*	*	*	*	..	S.	
,, *procera,* Spreng. .... to Summit.	*	*	*	*	*	*	S.	
Asplenium lunulatum, Sw......... to 7200 ft.	*	*	*	*	*	*	N.	*
,, *rhizophorum,* Kunze .... to Upper slopes.	*	*	*	*	*	*		Pacific.
,, *furcatum,* Thunb. ...... to 5400 ft.	*	*	*	*	*	*		*
,, *serra,* Langsd. & Fisch... Summit.	*	*	*	*	*			Africa.
Nephrodium conterminum, Desv..... to Summit.	*	*	*	*	*	*	N. & S.	
,, *denticulatum,* Hook. .. to Summit.	*							
,, *brachyodum,* Baker .. Upper slopes.								
,, *Leprieurii,* Hook. ..... to 5400 ft.	*	*						
,, *amplissimum,* Hook. .. to Upper slopes.	*	*						
Nephrolepis cordifolia, Presl ...... to 5400 ft.	*	*						*
Polypodium marginellum, Sw. .... to Summit.	*	*	*	*	*	*		
,, *Connellii,* Baker ...... Summit.	*							
,, *demeraranum,* Baker .. Upper slopes.								
,, *voraimense,* Baker ... Upper slopes.								
,, *trifurcatum,* Linn. ... to Upper slopes.								
,, *furcatum,* Mett. ...... to Summit.	*	*		*	*			
,, *serrulatum,* Mett. ..... to Summit.	*	*		*	*			*
,, *lanceolatum,* Klotzsch ... Upper slopes.	*	*	*	*	*			
,, *tenuicula,* Klotzsch ... Upper slopes.	*	*	*	*	*			
,, *squamulosum,* Lag. ... to Summit.	*	*	*	*	*			
,, *leptophyllum,* C. H. Wright Summit.								
,, *trichomanoides,* Sw.... to Upper slopes.	*	*	*	*	*	*	Juan F.	*
,, *taxifolium,* Linn....... to Upper slopes.	*	*	*	*	*			
,, *pectinatum,* Linn. .... to 5400 ft.	*	*	*	*	*	*	N.	
,, *cultratum,* Willd. .... to Upper slopes.	*	*	*	*	*	..		Africa.

	N. Brazil.	S. Brazil. Paraguay.	Colombia to Bolivia	Venezuela and Trinidad.	W. Indies.	Central America.	Elsewhere in America	Old World
FILICES (*cont.*).								
Polypodium xanthotrichum, Klotzsch — Upper slopes.								
" *capillare*, Desv. ...... to Upper slopes.	*	..	*	*	*			
" *Kathecyeei*, Baker .... Upper slopes.	..	..	*	*				
" *cinyscens*, Hory ...... to Summit.	*	*	..	*	*	*		*
" *flexuum*, Klotzsch...... Upper slopes.	*	..	..	*	*	*		
" *meridense*, Klotzsch.. Summit.	..	..	*	*	*			
" *subsessile*, Baker ...... Upper slopes.	..	..	*	*				
" *melanotrichum*, Baker .. at 5400 ft.								
" *loricum*, Linn. ...... to 7200 ft.	*	*	*	*	*	*	S.	
" *aureum*, Linn........ to 5400 ft.	*	*	*	*	*	*	N.	Australia.
" *angustifolium*, Sw. .... to 5400 ft.	*	*	*	*	*	*		
Gymnogramme lophoglossoides,								
Baker........ to Summit.								
" *cyclophylla*, Baker .. Summit.								
" *flexuosa*, Desv. .... to Summit.	*	*	*	*		..	*	
" *Schomburgkiana*,								
Kunze........... Upper slopes.								
" *hirta*, Desv. ...... Upper slopes.	*	*	*	*				
Enterosora Campbelliana, Baker ... Upper slopes.								
Vittaria lineata, Sw. .... to Upper slopes.	*	*	*	*	*	*	N. & S.	*
" *stipulata*, Kunze .... Upper slopes.	..	..	*	*		*		*
Acrostichum latifolium, Sw. ...... to Summit.	..	..	*	*		*		*
" *squamosum*, Sw....... to Upper slopes.	*	*	*	*	*	*		*
" *leptophlebium*, Baker .. Upper slopes.				*				
" *muscosum*, Sw. ...... to 5400 ft.	*	*	*	*	..	*		
" *stemplecis*, Klotzsch .. at 5400 ft.	*	*	*	*	*	*		
" *decoratum*, Kunze .... to 5400 ft.	*	*	*	*	*	*		
" *paltatum*, Sw....... .. to Upper slopes.	*	*	*	*	*	*		
Schizaea dichotoma, Sw. .... to 5400 ft.	*	*	*	*	*	*		*
" *elegans*, Sw. .... to 5400 ft.	*	*	*	*	*			
Aneimia tomentosa, Sw. .... to 5400 ft.	*	*	*	*	*	*	S.	
Total of PTERIDOPHYTA	55	50	67	59	55	45	17	25

BRYINEÆ.
Dicranum longisetum, Hook. ...... Ledge.	..	..	*	*				
Dicranodontium pulchroatrum, Broth. Ledge.				*				
Campylopus chlorophyllus, Mitt. .. Ledge.			*					
" *Kuraima*, Broth....... Ledge.								
" *atratus*, Broth. ..... Summit.								
Leucobryum auptophyllum, Mitt. .. Ledge.		*	*	*				
" *brevifolium*, Broth. .... Summit.	*	*	*	*				
Octoblepharum Mittenii, Jaeg....... Summit.	*	*	*		*			
Leptodontium circlifolium, Mitt..... Summit.	..	..	*					
Zygodon sublanticulatus, Hampe.... Summit.	..	..	*	*		*	N. & S.	*
Funaria calvescens, Schwaeg. ...... Ledge.	*	*	*	*	..	*		
Bartramia scoparia, Besch. .... Summit.	*	*	*	*				
Rhizogonium Lindigii, Mitt. ...... Summit.	..	..	*	*				
Mnium rostratum, Schrad. .... to Ledge.	*	*	*	*	*	*	*	*
Polytrichum aristiflorum, Mitt. ..... to 5400 ft.	*	*	*	*	..	*	S.	*
Rhacocarpus Humboldtii, Lindb..... Summit.	*	*	*	*				*
Hookeria pilotrichelloides, Broth. .. Ledge.								
" *crispa*, C. Muell. .... to 5400 ft.	..	*	*	*				
Ectropothecium unnabile, Mitt........ to Summit.		*	*	*				
Clenidium molluscles, Mitt.......... Ledge.	..	..	*					
Thuidiana pseudoprotensum, Mitt. .. Ledge.								
Hypopterygium tamarisci, Brid. ..... to 5400 ft.	*	*	*	*	*	*	S.	
SPHAGNACEÆ.								
Sphagnum sampinale, Warnst. .... Ledge.								N. & S.	*
" *medium*, Limpr. .... Ledge.	*		*	*				*
MARCHANTIACEÆ.								
Dumorticra hirsuta, Nees .... Ledge.	*	..	*	*	*			*

	N. Brazil.	S. Brazil, Paraguay.	Columbia to Bolivia.	Venezuela and Trinidad.	W. Indies.	Central America.	Elsewhere in America.	Old World.
JUNGERMANNIACEÆ.								
Aneura Schwaneckei, Steph........ Summit.	*			*				
,, *algoides*, Steph. .... Summit.			*					
,, *roraimensis*, Steph. .... Summit.								
,, *Brentelii*, Steph. .... Summit.							*	
,, *fucoides*, Steph. (*A. bipinnata*, Mitt.†)................. Ledge.	*				*		*	
Metzgeria inflata, Steph. .... Summit.								
,, *hamata*, Lindb.......... Ledge.		*			*	*	N. & S.	*
Pallavicinius Wallisii, Jack & Steph. Summit.		*				*	S.	*
Jamesoniella colorata, Spruce ...... Summit.		*				*		
Syzygiella Quelchii, Steph. .... Ledge.								
,, *perfoliata*, Spruce ..... Summit.				*	*			
Plagiochila area, Tayl. .... Ledge.				*		*		
,, *pavana*, Steph. .... Ledge.								
,, *remotifolia*, Hampe & Gottsche .... Ledge.				*				
,, *rutilans*, Lindb........ Ledge.						*		
,, *adiantoides*, Lindb. .... to Upper slopes.	*	*	*	*	*	*		
Leioscyphus fragilis, Jack & Steph. . Summit.			*		*	*		
Lophocolea Brentelii, Gottsche .... Ledge.						*		
Mastigobryum roraimense, Steph. ... Summit.								
,, *dissolutum*, Spruce... Summit.	*							
,, *vincentinum*, Lehm. & Lindenb. Ledge.					*			
,, *Krugianum*, Steph. .. Ledge.					*			
,, *gracile*, Hampe & Gottsche .... Ledge.					*			
Blepharozia Roraimae, Mitt. ...... Summit.					*			
Micropterygium grandistipulum, Steph. ...... Ledge.								
,, *pterygophyllum*, Spruce .... Summit.	*	*	*		*			
Lepidozia commutata, Steph. ...... Summit.					*			
Schisma juniperinum, Nees .... Summit.		*			*	*	N. & S.	*
,, *pensilis*, Steph. .... Ledge.			*					
,, *Durandii*, Steph. .... Ledge.			*			*		
,, *subdentatum*, Steph. ...... Ledge.			*					
Trichocolea sphagnoides. Steph. .... Ledge.		*						
Scapania portoricensis, Hampe & Gottsche .... Summit.				*		*		
Pharozia paradoxa, Jack .... Summit.				*		*		
Harpalejeunea tenax, Steph. ...... Ledge.				*				
Frullania mirabilis, Jack & Steph... Summit.								
,, *atrata*, Nees .... Summit.				*	*	*	*	
,, *longicollis*. Lindenb. & Gottsche .... Summit.				*		*		
Total of BRYOPHYTA........	7	17	31	13	25	17	8	9
Phoma Psammaisiae, Massee .... Summit.								
Echinobotryum roseum, Massee .... Summit.								*
Stenophyllium cricoctonum, R. Br. .. Summit.								*
Marcosporium ramulosum, Sacc..... Summit.			*					*
Capnodium fibrosum, Berk....... Summit.								*
Rhipidodema membranaceum, Sacc... Ledge.	*							Pacific.
Sphaerophora compressum, Achar. .. Summit.					*	*	N.	*
Cladonia rangiferina, Hoffm. ...... Summit.	*	*	*	*	*	*	N. & S.	*
Parmelia dictyorhiza, Massee ...... Summit.								
,, *perforata*, Achar. ...... Summit.						*	N.	Pacific.
Alectoria ochroleuca, Nyl. .... Summit.						*	N.	*
Total of THALLOPHYTA	2	1	2	1	2	3	4	8

CHIEF LITERATURE.

Schomburgks' journeys.

Sir Robert H. Schomburgk, in Proc. Roy. Geogr. Soc. x. 1840, pp. 196–242.

Sir Robert H. Schomburgk, 'Twelve Views in the Interior of Guiana' (London, 1841).

Sir Richard Schomburgk, ' Reisen in Britisch-Guiana' (Leipzig, 1847–48), ii. pp. 152–300; iii. pp. 1041–1104.

Sir Richard Schomburgk, ' Botanical Reminiscences of British Guiana' (Adelaide, 1876).

Sir Robert H. Schomburgk, in Verh. Gartenb. Ver. xv., 1841.

G. Bentham, in Ann. Nat. Hist. ii.–iii.; in Hooker's Journ. Bot. ii.–iv.; in Hooker's Lond. Journ. Bot. i.–vii.; in Trans. Linn. Soc. xviii. & xxii.; &c.

J. F. Klotzsch, in Verh. Gartenb. Ver. xviii., 1847; in ' Linnæa,' xxiv. 1851, p. 1; &c.

Various authors in Martius, ' Flora Brasiliensis' (Leipzig, 1840–1900).

Appun's journey.

K. Appun, ' Unter den Tropen' (Jena, 1871), ii. pp. 105–384.

Brown and Sawkins's journey.

C. B. Brown, ' Canoe and Camp-life, in Guiana,' 2nd edit. (London, 1877), pp. 118–124.

J. G. Sawkins, in Proc. Roy. Geogr. Soc. xv. 1870–71, p. 131.

C. B. Brown and J. G. Sawkins, ' Report on the Physical, Descriptive and Economic Geology of British Guiana' (London, 1875), pp 61–63.

Boddam-Whetham and McTurk's journey.

J. W. Boddam-Whetham, ' Roraima and British Guiana' (London, 1879), pp. 204–254.

im Thurn and Perkins's journey.

E. F. im Thurn, in Proc. Roy. Geogr. Soc. vii. 1885, pp. 497–521, and in ' Timehri,' iv. 1885, pp. 1–18 and 256–267.

H. I. Perkins, in Proc. Roy. Geogr. Soc. vii. 1885, pp. 529–530.

E. F. im Thurn, D. Oliver, and others in Trans. Linn. Soc. Ser. II. Bot. ii. pp. 249–300; reprinted in ' Timehri,' v. 1886, pp. 145–223.

Kromer's and Dressel's journeys.

' Timehri,' n. s., i. 1887, p. 330.

McConnell and Quelch's first journey.

J. J. Quelch in ' Timehri,' n. s., viii. 1894, p. 381; ix. 1895, pp. 107–188.

ENUMERATION OF THE PLANTS COLLECTED.

I. SPERMATOPHYTA.

By N. E. Brown, A.L.S. (the Orchids by R. A. Rolfe. A.L.S.).

SARRACENIACEÆ.

Heliamphora nutans, Benth. in Proc. Linn. Soc. i. (1840), p. 53, and in Trans. Linn. Soc. xviii. (1840), p. 429, t. 29; R. Schomb. Reisen in Brit.-Guiana, ii. p. 263, and iii. p. 1090; R. H. Schomb., Views in the Interior of Guiana, p. 15; Bot. Mag. t. 7093; Fl. des Serres, Sér. II. xi. (1875), p. 149, tt. 2246-47; Oliver, in Trans. Linn. Soc. Ser. II. Bot. ii. (1887), p. 271.

Summit of Mount Roraima, *McConnell & Quelch*, 78, 679; also collected on the lower slope in the " Eldorado Swamp " by all other collectors.—Endemic.

VIOLACEÆ.

Ionidium Ipecacuanha, Vent. Jard. Malm. sub t. 27.
Ireng Valley, *McConnell & Quelch*, 258.

Alsodeia flavescens, Spreng. Syst. i. p. 806.
Mazaruni River, 300 ft.. *McConnell & Quelch*, 715.

Salvagesia erecta. Linn. Sp. Pl. ed. i. p. 203; Oliver, in Trans. Linn. Soc. Ser. II. Bot. ii. (1887). p. 271.
Upper slopes and ledge of Mount Roraima, *McConnell & Quelch*, 7. Ireng Valley, *McConnell & Quelch*, 263. - Widely distributed in Tropical America.

Sauvagesia Sprengelii, A. St. Hil. in Mém. Mus. Par. xi. (1824), p. 97.
Savannahs generally, *McConnell & Quelch*, 330.

Leitgebia Imthurniana, Oliver, in Trans. Linn. Soc. Ser. II. Bot. ii. (1887), p. 271, t. 37A.
Summit of Mount Roraima. *McConnell & Quelch*, 97, 98, 316, 654. —Endemic.

POLYGALACEÆ.

Polygala glochidiata, H. B. & K. Nov. Gen. & Sp. v. p. 400.
Upper slopes of Mount Roraima, *McConnell & Quelch*, 38.—Widely distributed in Tropical America.

Polygala hygrophila, H. B. & K. Nov. Gen. & Sp. v. p. 395; Oliver, in Trans. Linn. Soc. Ser. II. Bot. ii. (1887). p. 271.
Upper slopes of Mount Roraima, *McConnell & Quelch*, 39. - Eastern Tropical America from Panama to Paraguay.

POLYGALA TIMOUTOU, Aubl. Pl. Guian. ii. p. 737, t. 295; R. Schomb. Reisen in Brit.-Guiana, iii. p. 1097.

Kotinga Valley, *McConnell & Quelch*, 196. Ireng Valley, *McConnell & Quelch*, 250.

POLYGALA CELOSIOIDES, Mart. *ex* A. W. Benn. in Mart. Fl. Bras. xiii. pt. iii. p. 35. Ireng Valley, *McConnell & Quelch*, 223.

SECURIDACA MARGINATA, Benth. in Hook. Journ. Bot. iv. (1842), p. 103. Kotinga Valley, *McConnell & Quelch*, 157.

MONNINA CACUMINA, N. E. Brown, sp. n. Folia oblonga, acuta vel obtusa, apiculata, exstipulata, glabra. Racemi densiflori, floribus breviter pedicellatis. Bracteæ lanceolatæ, acutæ, floribus breviores. Alæ ellipticæ, glabræ, basi ciliatæ. Carina glabra, ciliata. Petala lateralia utrinque pubescentia. Vagina staminea supra hirta. Fructus compresso-ellipsoideus, exalatus, unilocularis, glaber.

Stem subglabrous, or very thinly covered with very short hairs. Leaves about 2 in. long, ¾-1 in. broad, oblong or oblong-lanceolate, acute or obtuse and apiculate, rather thin in the dried state, exstipulate. Racemes 3-4, terminal, 2-4 in. long, rather densely many-flowered. Bracts 2 lin. long, ⅔ lin. broad, lanceolate, acute, caducous. Pedicels ½-1 lin. long. Dorsal sepal 1¼ lin. long, ⅔ lin. broad, ovate, acute, concave, ciliolate; the two lower sepals similar but rather smaller, connate to their middle; lateral sepals or alæ about 2¼ lin. long, 2 lin. broad, elliptic, obtuse, with incurved margins, glabrous, ciliate towards the base. Lower petal or keel 2½ lin. long, 2 lin. broad, obscurely 3-crenulate at the apex, glabrous ciliate along the sides. Lateral petals 2-2¼ lin. long, obliquely tapering from a broad base to an obtuse apex, adnate to the staminal tube, densely ciliate along the upper margin, pubescent along the middle of the outer side and more densely all over within. Staminal tube villose at the apex. Ovary elliptic, with a large unilateral gland at its base, glabrous; style thickened upwards, slightly incurved. Fruit 3-3½ lin. long, about 1¾ lin. broad, elliptic, subacute, compressed, not winged, 1-celled, glabrous.

Summit of Mount Roraima, 8600 ft. *McConnell & Quelch*, 615.

Allied to *M. cestrifolia*, H. B. & K., but differing in its much larger flowers.

KRAMERIA SPARTIOIDES, Klotzsch, *ex* O. Berg, in Bot. Zeit. xiv. (1856), p. 761. Ireng Valley, *McConnell & Quelch*, 244, 268.

VOCHYSIACEÆ.

TRIGONIA SUBCYMOSA, Benth. in Hook. Lond. Journ. Bot. ii. (1843), p. 373. Ireng Valley, *McConnell & Quelch*, 222.

PORTULACACEÆ.

PORTULACA SEDIFOLIA, N. E. Brown, sp. n. Caules humiles, diffusi. Folia parva, lineari-oblonga vel oblongo-lanceolata, breviter petiolata, axillis dense pilosa. Calycis lobi

D 2

late ovati, obtusi, apice inflexi, glabri.   Petala calyce duplo longiora.   Stamina 5.
Stylus 3-fidus.   Semina tuberculata.

A small succulent herb, branching at the base, with branches 2-3 in. long, glabrous,
with the exception of the tufts of long white hairs in the axils of the leaves and around
the flowers.   Leaves 1½-3 lin. long, ½-⅔ lin. broad, flattened, linear-oblong or oblong-
lanceolate, obtuse, tapering at the base into a short petiole, glabrous.   Flowers small.
Sepals ¾ lin. long, rather more than ½ lin. broad, broadly ovate, obtuse, inflexed at the
apex, concave, not keeled on the back, glabrous.   Petals 1¼ lin. long, only seen in a
withered state, apparently obtuse.   Stamens 5, shorter than the petals.   Style filiform,
with 3 filiform stigmas.   Upper half of the capsule broadly conical.   Seeds ¾ lin. diam.,
tuberculate, the tubercles on the sides very much larger than those on the back, black.

Ireng Valley, *McConnell & Quelch*, 237.

Allied to *Portulaca parvula*, A. Gray, but differing in its shorter leaves, fewer
stamens, and larger and more coarsely tuberculate seeds.

GUTTIFERÆ.

Clusia Planchoniana, Engl. (?) in Mart. Fl. Bras. xii. pt. 1. p. 431.

Kukenaam River, *McConnell & Quelch*, 130.

I am doubtful of my identification of this plant, and it may prove to be a new species,
but the specimen only consists of three flowers and two leaves, all detached.   They agree
fairly well with the flowers and leaves of *C. Planchoniana*, with the exception that the
leaves are rather more obtuse and have stouter petioles.

TERNSTRŒMIACEÆ.

Ternstrœmia Schomburgkiana, Benth. in Hook. Lond. Journ. Bot. ii. (1843), p. 362;
Appun, Unter den Tropen, ii. p. 292.

Kotinga Valley, *McConnell & Quelch*, 138.

Bonnetia sessilis, Benth. in Hook. Lond. Journ. Bot. ii. (1843), p. 363; Appun, Unter
den Tropen, ii. p. 292; R. Schomb. Reisen in Brit.-Guiana, ii. pp. 218, 251, and iii.
p. 1093.

Irengwatong Creek in the Ireng Valley, *McConnell & Quelch*, 269, 322.—Only known
from this western part of British Guiana.

Bonnetia Roraimæ, Oliver, in Trans. Linn. Soc. Ser. II. Bot. ii. (1887), p. 272, t. 37. f. B.

Summit of Mount Roraima, *McConnell & Quelch*, 84, 664.—Endemic.   According to
Mr. Quelch, "this is the commonest and most widely spread species on the summit,
rising to 35-40 ft. in height, where sheltered."

Archytæa multiflora, Benth. in Hook. Lond. Journ. Bot. ii. (1843), p. 363; R. Schomb.
Reisen in Brit.-Guiana, ii. p. 218, and iii. p. 1093.

Kotinga Valley, 3000 ft. *McConnell & Quelch*, 162; Ireng Valley, *McConnell & Quelch*,
311.

MAHURIA ENSTIPULATA, Benth. in Hook. Lond. Journ. Bot. ii. (1843), p. 365.
Silima Creek in the Ireng Valley, *McConnell & Quelch*, 270.

MALVACEÆ.

SIDA, sp. Specimen insufficient for determination, but apparently a new species.
Ireng Valley, *McConnell & Quelch*, 267.

PAVONIA SPECIOSA, H. B. & K. Nov. Gen. & Sp. v. p. 281.
Kotinga Valley, *McConnell & Quelch*, 176. Karona Falls on the Ireng River,
McConnell & Quelch, 228. Ireng Valley, *McConnell & Quelch*, 257.

PAVONIA CANCELLATA, Cav. Diss. iii. p. 135.
Ireng Valley, *McConnell & Quelch*, 248.

FUGOSIA CAMPESTRIS, Benth. in Hook. Journ. Bot. iv. (1842), p. 120.
Ireng Valley, *McConnell & Quelch*, 213, 239.

STERCULIACEÆ.

HELICTERES GUAZUMÆFOLIA, H. B. & K. Nov. Gen. & Sp. v. p. 304.
Ireng Valley, *McConnell & Quelch*, 212.

MELOCHIA MELISSÆFOLIA, Benth. in Hook. Journ. Bot. iv. (1842), p. 129.
Ireng Valley, *McConnell & Quelch*, 231.

MELOCHIA HIRSUTA, Cav. Diss. vi. p. 323.
Ireng Valley, *McConnell & Quelch*, 255.

WALTHERIA VISCOSISSIMA, A. St. Hil. Fl. Bras. Mer. i. p. 150.
Kotinga Valley, *McConnell & Quelch*, 168.

MALPIGHIACEÆ.

BYRSONIMA VERBASCIFOLIA, Rich. ex Juss. in Ann. Mus. Par. xviii. (1811), p. 481.
Ireng Valley, *McConnell & Quelch*, 226.

HETEROPTERIS OLEÆFOLIA, Griseb. in Linnæa, xxii. (1849), p. 19.
H. daphnoides, Griseb. in R. Schomb. Reisen in Brit.-Guiana, iii. p. 1096.
Upper slopes of Mount Roraima, *McConnell & Quelch*, 21, 319.—Endemic.

TETRAPTERIS SQUARROSA, Griseb. in Mart. Fl. Bras. xii. pt. t. p. 87.
Ireng Valley, *McConnell & Quelch*, 241.

GERANIACEÆ.

OXALIS DISTANS, A. St. Hil. Fl. Bras. Mer. i. p. 115.
O. Schomburgkiana, Prog. in Mart. Fl. Bras. xii. pt. 11. p. 500.
Ireng Valley, *McConnell & Quelch*, 202.

OCHNACEÆ.

POECILANDRA RETUSA, Tul. in Ann. Sc. Nat. Sér. III. viii. (1847), p. 342.
Kotinga Valley, *McConnell & Quelch*, 115, 167.   Ireng Valley, *McConnell & Quelch*, 325.

ILICACEÆ.

ILEX APICIDENS, N. E. Brown, sp. n. (Plate 1, figs. 1–6). Frutex glaber. Folia parva, coriacea, elliptica, obtusa vel emarginata, basi obtusa, apice denticulata. Cymæ axillares vel ad apices ramulorum aggregatæ, 2–3-floræ, vel flores solitarii, glabræ. Calyx 4-lobus, lobis brevissimis rotundatis. Petala 4, elliptica vel suborbiculata, obtusissima. Stamina 4.

A glabrous shrub; branches tuberculated with the scars of the fallen leaves. Leaves moderately crowded, coriaceous; petiole ½–2 lin. long; blade 5–11 lin. long, 4–7 lin. broad, elliptic or somewhat obovate, obtusely rounded or emarginate and with 5–9 small teeth at the apex, obtusely rounded or somewhat cuneate at the base, entire along the sides, with slightly revolute margins, not punctate-dotted beneath; primary lateral veins about 4 on each side, uniting in broad loops, impressed above, prominent beneath; stipules minute, about ⅓ lin. long, subulate. Flowers either solitary or in 2–3-flowered pedunculate cymes in the axils of the leaves, or crowded into a small, terminal, hemispherical corymb ½–¾ in. diam. Peduncles 1½–3 lin. long, glabrous. Pedicels of the solitary flowers 2–3½ lin. long, of those in cymes 1–2¼ lin. long, glabrous. Calyx about ½ lin. long, cupular, shortly 4-lobed, lobes broadly rounded, obtuse, glabrous. Petals 4, 1¼–1½ lin. long, 1¼–1½ lin. broad, elliptic or suborbiculate, very obtuse, concave, glabrous. Stamens 4, a little shorter than the petals. Pistillode globose, glabrous. Female flowers not seen.

Summit of Mount Roraima, 8600 ft., *McConnell & Quelch*, 634.

Allied to *I. obcordata*, Sw., but differing in the apically toothed leaves, with the midrib and veins much more prominent beneath.

ILEX RETUSA, Klotzsch, in R. Schomb. Reisen in Brit.-Guiana. iii. p. 1097; Oliver, in Trans. Linn. Soc. Ser. II. Bot. ii. (1887), p. 273.

Summit of Mount Roraima, *McConnell & Quelch*, 655. Collected by Schomburgk on the bank of a mountain-stream in the vicinity of Roraima.—Endemic.

CYRILLACEÆ.

CYRILLA ANTILLANA, Michx. Fl. Bor.-Am. i. p. 158.

Stachyanthemum Schomburgkii, Klotzsch, in R. Schomb. Reisen in Brit.-Guiana. iii. p. 1097, *et* Loesener, in Engler & Prantl, Pflanzenfam. iii. pt. 5, p. 159.

Kotinga Valley. 3000 ft., *McConnell & Quelch*, 193.   Ireng Valley, *McConnell & Quelch*, 203.

CYRILLA BREVIFOLIA, N. E. Brown, sp. n. (Pl. 1, figs. 7–10.) Folia lanceolato-elliptica vel obovato-elliptica vel lanceolata, obtusa vel acuta, glabra, rigide coriacea, costa infra vix prominente. Racemi 1–2 poll. longi, dense multiflori. Sepala lanceolata, acuminata, glabra. Petala lanceolata, involuto-acuminata, glabra.—*C. antillana*, Michx., var. *brevifolia*, Oliver, in Trans. Linn. Soc. Ser. II. Bot. ii. (1887) p. 273.

Leaves crowded towards the ends of the branches, glabrous; petiole 2-2½ lin. long ; blade ¾-1¼ in. long, 4-8 lin. broad, lanceolate-elliptic or slightly obovate-elliptic and obtuse, or occasionally lanceolate and acute, sometimes minutely apiculate, rigidly coriaceous, entire, shining and smooth or coarsely pitted above, coarsely pitted between the veinlets beneath ; midrib impressed above, prominent and keeled beneath at the basal part only, not raised above the general surface in the apical half. Racemes 1-2 in. long, 3-4 lin. diam., densely many-flowered, erect, glabrous. Bracts 1½-2 lin. long, subulate, very acute. Pedicels ¾-1 lin. long, ascending curved, glabrous. Sepals 1-1¼ lin. long, acuminate from an ovate base, glabrous. Petals 1½-1¾ lin. long, ½ lin. broad, lanceolate, acuminate from the margins being inrolled, subacute when expanded, glabrous. Stamens about ¾ as long as the petals. Ovary oblong, irregularly wrinkled in the dried state, 2-3-celled, glabrous; style very short and stout; stigmas 2-3. Ovules 2, pendulous from the apex of each cell.

Summit of Mount Roraima, 8600 ft., *im Thurn*, 334 ; *McConnell & Quelch*, 88, 318, 638.

This species differs from *Cyrilla antillana*, Michx., in having smaller and more rigidly coriaceous leaves, with the midrib not prominent beyond the middle on the underside, shorter and denser racemes, and longer and more acuminate sepals and petals.

LEGUMINOSÆ.

CROTALARIA ANAGYROIDES, H. B. & K. Nov. Gen. & Sp. vi. p. 404.
Kotinga Valley. *McConnell & Quelch*, 169.

TEPHROSIA ADUNCA, Benth. in Ann. Nat. Hist. Ser. I. iii. (1839), p. 432.
Kotinga Valley, *McConnell & Quelch*, 131, 199.

CLITORIA GUYANENSIS, Benth. in Journ. Linn. Soc., Bot. ii. (1858), p. 40.
Kotinga Valley, *McConnell & Quelch*, 155 ; Ireng Valley, *McConnell & Quelch*, 209.

DIOCLEA GUIANENSIS, Benth. in Ann. Wien. Mus. ii. (1838), p. 134.
Kotinga Valley, *McConnell & Quelch*, 158.

PHASEOLUS SEMIERECTUS, Linn. Mant. i. p. 100, var.
Kotinga Valley, *McConnell & Quelch*, 171.

PHASEOLUS LASIOCARPUS, Mart. (?) ex Benth. in Ann. Wien. Mus. ii. (1838), p. 140,
Kotinga Valley, *McConnell & Quelch*, 177.

ERIOSEMA CRINITUM, Benth. in Hook. Journ. Bot. ii. (1840), p. 62.
Kotinga Valley, *McConnell & Quelch*, 186.

DIPTERYX OPPOSITIFOLIA, Willd. Sp. Pl. iii. p. 910.
Arabapu River, *McConnell & Quelch*, 143, 303. Roraima Range, 3500 ft., *McConnell & Quelch*, 717.—Guiana and Brazil.

CASSIA INSIGNIS, N. E. Brown, sp. n. Foliola bijuga, ampla, oblique oblonga vel elliptico-oblonga, breviter obtuse acuminata, venosa, glandula magna inter inferiora. Stipulæ foliaceæ, falcato-lanceolatæ. Racemi laxe subcorymbosi. Pedicelli elongati. Stamina perfecta 7; staminodia 3. Antheræ perfectæ subæquales, 3 inferiores breviter rostratæ.

Leaves large, bijugate; petiole below the basal pair of leaflets, $\frac{3}{4}$-1 in. long, minutely puberulous, becoming nearly glabrous; leaflets obliquely oblong or elliptic-oblong, shortly and obtusely acuminate, obliquely rounded at the base, glabrous to the eye, but with a minute scattered pubescence as seen under a lens, with the veins and veinlets very conspicuous on both sides; the basal pair $1\frac{1}{2}$-$3\frac{1}{4}$ in. long, $\frac{3}{4}$-$1\frac{3}{4}$ in. broad; the terminal pair 4-9 lin. distant, $2\frac{3}{4}$-$4\frac{1}{2}$ in. long, 1-2 in. broad; gland $1\frac{1}{2}$ lin. long, 1 lin. thick, erect, ovoid, obtuse, placed between the basal pair of leaflets. Stipules leafy, $\frac{1}{2}$-$\frac{3}{4}$ in. long, 2-4 lin. broad, falcate-lanceolate, obtuse or acute, tapering at the base into a curved petiole. Racemes loosely subcorymbose at the ends of the branches, solitary or in pairs from the axils of the uppermost reduced leaves, $1\frac{1}{2}$-3 in. long, 7-14-flowered, softly and minutely pubescent. Pedicels 1-$1\frac{1}{4}$ in. long, pubescent. Sepals about $5\frac{1}{2}$ lin. long, $\frac{1}{4}$ in. broad, obovate, obtuse, puberulous, minutely ciliate towards the apex. Petals 8-11 lin. long, 4-8 lin. broad, elliptic or elliptic-obovate, very distinctly clawed, minutely puberulous on both sides. Stamens with 7 subequal perfect and 3 reduced abortive anthers, 3 of the perfect anthers shortly beaked. Ovary linear, curved, densely pubescent with yellowish adpressed hairs. Legume not seen.

On the upper slopes of Mount Roraima, *McConnell & Quelch*, 23.

Allied to *C. latifolia*, G. F. W. Mey., but may be at once distinguished by its narrow-based, petiolate stipules, and much longer pedicels.

CASSIA APOUCOUITA, Aubl. Pl. Guian. i. p. 379, t. 146.

Mazaruni River, 300 ft., *McConnell & Quelch*, 716.

This appears to be the true plant of Aublet, which is easily distinguished from the Brazilian plants described by Bentham as *C. Apoucouita*, by its narrowly winged petiole and differently shaped leaflets. The *C. Apoucouita* of Bentham appears to me to include 2 or 3 perfectly distinct species.

CASSIA HISPIDULA, Vahl, Eclog. Am. iii. p. 10.

Kotinga Valley, *McConnell & Quelch*, 170. Ireng Valley, *McConnell & Quelch*, 246.

CASSIA POLYSTACHYA, Benth. in Hook. Journ. Bot. ii. (1840), p. 77; R. Schomb. Reisen in Brit.-Guiana, ii. pp. 187, 207, and iii. p. 1207.

Ireng Valley, *McConnell & Quelch*, 229. Upper slopes of Mount Roraima, *McConnell & Quelch*, 317.—Only known from this western corner of British Guiana.

CASSIA UNIFLORA, Spreng. Neue Entdeck. i. p. 291.

Kotinga Valley, near Roraima, *McConnell & Quelch*, 133. Kotinga Valley. *McConnell & Quelch*, 151. Savannahs generally, *McConnell & Quelch*, 320.

CASSIA RORAIMÆ, Benth. in Trans. Linn. Soc. xxvii. (1871), p. 574; Oliver in Trans. Linn. Soc. Ser. II. ii. (1887) p. 273.

Kotinga Valley, *McConnell & Quelch*, 140. Roraima Range, 3500 ft., *McConnell & Quelch*, 719.—Only known from this region.

MIMOSA MICROCEPHALA, Humb. & Bonpl. *ex* Willd. Sp. Pl. iv. p. 1039.

Kotinga Valley, *McConnell & Quelch*, 173.

PITHECOLOBIUM FERRUGINEUM, Benth. in Hook. Lond. Journ. Bot. iii. (1844), p. 208; R. Schomb. Reisen in Brit.-Guiana, iii. p. 1038.

Upper and lower slopes of Mount Roraima, *McConnell & Quelch*, 19. Roraima Range, 3500 ft., *McConnell & Quelch*, 712.—Endemic.

The fruit described by Bentham under *P. ferrugineum* in Trans. Linn. Soc. xxx. (1875) p. 584, does not belong to that species, but to some totally different plant.

ROSACEÆ.

MOQUILEA TURIUVA, Hook. f. in Mart. Fl. Bras. xiv. pt. II. p. 25.

Savannahs generally, *McConnell & Quelch*, 308.

HIRTELLA AMERICANA, Linn. Sp. Pl. ed. 1. p. 34.

Savannahs generally, *McConnell & Quelch*, 309.

RUBUS URTICÆFOLIUS, Poir. Encycl. vi. p. 246.

Upper slopes of Mount Roraima, *McConnell & Quelch*, 11.—Widely dispersed throughout Tropical America.

It is uncertain whether *R. Schomburgkii*, Klotzsch, in R. Schomb. Reisen in Brit.-Guiana, iii. p. 1102, is a synonym of this species or identical with *R. guyanensis*, Focke. in Brem. Abh. iv. (1874), p. 160, as no description is given by Klotzsch, and Schomburgk collected both species.

SAXIFRAGACEÆ.

WEINMANNIA GUYANENSIS, Klotzsch, in R. Schomb. Reisen in Brit.-Guiana, iii. p. 1089; Engler, in Linnæa, xxxvi. (1870), p. 605; Oliver, in Trans. Linn. Soc. Ser. II. Bot. ii. (1887), p. 273.

Summit of Mount Roraima, *McConnell & Quelch*, 92, 636.—Endemic.

The foliage of this plant is somewhat variable. In some examples the leaves are all trifoliolate, this being the typical form; in others they all consist of one leaflet only, whilst others have trifoliolate and unifoliolate leaves on the same branch.

WEINMANNIA FAGARIOIDES, H. B. & K. Nov. Gen. & Sp. vi. p. 54.

W. glabra, Linn. f. *var.* ?, Oliver, in Trans. Linn. Soc. Ser. II. Bot. ii. (1887), p. 273.

Summit of Mount Roraima, *McConnell & Quelch*, 639.—Also on the Andes of Peru, Bolivia, and Ecuador, from 6000–10,000 ft. elevation.

The specimens collected by im Thurn upon Roraima have longer leaves, with more numerous and narrower leaflets and longer and more lax racemes than those of the present collections; but I believe both forms belong to *Weinmannia fagarioides*, H. B. & K., which seems to be somewhat variable in the characters mentioned.

DROSERACE.E.

DROSERA COMMUNIS, A. St. Hil. Pl. Rem. Bres. p. 267; Oliver, in Trans. Linn. Soc. Ser. II. Bot. ii. (1887), p. 273.

D. Roraimæ, Klotzsch, in R. Schomb. Reisen in Brit.-Guiana, iii. p. 1090.

Upper slopes of Mount Roraima, *McConnell & Quelch*, 42. Summit of Mount Roraima, *McConnell & Quelch*, 85, 681. Arabapu River, *McConnell & Quelch*, 154.— Widely distributed in eastern South America, westward to New Granada, and southward to Paraguay.

MYRTACE.E.

CAMPOMANESIA COÆTANEA, Berg, in Mart. Fl. Bras. xiv. pt. i. p. 44.

Kanuku Mountains, *McConnell & Quelch*, 275.

MYRTUS MYRICOIDES, H. B. & K. Nov. Gen. & Sp. vi. p. 131, t. 539.

M. sp. nov. aff. myricoides, Oliver, in Trans. Linn. Soc. Ser. II. Bot. ii. (1887), p. 273.

Summit of Mount Roraima, *McConnell & Quelch*, 195.—Also in the Andes of Colombia up to 11,000 ft. elevation.

This was considered to be a new species by Prof. Oliver, but I cannot distinguish it by any specific character from *M. myricoides*, H. B. & K.

MYRTUS RORAIMENSIS, N. E. Brown, sp. n. Omnino glabra. Folia parva, anguste oblonga vel oblongo-lanceolata, obtusa, coriacea, utrinque glanduloso-punctata, supra nitida, rugulosa. Flores axillares. Petala orbicularia, glanduloso-punctata. Stamina quam petala breviora. Ovarium 3-loculare.

A branching shrub, quite glabrous in all parts. Leaves small, 4–6 lin. long, including the $\frac{1}{2}$–1 lin. long petiole, $1\frac{1}{2}$–$3\frac{1}{2}$ lin. broad, usually narrowly oblong or oblong-lanceolate, occasionally ovate, obtuse, rounded at the base, rigidly coriaceous, shining and rugulose above in the dried state, pale beneath, gland-dotted on both sides. Flowers axillary, solitary. Pedicels $1\frac{1}{2}$–3 lin. long, bibracteolate at the apex. Bracteoles $1\frac{1}{2}$–$1\frac{3}{4}$ lin. long, $\frac{1}{4}$–$\frac{1}{2}$ lin. broad, linear or linear-lanceolate, obtuse, coriaceous, gland-dotted. Calyx-tube $\frac{3}{4}$ lin. long, hemispherical; lobes about 1 lin. long, $\frac{3}{4}$–$\frac{4}{5}$ lin. broad, oblong or ovate-oblong, obtuse, gland-dotted. Petals about 2 lin. long and broad, suborbicular, very obtuse, gland-dotted. Stamens shorter than the petals. Ovary 3-celled; ovules several in each cell. Berry drooping, globose, about 3 lin. diam., crowned with the calyx-lobes. Summit of Mount Roraima, 8600 ft., *McConnell & Quelch*, 635, 641.

This species somewhat resembles *M. myricoides*, H. B. & K., but differs in having perfectly glabrous stems, smaller, narrower, and less acute leaves, shorter pedicels, and smaller calyx-lobes.

LECYTHIS VENUSTA, Miers, in Trans. Linn. Soc. xxx. (1874), p. 214.

Mazaruni River, 200 ft., *McConnell & Quelch*, 713.

MELASTOMACE.E.

MICROLICIA BRYANTHOIDES, Oliver, in Trans. Linn. Soc. Ser. II. Bot. ii. (1887), p. 274
t. 39. f. B; Cogn. in DC. Monog. Phan. vii. p. 49.
Summit of Mount Roraima, *McConnell & Quelch*, 630.—Endemic.

RHYNCHANTHERA GRANDIFLORA. DC. Prod. iii. p. 107.
Ireng Valley, *McConnell & Quelch*, 230.

SIPHANTHERA MICROLICIOIDES. Cogn. in Mart. Fl. Bras. xiv. pt. iii. p. 199; and in DC.
Monog. Phan. vii. p. 113.
Meisneria cordifolia, Benth. in Hook. Journ. Bot. ii. (1840), p. 299; R. Schomb. Reisen in Brit.-
Guiana, iii. p. 1101.
M. microlicioides, Naud. in Ann. Sc. Nat. Sér. III. xii. (1849), p. 204; Oliver, in Trans. Linn. Soc.
Ser. II. Bot. ii. (1887), p. 274.
Upper slopes of Mount Roraima, *McConnell & Quelch*, 8. Kotinga Valley, *McConnell
& Quelch*, 182.—Apparently endemic in the Roraima region.

DESMOSCELIS VILLOSA, Naud. in Ann. Sc. Nat. Sér. III. xiii. (1850), p. 30.
Kotinga Valley, *McConnell & Quelch*, 195.

MACAIREA ASPERA, N. E. Brown, sp. n. (Plate 2.) Folia oblonga, obtusa, supra scaberrima,
subtus appresse rufo-tomentosa. Calyx appresse pubescens et glandulosus. Petala
obovato-oblonga, obtussisima, glanduloso-ciliata. Staminum filamenta superne
glandulosa. Ovarium superne dense glandulosum, stylo parce glanduloso.
A branching shrub; clothed on the young shoots, branches of the panicle, pedicels
and calyx with rather long, rust-coloured, adpressed hairs. Leaves opposite;
petiole 4–6 lin. long, pubescent like the stems; blade 1¼–3 in. long, 8–17 lin. broad,
oblong, obtuse, or shortly and stoutly apiculate, cuneately rounded into the petiole
at the base, coriaceous, 3-nerved, with the lateral nerves close to the revolute margin,
scabrid with minute, conical, hair-tipped tubercles on the upper surface, tomentose
beneath with a dense adpressed pubescence of rust-coloured hairs. Panicles 4–6 in.
long, 2–3½ in. broad, many-flowered. Pedicels 1–2½ lin. long, minutely bibracteolate in
the middle. Calyx with sessile glands mingled with the hairs outside; tube campanulate,
1½ lin. long; lobes 1½ lin. long, deltoid, acuminate. Petals 3–4 lin. long, 2½–3 lin. broad,
oblong-ovate, very obtuse, minutely gland-ciliate, glabrous. Stamens glandular on the
apical part of the filaments. Anthers with the connective dilated at the base into a
cordate-orbicular shield. Ovary free, densely covered with glands on the upper part;
style filiform, sparsely glandular.
Upper slopes of Mount Roraima, *McConnell & Quelch*, 31.
Another specimen (no. 24, *McConnell & Quelch*), collected at the same place as no. 31,
is identical with it in all particulars excepting the anthers, in which the portion of the
connective between the pollen-cells and the dilated base is very much longer than in 31,

as shown in figs. 6–7, but I cannot consider this variation of sufficient importance to separate the two specifically.

Allied to *Macairea thyrsiflora*, DC., and *M. albiflora*, Cogn.; differing in the very much rougher upper surface and different indumentum of the lower surface of the leaves and in the stouter anthers. *M. albiflora*, Cogn., according to Spruce's label, has purple flowers, not white as described by Cogniaux.

MACAIREA PACHYPHYLLA, Benth. in Hook. Journ. Bot. ii. (1840), p. 292; R. Schomb. Reisen in Brit.-Guiana, iii. pp. 1100, 1192; Cogn. in DC. Monog. Phan. vii. p. 178.

Kotinga Valley. *McConnell & Quelch*, 181.—Apparently endemic to the vicinity of Roraima.

TIBOUCHINA FRATERNA, N. E. Brown, sp. n.   Folia anguste elliptica, utrinque æqualiter subacuta, 3-nervia, subtus appresse squamosa, supra striolata, et marginibus et secundum lineas duas inter nervos squamosa. Bracteæ liberæ, oblongæ, obtusæ. Calyx appresse squamosus, 5-lobus, tubo cylindrico quam lobis longiore. Petala elliptico-obovata, unguiculata, glanduloso-ciliata.

Branchlets densely clothed with imbricating, lanceolate, acuminate, brownish scales about ½ lin. long, those at the nodes about twice as long and more acuminate. Leaves spreading; petiole 1–1½ lin. long, scaly; blade ¾–1 in. long, 4–6 lin. broad, narrowly elliptic, about equally acute or subacute at both ends, apiculate, 3-nerved, the underside clothed with adpressed acuminate scales, those on the nerves much larger than the rest, the upper surface finely striate, with a longitudinal row of minute scales near each of the lateral nerves and along the margins. Cymules 2–3-flowered, subsessile or with peduncles up to 3½ lin. long, axillary and terminal, forming a terminal inflorescence 1–2 in. long, 1 in. broad, clothed to the tips of the calyx-lobes with pale, rosy-tinted acuminate scales. Bracts free, 2–4 lin. long, about 1½ lin. broad, oblong, obtuse, resembling reduced leaves; bracteoles smaller, thinner, more glabrous, free, ciliate with long hair-like scales. Pedicels very short, scarcely 1 lin. long. Calyx-tube 3 lin. long and about 1½ lin. diam., cylindric-campanulate; lobes 2 lin. long, 1½ lin. broad at the base, whence they gradually taper in a nearly straight line to an acute point, erect or very slightly spreading, glabrous inside, ciliate. Petals 7 lin. long, 3½ lin. broad, elliptic-obovate, very obtuse, clawed, minutely ciliate with gland-tipped hairs, and with a few long simple hairs at the apex, otherwise glabrous. Stamens 10, unequal, glabrous; the longer anthers 5 lin. long, the shorter 4 lin. long, all attenuate to a subulate point, opening by one terminal pore; connective bifid at its insertion on the filament. Ovary free, oblong, densely covered with hair-like scales; style slender, glabrous.

Upper slopes of Mount Roraima, *McConnell & Quelch*, 17.

A very distinct species, which, according to the arrangement of Cogniaux, I think should be placed in the section *Lepidotæ*, although it bears very little resemblance to the only two species (*T. lepidota*, Baill., and *T. paleacea*, Cogn.) at present placed under that section. It has much more resemblance to *T. Spruceana*, Cogn., and *T. aspera*, Aubl., but the free (not connate) bracts and bracteoles at once separate it from the section to which they belong.

TIBOUCHINA LASIOPHYLLA, Cogn. in Mart. Fl. Bras. xiv. pt. III. p. 297; and in DC. Monog. Phan. vii. p. 270.

Pterolepis lasiophylla, Triana, in Trans. Linn. Soc. xxviii. (1871), p. 40; Oliver, in Trans. Linn. Soc. Ser. II. Bot. ii. (1887), p. 274.

Kotinga Valley, *McConnell & Quelch*, 183, 197.   Ireng Valley, *McConnell & Quelch*, 205.   Slope of Mount Roraima, at 5400 ft. *im Thurn*, 59.—Only known from the above localities.

TIBOUCHINA ASPERA, Aubl. Pl. Guian. i. p. 446, t. 177; R. Schomb. Reisen in Brit.-Guiana, iii. pp. 1100, 1191.

Pleroma tibouchinum, Triana, in Trans. Linn. Soc. xxviii. (1871), p. 45, t. 3; Oliver, in Trans. Linn. Soc. Ser. II. Bot. ii. (1887), p. 274.

Ireng Valley, *McConnell & Quelch*, 217.—Widely spread in Tropical South America, extending westward to Colombia and Peru.

MARCETIA TAXIFOLIA, DC. Prod. iii. p. 124; R. Schomb. Reisen in Brit.-Guiana, ii. p. 216, and iii. p. 1100; Oliver, in Trans. Linn. Soc. Ser. II. Bot. ii. (1887), p. 273. Upper slopes of Mount Roraima, *McConnell & Quelch*, 13, 20; *im Thurn.* 68; *Appun*, 1114, 1153.   Kotinga Valley near Roraima, *McConnell & Quelch*, 149.

With the exception of the above localities, this species is only known from Brazil, where it is a common and widely spread plant.

MARCETIA JUNIPERINA, DC. Prod. iii. p. 125 ; Oliver, in Trans. Linn. Soc. Ser. II. Bot. ii. (1887), p. 274.

Summit of Mount Roraima, *McConnell & Quelch*, 86, 644.—Also in Venezuela at Cumana and Merida.

CHAETOLEPIS ANISANDRA, Naud. in Ann. Sc. Nat. Sér. III. xiv. (1850), p. 140; Cogn. in DC. Monog. Phan. vii. p. 171.

On the face of the cliff of Mount Roraima, at 7000–8000 ft., *McConnell & Quelch.* 22.—Endemic.

MONOCHAETUM BONPLANDII, Naud. in Ann. Sci. Nat. Sér. III. xiv. (1850), p. 51; Oliver, in Trans. Linn. Soc. Ser. II. Bot. ii. (1887), p. 274; Cogn. in DC. Monog. Phan. vii. p. 393.

Kotinga Valley, *McConnell & Quelch*, 189.—Also in Venezuela. Colombia, Ecuador, and Peru.

MICONIA HOLOSERICEA, DC. Prod. iii. p. 181.

M. albicans, Steud. Nom. ed. 2, ii. p. 139.

Upper slopes of Mount Roraima, *McConnell & Quelch*, 28.—Throughout Tropical America from Mexico to Paraguay.

MICONIA TINIFOLIA, Naud. in Ann. Sc. Nat. Sér. III. xvi. (1851), p. 225.
Kotinga Valley, *McConnell & Quelch*, 191. Summit of Mount Roraima, *McConnell & Quelch*, 633.— Also in Venezuela.

LYTHRACEÆ.

CUPHEA GRACILIS, H. B. & K. Nov. Gen. & Sp. vi. p. 199, var. MEDIA, Koehne. in Mart. Fl. Bras. xiii. pt. II. p. 284.
Ireng Valley, *McConnell & Quelch*, 225.

ONAGRACEÆ.

JUSSIEA LONGIFOLIA, DC. in Mém. Soc. Phys. Genèv. ii. pt. II. (1824). p. 141.
Ireng Valley, *McConnell & Quelch*, 208. 214, 227.

TURNERACEÆ.

TURNERA ULMIFOLIA, Linn. Sp. Pl. ed. 1, p. 271.
Kotinga Valley. *McConnell & Quelch*, 174. Ireng Valley. *McConnell & Quelch*, 256. 260.

TURNERA VELUTINA, Benth. in Hook. Journ. Bot. iv. (1842). p. 116.
Ireng Valley, *McConnell & Quelch*. 240.

PIRIQUETA GUIANENSIS, N. E. Brown, sp. n.   Perennis, caulibus simplicibus, pilis stellatis cum setulis intermixtis tomentosa.   Folia petiolata, anguste vel oblongo-lanceolata, obtusa, obtuse dentata, dense tomentosa.   Flores axillares, solitarii.   Pedicelli 4-10 lin. longi, supra medium articulati.   Petala purpurea ?, glabra.   Fructus globosus, dense appresse pubescens.   Semina oblonga, reticulato-foveolata.

A perennial herb growing to about 1 ft. high.   Stems several from the same rootstock, rather slender, usually simple, tomentose with a short down of stellate hairs intermingled with longer spreading hairs.   Leaves petiolate ; petiole 1-2 lin. long, blade ½-1 in. long, 1½-4 lin. broad, narrowly oblong or oblong-lanceolate, obtuse, obtusely 3-6-toothed on each side, densely stellate tomentose on both sides.   Flowers axillary, solitary.   Pedicels 4-10 in. long, jointed above the middle, stellate-tomentose.   Calyx 3-4½ lin. long, stellate-tomentose outside ; tube about 1 lin. long, shortly obconical, lobes 2-3½ lin. long, 1-1½ lin. broad, ovate-lanceolate or lanceolate, acute.   Petals much longer than the calyx, obovate, glabrous, with a fringed scale at their base, apparently purple.   Stamens about 2¼ lin. long, with glabrous filaments.   Ovary ovoid, densely adpressed-pubescent, not tubercled ; styles 2 lin. long, with a few scattered hairs or almost glabrous ; stigmas dilated.   Capsule globose, about 2 lin. diam., 3-valved, densely covered with adpressed, rather silky hairs.   Seeds 1 lin. long, oblong, rather coarsely pitted, pale reddish brown.

British Guiana ; without precise locality. *Appun*, 1858. Ireng Valley, *McConnell & Quelch*, 264.

Allied to *P. Duarteana*, Urb.

Piriqueta villosa, Aubl. Pl. Guian. i. p. 298, t. 117.

P. cistoides, Mey. ex Steud. Nom. ed. 2, ii. p. 344.

Kotinga Valley, McConnell & Quelch, 178.

PASSIFLORACEÆ.

Passiflora Quelchii, N. E. Brown, sp. n. (Plate 3.) Frutex vel arbor, glaber. Folia petiolata, cuneato-oblonga, acuta vel obtusissima, undulata, coriacea; petiolus apice biglandulosus. Stipulæ minutæ, subulatæ, deciduæ. Cirrhi nulli. Flores in racemum abbreviatum dispositi, glabri. Calycis tubus elongatus, cylindricus. Sepala petalis subconformia, oblongo-lanceolata, obtusa. Corona faucialis uniserialis, multipartita, segmentis complanatis prope apicem dilatatis oblique acuminatis; corona interior e tubo versus basin emergens, multipartita, segmentis complanatis lineari-falcatis.

Shrubby or arborescent, not climbing; branches woody, glabrous. Leaves simple, entire, very coriaceous, 2-4 lin. distant, spreading, glabrous; petiole 4-6 lin. long, moderately stout, with two large sessile glands at the apex; blade 3-5 in. long, ¾-1½ in. broad, cuneately oblong, gradually tapering from ¾ the way up in a slightly curved line to an acute base, shortly acute or very obtuse and slightly emarginate with an apiculus in the notch, with strongly undulated margins; primary lateral veins 12-15 on each side of the midrib, very spreading, uniting close to the margin in a series of broad loops; secondary veins much reticulated, all prominent on both sides. Stipules minute, subulate, very deciduous. Tendrils none. Flowers in short racemes or clusters, probably on the older parts of the branches; axis of the inflorescence ½-¾ in. long, several-flowered, glabrous. Pedicels 1-2 lin. long, glabrous. Calyx-tube about 1 in. long, 1½-2 lin. diam. in the dried state, cylindric, slightly enlarged at the mouth, glabrous; the lobes 10-12 lin. long, 2¼-3½ lin. broad, oblong-lanceolate, obtuse or subacute. Petals similar to the calyx-lobes and of about the same size. Corona in two series; one placed towards the bottom of the calyx-tube, consisting of numerous linear-falcate, acute, erect filaments about 1½ lin. long; the other at the mouth of the tube, consisting of numerous flattened, somewhat hatchet-shaped segments rather more than ½ in. long, with the dilated part slightly toothed and dorsally produced into a short point. Gynophore nearly 1½ in. long, terete or perhaps sulcate at the base, glabrous. Filaments of the stamens 2 lin. long. Ovary oblong, 9-striate; styles 2 lin. long, stigmas capitate.

Ireng Valley, McConnell & Quelch, 207.

A very distinct species, easily distinguished from all the others of shrubby habit by its cuneately oblong, undulated leaves, shortly racemose flowers, and long calyx-tube, besides other characters.

ARALIACEÆ.

Didymopanax rugosum, N. E. Brown, sp. n. Folia 3-foliolata, foliolis ellipticis vel elliptico-oblongis utrinque obtusis, rigide coriaceis, supra glabris rugosis, subtus dense tomentosis. Umbellæ compositæ, longe pedunculatæ, fulvo-tomentosæ, multifloræ. Petala ovata, acuta. Drupa immatura valde compressa, suborbiculata,

Leaves digitately trifoliolate; petiole stout, $\frac{1}{4}$ in. thick, tomentose, broken in the only specimen seen and about $3\frac{1}{2}$ in. long; leaflets rigidly coriaceous, above glabrous and rugose, with a narrow prominent midrib and impressed veins and veinlets, beneath tomentose on the very stout prominent midrib and the primary veins, and covered with a dense blanket-like tawny tomentum between them ; the lateral pair $3\frac{1}{2}$-4 in. long, $2\frac{1}{2}$-$2\frac{3}{4}$ in. broad, elliptic, obtuse at both ends, mucronulate, with stout petiolules about 2 lin. long ; the terminal leaflet $4\frac{3}{4}$ in. long, $2\frac{3}{4}$ in. broad, elliptic-oblong, slightly emarginate at the obtuse apex, mucronulate, with a stout petiole 4 lin. long.   Umbel very compound, 6-8-rayed, many-flowered, $2\frac{3}{4}$-$3\frac{1}{2}$ in. diam., with a stout, more or less flattened peduncle 4-7 in. long, 2-3 lin. thick, everywhere, to the outside of the petals, densely covered with a tawny tomentum, becoming greyish with age.   Secondary umbels 6-7-rayed, some of the rays bearing a single flower, others dividing into tertiary umbels, some of which again divide in a similar manner, forming 2-4-flowered umbels of a fourth order.   Bracts and bracteoles suborbicular, about $\frac{1}{2}$-1 lin. diam.   Pedicels $1\frac{1}{2}$-2 lin. long, stout. not jointed. Calyx-limb shortly cupular, 5-toothed ; teeth $\frac{1}{4}$-$\frac{1}{3}$ lin. long, deltoid, acute.   Bud globose. Petals 5, about $\frac{3}{4}$ lin. long, and nearly as broad, deltoid-ovate, acute, rather thick, glabrous within.   Stamens 5, not longer than the petals.   Ovary 2-celled ; styles 2, somewhat flattened, divergent in young fruit, which is suborbicular in outline and compressed.

Summit of Mount Roraima, 8600 ft . *McConnell & Quelch*, 663.

A most distinct species, in general habit more like *Didymopanax Spruceanum*, Seem., than any other; but the very thick rigid leaves, rugose above and tomentose beneath, at once distinguish it from that and all others.

SCIADOPHYLLUM UMBELLATUM, N. E. Brown, sp. n.   Folia digitata, foliolis 6-8 petiolulatis oblongo-lanceolatis vel oblanceolato-oblongis obtuse acutis basi cuneatis supra glabris subtus tomento appresso pallido vestitis.   Umbellæ compositæ, longissime pedunculatæ, multifloræ.   Petala ovata, acuta.   Fructus immaturus 5-angularis, compressus.

Leaves digitately 6-8-foliolate; petiole 4-6 in. long, $1\frac{1}{2}$-2 lin. thick, glabrous ; leaflets coriaceous, unequal, $2\frac{1}{2}$-6 in. long, excluding the 2-7 lin. long petiolules, 1-$2\frac{1}{4}$ in. broad, oblong-lanceolate or oblanceolate-oblong, obtusely pointed at the apex, cuneate at the base, entire or very slightly repand, slightly revolute along the margins, glabrous above, with a thin layer of pale close tomentum beneath ; midrib prominent on both sides, stouter beneath ; primary lateral veins 9-16 on each side of the midrib, rather slender and not very prominent.   Umbel compound, 2-3 in. diam., on a peduncle 9-12 in. long, $2\frac{1}{2}$ lin. thick : rays numerous, unequal, $\frac{1}{2}$-$1\frac{1}{4}$ in. long. $\frac{3}{4}$-1 lin. thick.   Bracts minute, rounded.   Secondary umbels 10-16-flowered.   Pedicels 1-$1\frac{3}{4}$ lin. long.   Calyx-limb annular, entire or very minutely 5-toothed.   Petals 5, acute.   Stamens 5, not exceeding the petals.   Ovary 3-5-celled ; style or column of united styles $1\frac{1}{4}$ lin. long, minutely 3-5-fid at the apex.   Young fruit deeply 3-5-angled, angles compressed.

Summit of Mount Roraima, 8600 ft. *McConnell & Quelch*, 666. .

- Allied to *S. coriaceum*, Marchal, from which it differs in its more pointed leaves, very much shorter and stouter pedicels, and different indumentum. The indumentum which covers the whole of the inflorescence is rather peculiar, and is neither scurfy nor hairy, and when highly magnified seems to consist of a very thin dense covering of very minute, flattened, and very closely adpressed hairs, producing a greyish hue.

This species and *Sciadophyllum coriaceum* differ from all the others in the genus in having the flowers collected into a compound umbel terminating a long peduncle, and not paniculate; for although *S. coriaceum* has a second whorl of umbels below the terminal one, they all spring from one level, and the inflorescence cannot be called a panicle. The styles also of these two species are united in a column, and in this character, and indeed in their entire floral structure, they quite agree with *Heptapleurum*, a genus that is only artificially separated from *Sciadophyllum* by this one point, as has already been pointed out in Benth. & Hook. f. Genera Plantarum, i. pp. 940, 942. As there are some species of *Heptapleurum* in which the styles are at first united in a column and during the growth of the young fruit become free, it appears to me that *Sciadophyllum* should include *Heptapleurum*, when it would form a genus fairly uniform in character and of world-wide distribution within the tropics.

RUBIACEÆ.

HENRIQUEZIA JENMANI, K. Schum. in Mart. Fl. Bras. vi. pt. vi. p. 135. (Plate 4.)

Mazaruni River. *McConnell & Quelch*, 711; *Jenman*, 629.

This handsome tree appears only to have been collected in this single locality.

CHALEPOPHYLLUM SPECIOSUM, N. E. Brown, sp. n. (Plate 5, figs. 10–17.) Frutex glaber, ramis tetragonis. Folia opposita ad apicem ramorum subconferta, coriacea, sessilia, obovata, obtusa, subapiculata. Flores in axillis supremis (foliis delapsis) solitarii, breviter pedicellati, bibracteati. Calycis lobi æquales vel inæquales, lineares vel oblongi, acuti. Corolla hypocrateriformis, 5-lobata, tubo longissimo, lobis anguste lanceolatis vel oblongis acutis. Stamina inclusa. Stylus sæpius inclusus.

A stoutly-branched shrub, glabrous in all parts excepting the inside of the corolla. Branches 4-angled, 2 lin. thick; internodes very short, $1\frac{1}{2}$–5 lin. long. Leaves opposite, in a cluster of 3–5 pairs at the tips of the branches, subsessile, $1\frac{1}{4}$–2 in. long, $\frac{1}{2}$–1 in. long, more or less obovate, obtuse, bluntly apiculate, cuneate at the base, rigidly coriaceous in the dried state, shining above, pale beneath, slightly revolute along the margins; midrib stout and conspicuous beneath; veins inconspicuous or not at all visible. Stipules broad-based, abruptly contracted into a linear point about $1\frac{1}{2}$ lin. long, persistent long after the leaves have fallen. Flowers usually 2 to each shoot, or sometimes 1 only, arising immediately below the terminal tuft of leaves in the axils of fallen leaves or in those of the lowest pair, solitary in each axil. Pedicels 1–4 lin. long, stout, flattened, bibracteate at the base of the ovary. Bracts 4–8 lin. long, $1\frac{1}{2}$–5 lin. broad, of the form and substance of reduced leaves. Calyx-lobes 5–10 lin. long, 1–$2\frac{1}{2}$ lin. broad, equal or unequal, varying from linear to oblong, acute, erect, coriaceous. Corolla very variable in size, hypocrateriform, regular, 5-lobed; tube $1\frac{3}{4}$–$3\frac{1}{2}$ in. long, about $1\frac{1}{2}$ lin.

diam., cylindric, 5-grooved, slightly enlarged and densely hairy inside at the throat around the anthers; lobes spreading or recurved, 1-2 in. long, 2-6 lin. broad, linear-lanceolate or oblong, acute, glabrous, contorted in the bud.   Stamens 5, included. inserted in the throat of the corolla-tube; filaments about 2½ lin. long; anthers 3-3½ lin. long, dorsifixed, with a rather long and broad attachment to the filaments, linear, acute, bifid at the base, glabrous.   Ovary 2½-3 lin. long, stoutly obconical, 2-celled; style about as long as the corolla-tube, or shorter than the anthers or rarely exserted, glabrous; stigma of two oblong obtuse lobes about 1 lin. long.   Ovules numerous, flattened, on broad placentas that are peltately attached along their middle by a very short narrow plate to the septum.   Fruit not seen.

Summit of Mount Roraima, 8600 ft., *McConnell & Quelch*, 100, 305, 653.

The variation in the length of the style would seem to imply that the flowers are heterostyled, but it may be due to a lengthening at various periods of development. The stems in the figure on Plate 5 are not represented of sufficient stoutness.

SIPANEA PRATENSIS, Aubl. Pl. Guian. i. p. 147, t. 56; im Thurn & Oliver, in Trans. Linn. Soc. ser. 11. ii. (1887), pp. 261, 276.

Kotinga Valley, *McConnell & Quelch*, 175, 185, 198.—Widely distributed in eastern Tropical America from Trinidad to Minas Geraes and westward to Colombia.

DIDYMOCHLAMYS CONNELLII, N. E. Brown, sp. n.   (Plate 5, figs. 1-9.)   Folia alterna, oblique oblanceolata, subabrupte acuta, glabra.   Bracteæ exteriores suborbiculares, brevissime cuspidatæ.   Corollæ tubus supra medium ampliatus, ore contractus; lobi infra medium bilobulati lobulis lineari-oblongis undulatis subtortis.

A small herb, with a simple stem 1¼-6 in. long.   Leaves alternate, distichous, 1-1¼ in. long, including the very short petiole, 2½-4½ lin. broad, obliquely or subfalcately oblanceolate, acute or rounded in at the apex to a very short cuspidate point, tapering from above the middle to an unequal base, the upper side of which is very narrow and acute, and the lower side broadly rounded or subtruncate, glabrous on both sides; under surface pale, densely covered with large stomata, which appear as whitish dots under a lens; stipule solitary, 3-4 lin. long, linear, acuminate, glabrous.   Peduncle terminal, about ¼ in. long, bearing two suborbicular, apiculate, glabrous bracts, about ½ in. in length and breadth, enclosing 2 (or more?) shortly pedicellate flowers and 1 (or more?) linear acute bracteole.   Calyx-lobes slightly unequal, ¾-1 lin. long, lanceolate, acute, erect, glabrous.   Corolla-tube about ½ in. long, probably somewhat compressed, dilated a little above the middle, then narrowed to the mouth, glabrous, with the exception of a ring of hairs inside near the base; lobes divided to slightly below the middle into two diverging, linear-oblong, obtuse, undulated and somewhat twisted lobules 1½ lin. long and rather more than ½ lin. broad, the basal entire part being about 1 lin. long and broad, deltoid-ovate, slightly concave, with a minute, obtuse, incurved point at the apex between the lobules.   Stamens 5, included, inserted below the middle of the corolla-tube, unequal, 2 longer than the rest and inserted higher up, having on one side a pair and on the other side one of the shorter stamens alternating with them; filaments glabrous, anthers linear. Glands of the disk 4, in 2 opposite pairs, the larger pair partly enclosing the smaller pair. Ovary inferior, laterally compressed, 2-celled; style included, filiform; stigma of 2 short oblong lobes; placenta ascending from near the base of the septum, thin; ovules numerous, flat.

On the Roraima Range at 3500 ft., *McConnell & Quelch*, 714; Kaieteur Falls on the Potaro River, *Jenman*, 7462.

This is one of the most remarkable plants in the collection; its alternate leaves and general habit give it the appearance of a Gesneraceous rather than of a Rubiaceous plant. The two large bracts enclosing the flowers and the bilobed corolla-lobes are very remarkable characteristics. It is very closely allied to *Didymochlamys Whitei*, Hook. f., from New Granada, the only other known species, but differs in its much smaller leaves and very much longer corolla-lobules. In *D. Whitei* the leaves are 1¾–3½ in. long, 4–11 lin. broad, and taper at the apex into a long acuminate point, and the subquadrate lobules of the corolla are only about ¾ a line long and the same in breadth.

To the generic characters of *Didymochlamys* may be added the following description of the fruit, taken from a specimen of *D. Whitei* sent to Kew by Mr. R. B. White in 1882:—Fruit a laterally-compressed 2-celled capsule, dehiscing at the apex between the glands; placentas ascending from near the base of the septum, thin; seeds numerous, minute, ovate, flattened, thinly covered with rather long hairs, with a dense tuft at the narrower (micropyle ?) end; testa rather coriaceous, moderately thin; albumen copious, oily; embryo minute.

The two smaller glands of the disk in the fruiting stage of *D. Whitei* are a little longer than the larger glands, they are tubular in the upper part and may assist in the dispersion of the seeds.

TOCOYENA NEGLECTA, N. E. Brown, sp. n. Folia breviter petiolata, lanceolata vel elliptico-lanceolata, acuta, basi cuneata, supra pubescentia, subtus tomentosa. Cymae terminales, subsessiles, 9–20-florae. Calyx acute 5-dentatus, plus minusve tomentosus. Corollae tubus 3–3½ poll. longus, extra tomentosus, intra glaber, fauce hirtus; lobi oblique oblongo-lanceolati, subacuti, glabri, ciliati.

Branches subterete or obscurely 4-angled, with a light brown bark, tomentose when young. Leaves opposite, 3–7 in. long, 1¾–3½ in. broad, lanceolate, elliptic-lanceolate or slightly obovate, acute, cuneately tapering at the base into a petiole 1½–3 lin. long, somewhat harshly pubescent above, densely tomentose beneath, with the hairs along the veins distinctly diverging on either side; primary veins 9–13 on each side of the midrib, and together with the reticulated veinlets impressed above, prominent beneath. Stipules about 2 lin. long, triangular, acute, at first tomentose, becoming glabrous with age. Cymes terminal, subsessile, about 9–20-flowered. Flowers sessile. Calyx more or less tomentose; the tube 1½–2½ lin. long, oblong, slightly tapering downwards; the limb cup-shaped, with 5 deltoid acuminate teeth ¾–2 lin. long. Corolla hypocrateriform, 5-lobed, white; the tube 3–3½ in. long, about 1¼ lin. diam., slightly enlarged at the mouth, tomentose outside, glabrous within, except in the throat, which is densely hairy; the lobes 10-12 lin. long, 5-6 lin. broad, obliquely oblong-lanceolate, subacute, glabrous on both sides, ciliate along the outer margin, but in the younger stage, when contorted into the lanceolate acuminate bud, the outside towards the base is more or less pubescent or tomentose. Anthers sessile at the mouth of the corolla-tube, partly exserted, ⅓ lin. long, oblong-lanceolate, obtuse. Ovary 2-celled; style as long as the corolla-tube, slender, glabrous; stigma of 2 oblong obtuse lobes, about 2 lin. long. 1 lin. broad. Fruit globose, about ¾ in. diam., thinly pubescent or subglabrous.

British Guiana : Maimatta on the Rupununi River, *Jenman*, 5525, 5742 ; Kotinga Valley, *McConnell & Quelch*, 163; Roraima, *Schomburgk*, 478 ; Surumu River, *Schomburgk*, 772 B.

Allied to *Tocoyena fœtida*, Poepp. & Endl., but differs in its much shorter petioles and corolla-tube. From *T. velutina*, Spruce (which is a very distinct species, wrongly referred to *T. fœtida* by K. Schumann), it differs in the less elliptic form of the leaves, in the indumentum, and very different calyx-limb. Schomburgk's specimens are quoted by K. Schumann in the 'Flora Brasiliensis,' vi. pt. vi. p. 318, under *T. formosa*, K. Schum., which is a quite different species, with orbicular leaves and short, ellipsoidal, obtuse buds.

RETINIPHYLLUM LAXIFLORUM, N. E. Brown. (Plate **6**.) Folia petiolata, elliptica vel elliptico-oblonga, obtusa basi subcuneata, glabra. Racemus terminalis, 3-9-florus, floribus longe pedicellatis. Bracteoli sub ovario in cupulam disciformem minute denticulatam connati. Calyx non costatus, truncatus, minutissime 5-dentatus. Corolla utrinque sericeo-puberula, lobis reflexis tubo brevioribus.— *Patima laxiflora*, Benth. in Hook. Journ. Bot. iii. (1841) p. 220; R. Schomb. Reisen in Brit.-Guian. iii. p. 1142. *Synisoon Schomburgkianum*, Baill. in Bull. Soc. Linn. Paris (1879), p. 208 ; Baill. Hist. Pl. vii. p. 433 ; K. Schum. in Mart. Fl. Bras. vi. pt. vi. p. 398.

A shrub or tree, glabrous in all parts excepting the flowers, and exuding a varnish-like resin on various parts of the young branches and inflorescence. Branches moderately slender, with a brown bark. Leaves opposite, petiolate, thinly coriaceous ; petiole 2-8 lin. long ; blade 1½-4¾ in. long, 1-2¼ in. broad, shining above, paler beneath with distinctly reticulated veins. Stipules subtruncate, minutely apiculate. Raceme erect, terminal, very lax, 2-2¾ in. long, consisting of 1-4 pairs of opposite flowers and one terminal one. Bracts reduced to a minutely denticulate raised line. Pedicels 6-8 lin. long, ascending, slender. Bracteoles beneath the ovary connate into a very small, disk-like, minutely-denticulate involucel. Calyx 3½-4 lin. long, with the limb produced for 2-2¾ lin. above the ovary, tubular, truncate, with 5 very minute distant teeth, glabrous, but more or less coated with the varnish-like secretion. Corolla erect, 5-lobed, minutely adpressed-pubescent outside and inside, with a dense ring of white hairs near the base of the tube inside, below which it is glabrous; tube 8-9 lin. long, 1¼-1¾ lin. diam., cylindric; lobes pendulous, reflexed from their base, 7 lin. long, 1¼ lin. broad, linear-oblong, obtuse, nearly straight along one margin curved along the other, strictly contorted in the bud. Stamens inserted at the mouth of the tube, reflexed with the corolla-lobes; filaments 5 lin. long, pubescent ; anthers 2 lin. long, dorsifixed, lanceolate, produced beyond the cells into a subulate point at the apex and into an oblong, emarginate, membranous appendage at the base, glabrous; pollen apparently red. Ovary 5-celled, surmounted by a rather deep ring-like disk; style much exserted, 1¾ in. long, rather slender, pubescent; stigma slightly thickened, ovoid-conical, tipped with 5 minute points. Ovules 2 in each cell, collateral, axile, pendulous from near the top of the cell, and partly covered at the top by a cap-like outgrowth of the funicle-like placenta. Fruit a globose, ribbed berry about ¼ in. diam., crowned with the calyx-tube; endocarp hardened into 5 separable nutlets, 3-keeled on the back, triangular in transverse section, with a false cell under each lateral wing. Seeds not seen.

Aroie Creek, *im Thurn*, 6. Upper slopes of Mount Roraima, *McConnell & Quelch*, 18; *Appun*, 1175; *Schomburgk*, 724 (815 B), 158.

This very distinct species of *Retiniphyllum* appears to have been misunderstood by all authors. Originally it was doubtfully referred by Bentham to the genus *Patima*, and erroneously described as having very numerous seeds. Next, in Bentham and Hooker's 'Genera Plantarum,' ii. p. 98, it is confused with *Kutchubaea insignis*, Fisch., and the part of the generic description in that work, relating to the fruit, is drawn up from the present plant and not from the true *Kutchubaea*, which indeed it greatly resembles in habit, but differs in having a 5-lobed corolla, 5 exserted, reflexed stamens, with long filaments, a long exserted style, and in the presence of a minute disk-like involucel at the apex of the pedicel. which is jointed to the calyx; whilst in *Kutchubaea* the corolla is 8-lobed, the stamens are 8, with the anthers almost sessile and included in the throat of the corolla-tube, the style is included, and the pedicel is continuous with the calyx, without any trace of an involucel; the foliage and stipules of the two plants are also very different, besides disagreeing in several minor details. Finally Baillon made a distinct genus of it, which he placed next to *Knoxia*, where it has no affinity, for it is undoubtedly a true *Retiniphyllum*, allied to *R. scabrum*, Benth., but differing from that and all others of the genus by the long slender pedicels of its lax, few-flowered inflorescence. The involucel is characteristic of the genus *Retiniphyllum*.

PSYCHOTRIA CONCINNA, Oliver, in Trans. Linn. Soc. Ser. II. ii. (1887) p. 276, t. 42. f. B. Summit of Mount Roraima, *McConnell & Quelch*, 80, 89, 667.—Endemic.

PSYCHOTRIA CRASSA, Benth. in Hook. Journ. Bot. iii. (1841), p. 227; im Thurn & Oliver, in Trans. Linn. Soc. Ser. II. Bot. ii. (1887). pp. 265, 276; R. Schomb. Reisen in Brit.-Guiana, iii. p. 945.

Summit of Mount Roraima, *McConnell & Quelch*, 632. Also collected on Roraima by *Appun*, 1112.—Kanuku Mountains.

DIODIA HYSSOPIFOLIA, Cham. & Schlecht. in Linnæa, iii. (1828), p. 350. Kotinga Valley, *McConnell & Quelch*, 190.

COMPOSITÆ.

VERNONIA ACUTA, N. E. Brown, sp. n. Rami tomentosi. Folia alterna, brevissime petiolata, lanceolata, acutissima vel subpungentia, basi acuta, supra glabra, subtus tenuiter et appresse pubescentia, glanduloso-punctata ; petiolus tomentosus. Capitula in axillis aggregata, sessilia, sub-10-flora. Involucri squamæ 5–6 seriatæ, imbricatæ, lanceolatæ, acuminatæ, pungentes, subtomentosæ, exteriores gradatim minores. Achænia appresse pubescentia. Pappus biserialis, squamis exterioribus linearibus acutis quam setis interioribus multo brevioribus.

Branchlets densely tomentose. Leaves alternate, spreading ; petiole 1–2 lin. long, tomentose ; blade 1¼–2 in. long, ¼–½ in. broad, lanceolate, very acute and subpungent at the apex, acute at the base, entire, with revolute margins, rather rigid, glabrous above, except the midrib, which is pubescent, thinly covered with short adpressed hairs and gland-dotted beneath, with the veins and reticulated veinlets impressed above, prominent beneath. Heads in clusters of 3 or 4, sessile in the axils of the leaves at the ends of the branchlets, about ¼ in. diam., and about 10-flowered. Involucre-scales in 5 6 series, adpressed, lanceolate, acuminate, pungent-pointed, adpressed-pubescent or subtomentose, the innermost about 3 lin. long, ½–⅔ lin. broad, the others gradually smaller Corolla ¼ in. long, 5-lobed, with the linear acute lobes of equal length with the tube, glabrous. Style-branches only about ½ lin. longer than the stamens. Achenes rather more than 1 lin. long, adpressed-pubescent. Pappus in two series, white ; the outer of numerous linear acute scales, the inner of numerous bristles, slightly scabrous, much longer than the outer series.

Kotinga Valley, *McConnell & Quelch*, 192.

EUPATORIUM IVÆFOLIUM, Linn. Syst. ed. 10, p. 1205, var. GRACILLIMUM, Baker, in Mart. Fl. Bras. vi. pt. II. p. 290.

Ireng Valley, *McConnell & Quelch*, 242.

EUPATORIUM SUBOBTUSUM, DC. Prod. v. p. 161.

Ireng Valley, *McConnell & Quelch*, 211, 304.

EUPATORIUM RORAIMENSE, N. E. Brown, sp. n. Herbacea, ramis breviter pubescentibus. Folia opposita, petiolata, ovato-lanceolata, acuminata, glabra, crenato-dentata, petiolo pubescente. Capitula corymbosa, circa 20-flora. Involucri squamæ lineares, acutæ, glabræ. Corollæ 5-dentata, glabra, tubo supra medium ampliato, campanulato, dentibus ovatis, acutis. Achænia 5-angulata, angulis scaberulis. Pappi setæ scaberulæ, roseo-purpureæ.

Stems herbaceous, with a very fine spreading pubescence. Leaves opposite; petiole 4–6 lin. long, pubescent ; blade 1¼–2½ in. long, ½–1 in. broad, ovate-lanceolate, acuminate, crenately toothed, with teeth 1–2 lin. broad, glabrous on both sides, rather thin and submembranous in texture in the dried state. Corymbs terminal, compact, 2–2¼ in. diam., its branches ¼–1 in. long, and, together with the slender 1½–3 lin. long pedicels, pubescent like the stem. Bracteoles almost filiform. Heads about 2½ lin. diam., about 20-flowered. Involucre-scales 2-seriate, 2–2¼ lin. long. linear, acute, nearly or quite glabrous. Corolla glabrous, the tube 1 lin. long, slender below, dilated into a campanulate cup above the middle, with 5 ovate acute teeth ½ lin. long. Achenes 1 lin. long, 5-angled, slightly scabrous along the angles, blackish. Pappus-bristles slightly scabrous, rosy-purple.

Summit of Mount Roraima, *McConnell & Quelch*, 640.

This somewhat resembles *Eupatorium Pentlandianum*, DC. (*Maudon*, 259), but the corolla, pappus, and achenes are all much shorter, the corolla is very different in form, the involucre-scales are longer and narrower, and the leaves are less sharply toothed.

EUPATORIUM FUSCUM, N. E. Brown, sp. n. Rami validi, cum petiolis et corymbis nigrescente-tomentosi. Folia breviter petiolata, late ovata, obtusa, basi rotundata vel subcordata, irregulariter et obtuse dentata, subcoriacea, supra glabra, glanduloso-punctata, subtus fusco-pubescentia. Corymbi compacti. Capitula 15–16-flora. Involucri squamae biseriatae, interiores lineari-oblongae acutae, exteriores minores. Corolla subcylindrica, breviter 5-dentata, tubo glabro, dentibus dorso minute papillatis. Pappi setae scabridae, plus minusve flexuosae, subfulvescentes.

Flowering branches stout, 2–2½ lin. thick, densely covered with a short blackish tomentum. Leaves opposite, rather crowded, 4–9 lin. distant; petiole 2–3 lin. long, stout, with a blackish tomentum, which spreads along the veins of the leaf; blade 1–1¾ in. long, 10 lin. to 1¾ in. broad, broadly ovate, obtuse, rounded or subcordate, very shortly and irregularly dentate, with subobtuse teeth, or nearly entire, somewhat coriaceous, glabrous (except along the veins,) and densely gland-dotted above, with a brownish or fuscous pubescence beneath; primary lateral veins 4–5 on each side of the midrib, 2–3 of them arising close to the base, the others at or above the middle, prominent beneath. Corymbs terminal, 1½–2½ in. diam., compact, with short branches, clothed with the blackish tomentum as are also the pedicels and involucres. Heads about ¾ in. diam., 15–16-flowered. Involucral-scales in two series; the inner about 2 lin. long, ½ lin. broad, linear-oblong acute; the outer a little shorter, narrower and tapering from the base to an acute point. Corolla 2 lin. long, tubular, subcylindric, 5-toothed, glabrous, with some minute papillae on the back of the ½ lin. long, acute teeth. Ovary pubescent in the upper part with short fuscous subglandular hairs. Pappus-bristles numerous, scabrid, more or less flexuose, dull tawny. Ripe achenes not seen.

Summit of Mount Roraima, 8600 ft., *McConnell & Quelch*, 618.

A very distinct species, which would appear to be best placed near *E. nummularia*, Hook. & Arn.

BACCHARIS VITIS-IDÆA, Oliver, in Trans. Linn. Soc. Ser. II. Bot. ii. (1887), p. 277, t. 43. f. A. Upper slopes and summit of Mount Roraima, *McConnell & Quelch*, 27, 91, 650.—Endemic.

HETEROTHALAMUS DENSUS, N. E. Brown, sp. n. (Plate 7, figs. 1–7.) Planta nana, perennis, dioica, dense foliosa. Folia patentia, lanceolata, acuta vel obtusa, basi in petiolum attenuata, integra, coriacea, nitida. Capitula sessilia, 2 4-na ad apices ramorum conferta vel solitaria, discoidea. Flores hermaphroditi steriles, corollae tubo anguste infundifuliformi, lobis 5 linearibus acutis patentibus. Florum fœmininorum corolla angustissime tubulosa, truncata, vel oblique truncata, minutissime denticulata, stylo multo brevior.

A dwarf diœcious perennial with erect woody stems, apparently about 3–5 in. high, rooting at the base, sparingly branched in the upper part, densely leafy to the top, quite glabrous in all parts. Leaves densely crowded, spreading, ⅓–⅔ in. long (including the petiole), 1–2 lin. broad, lanceolate, acute or obtuse, tapering at the base into a linear petiole, entire, coriaceous, shining above, wrinkled from shrinkage in drying, veinless. Heads subunisexual, solitary or 2–4 together, sessile at the apex of the branches, and surrounded, but not overtopped by the leaves, about 2½ lin. diam., discoid, many-flowered. Involucre campanulate, a little shorter than the florets, its scales in 2–3 series, subequal, about 1½ lin. long, ⅜ lin. broad, oblong or lanceolate, obtuse or acute, ciliate. Receptacle naked in the sterile heads, but with several linear or linear-lanceolate acute scales in the female heads, scattered among, and about as long as, the florets. Florets of the sterile heads structurally hermaphrodite, but with barren ovaries; corolla with a tube 1 lin. long, gradually widening at the mouth, and 5 linear, acute, spreading lobes ½ lin. long, glabrous. Florets of the female heads with a very slender tubular corolla, truncate or oblique and very minutely 5-toothed at the apex, much shorter than the shortly bifid style, glabrous. Ovary glabrous. Pappus-bristles numerous and alike in both kinds of flowers, equalling the style in the female florets, slightly scabrid, whitish.

Summit of Mount Roraima, 8600 ft., *McConnell & Quelch*, 631.

PTEROCAULON VIRGATUM, DC. Prod. v. p. 454, var.

Kotinga Valley, *McConnell & Quelch*, 159. Savannahs generally, *McConnell & Quelch*, 306.

STIFFTIA CONDENSATA, Baker, in Mart. Fl. Bras. vi. pt. III. p. 351; im Thurn & Oliver, in Trans. Linn. Soc. Ser. II. ii. (1887), pp. 254, 278.

Summit of Mount Roraima, *McConnell & Quelch*, 87, 651.—Endemic.

STIFFTIA CONNELLII, N. E. Brown, sp. n. (Plate **8**.) Rami 2–3 lin. crassi, tomento compacto cinereo dense obtecti. Folia petiolata, coriacea, oblonga vel oblongo-obovata, obtusa, basi cuneato-rotundata, supra glabra, subtus tomento deciduo vestita. Capitula solitaria, magna. Involucri subinfundibuliformis bracteae multiseriatae; interiores ligulatae obtusae; exteriores gradatim minores, ovatae, obtusae, subtomentosae. Receptaculum bracteis linearibus minute dentato-ciliatis paucis onustum. Corolla infra medium 5-loba, glabra, lobis linearibus acutis spiraliter revolutis. Stylus longe exsertus, apice minute bifidus.

Branches woody, 2–3 lin. thick, covered with a dense, felt-like, greyish tomentum. Leaves alternate, petiolate, coriaceous; petiole ¼–¾ in. long, tomentose; blade 3½–5½ in. long, 1½–2½ in. broad, oblong or obovate-oblong, obtuse, somewhat cuneately rounded at the base, entire, glabrous above, clothed with a deciduous tomentum beneath, which falls away in patches; midrib and veins about equally prominent on both sides. Heads solitary, terminal, about 2½ in. long and 2 in. diam. Involucre somewhat funnel-shaped, shorter than the florets, with imbricating bracts in 10 or 12 series, the innermost about 1¾ in. long, 1¾–3½ lin. broad, strap-shaped to lanceolate-oblong, obtuse, the outer gradually smaller, ovate, obtuse, tomentose on the back. Receptacle with a few deciduous bracts, scattered among the florets, about 1¼ in. long, linear, obtuse, sparsely and minutely denticulate-ciliate. Corolla glabrous, with a tube about ½ in. long, slightly enlarging upwards, and spirally revolute linear-acute lobes, about 8 lin. long, ½–¾ lin. broad. Anthers about 7 lin. long, with the tails connate in pairs. Ovary ¼ in. long, compressed, glabrous. Style much exserted, minutely bifid at the apex. Pappus-bristles copious, unequal, the longest about 10 lin. long, minutely adpressed pubescent, dull straw-coloured, or pale tawny.

Summit of Mount Roraima, 8600 ft., *McConnell & Quelch*, 661.

A very distinct species, readily distinguished by its large heads, and the very long exserted styles. It appears to be a connecting link between *Stifftia* and *Wunderlichia*. The presence of bracts upon the receptacle and the minutely bifid stigma, technically place it in the genus *Wunderlichia*, Riedel, but the plant has a different appearance, and the receptacular bracts are not persistent and not of the same character or scarious texture as those of *Wunderlichia*. In all probability when more species are discovered it will be found that the two genera will have to be united.

QUELCHIA, N. E. Brown, gen. nov.

Capitula 1-flora in glomerulum vel cymam densam aggregata. Involucrum conico-tubulosum, bracteis imbricatis interioribus elongatis, exterioribus gradatim brevioribus ovatis. Receptaculum parvum, nudum. Corolla regularis, profunde 5-loba, tubo brevissimo, lobis linearibus. Antherae basi caudato-sagittatae, caudis retrorsim subbarbatis. Styli rami breves, erecti, truncati. Achaenia subteretia, leviter costata. Pappi setae copiosae. —Frutex, foliis alternis integris coriaceis. Capitulorum glomeruli pedunculati.

QUELCHIA CONFERTA, N. E. Brown. (Plate 7, figs. 8–14.) Rami apice tomentosi. Folia petiolata, obovata vel oblongo-oblanceolata, obtusa vel apiculata basi cuneato-acuta, primum subtomentosa, demum glabrata. Glomeruli vel corymbi ¾–1 poll. diam. Pedunculi tomentosi. Capitula sessilia, 1-flora, conferta. Involucri bracteae interiores anguste lanceolatae, obtusae, glabrae; exteriores ovatae, dorso tomentosae. Corolla glabra. Achaenia 2½ lin. longa, glabra. Pappi setae 3–4 lin. longae vix vel leviter scabridae.

Apparently a shrub, densely tomentose on the youngest parts of the shoots. Leaves alternate, coriaceous, petiolate; petiole 2–6 lin. long, tomentose in the young state becoming glabrous; blade 1–2½ in. long, 5–10 lin. broad, obovate or oblong-oblanceolate, obtuse or more or less apiculate, cuneate-acute at the base, entire, at first with a thin tomentum on both sides, which soon disappears and the leaf becomes glabrous; midrib impressed and pubescent above, very prominent beneath, veins reticulated, impressed above, scarcely prominent beneath. Corymbs pedunculate, small, hemispherical or subglobose, very densely many-headed, ¾–1 in. diam. Peduncles ½–1½ in. long, tomentose, bearing a few small leaf-like bracts at the base of the very short branches of the corymb. Heads sessile, densely crowded, about 4 lin. long, 1-flowered. Involucre cylindric-conical, with 12–16 spirally imbricating scales, the innermost about 3½ lin. long, ½–1 lin. broad, narrowly lanceolate obtuse, glabrous, the outer gradually shorter and more and more ovate, and more or less tomentose on the back. Floret not exceeding the involucre (?), hermaphrodite. Corolla regular, very deeply 5-lobed, glabrous, the lobes about 2½ lin. long, linear, acute, incurved at the apex. Stamens with free filaments and syngenesious anthers, which are produced at the base into long, slightly barbed tails. Achenes 2½ lin. long, subterete, slightly grooved, glabrous. Pappus-bristles copious, 3–4 lin. long, nearly smooth or very slightly scabrid, pale tawny-white.

Summit of Mount Roraima, 8600 ft., *McConnell & Quelch*, 652.

This plant appears to be nearly allied to the genus *Moquinia*, DC., but differs in habit and in its 1-flowered, densely-crowded heads. I am somewhat doubtful as to the exsertion of the floret from the involucre during flowering, as I have only seen the corollas in the bud state; when in fruit the achene is as long as the involucre and the pappus is entirely exserted.

CAMPANULACEÆ.

CENTROPOGON SURINAMENSIS, Presl, Prod. Monog. Lobel. p. 48; im Thurn & Oliver, in Trans. Linn. Soc. Ser. II. Bot. ii. (1887), pp. 261, 278.

Kotinga Valley, *McConnell & Quelch*, 156.—Widely dispersed throughout Tropical America except on the west of the Andes.

VACCINIACEÆ.

PSAMMISIA CORIACEA, N. E. Brown, sp. n. Frutex glaber. Folia breviter petiolata, obovata, oblonga vel orbiculata, crasse coriacea, integra, infra reticulato-venosa. Flores in axillis aggregati, penduli. Pedicelli recurvi, bibracteolati. Calyx cum pedicello articulatus, limbo breviter 4–5-dentato. Corolla ½ poll. longa, tubulosa, ore angustata, breviter 4–5-loba, lobis erectis lineari-oblongis obtusis. Stamina inclusa, biseriata, libera, glabra, antheris longe bitubulosis. Ovarium subglobosum. Stylus corolla subæquilongus, nec exsertus.

A shrub with a greyish-brown bark. Leaves shortly petiolate, thick and rigidly coriaceous, glabrous; petiole 1–2 lin. long, stout; blade ¾–1½ in. long, ½–1¼ in. broad, varying from obovate to orbicular, obtuse, entire, reticulately veined beneath. Flowers in clusters of 3–9 in the axils of the leaves, pedicellate, drooping. Pedicels about 4 lin. long, curved, bibracteolate at the middle or below, glabrous. Bracteoles opposite or sub-opposite, ¼–⅓ lin. long, broadly ovate, obtuse or subapiculate, very minutely ciliate. Calyx about 2¼ lin. long, glabrous, jointed to the pedicel, truncate at the base, with a subglobose tube and a cup-shaped shortly 4–5-toothed limb, the teeth very much broader than long, acute or apiculate. Corolla ½ in. long, about 2 lin. diam., tubular, narrowed at the mouth, 4–5-lobed, glabrous inside and outside; lobes 1 lin. long, erect, linear-oblong, obtuse. Stamens 8–10, included, biseriate, glabrous; the shorter filaments 1½ lin. long, the longer 1⅞ lin. long; anthers ¼ in. long, with the cells passing into two

MOUNT RORAIMA IN BRITISH GUIANA.   13

long tubes about 3 times as long as the united part, opening by long oblique slits
Ovary subglobose, 4–5 celled ; style 5½–6 lin. long, not exserted, filiform, glabrous ; stigma
small, discoid. Ovules numerous in each cell. Berry globose, many-seeded ; seeds about
⅜ lin. long, variable in form, with a pale brown reticulated testa.
Summit of Mount Roraima, 8600 ft., *McConnell & Quelch*, 662.

VACCINIUM RORAIMENSE, N. E. Brown, sp. n. Fruticulus, ramis patente pubescentibus
foliosis. Folia parva, breviter petiolata, rigide coriacea, lanceolata obovata vel
elliptica, obtusa vel rare acuta, crenato-dentata vel integra, glabra, marginibus subtus
incrassata. Racemi breves, terminales, bracteati. Pedicelli bracteolati, pubescentes.
Bracteolæ lanceolatæ, acutæ, tenuiter glanduloso-ciliatæ. Calyx glaber, lobis
deltoideo-ovatis acutis. Corolla 2¾ lin. longa, urceolata, breviter 5-loba. Stamina
10, inclusa, filamentis a basi attenuatis ciliatis, antheris acutis nec aristatis.
Ovarium obconicum, 5-loculare, glabrum, loculis 2–3-ovulatis.—*Vaccinium, an
V. floribundum*, H. B. & K.?, Oliver, in Trans. Linn. Soc. Ser. II. Bot. ii. (1887) p. 278.

A small branching shrub, probably of dwarf habit. Branches rather slender, very
leafy, pubescent with short spreading hairs. Leaves small, petiolate, thick, rigidly
coriaceous, glabrous ; petiole ½–1¼ lin. long ; blade 3½–7 lin. long, 2–5½ lin. broad,
varying from lanceolate to elliptic, obtuse or bluntly pointed, rarely acute, crenately
toothed or entire, with the margins much thickened beneath, and the veins usually
inconspicuous above, more or less evident beneath. Flowers in short terminal bracteate
racemes, or aggregated at the apex of the branches. Pedicels 1½–3, rarely 4–5 lin. long,
pubescent, bracteolate. Bracts and bracteoles similar, 1–1½ lin. long, lanceolate,
acute, or occasionally the bracts are larger and resemble very small leaves, glabrous,
more or less gland-ciliate. Calyx jointed to the pedicel, with a 5-lobed limb, glabrous ;
lobes 1 lin. long, deltoid-ovate, acute. Corolla 2¾ lin. long, urceolate, 5-lobed,
glabrous ; lobes about ¾ lin. long, broadly ovate, obtuse. Stamens 10, included ;
filaments 1 lin. long, tapering upwards from a broad base, ciliate ; anthers acute but not
aristate. Ovary obconical, surmounted by a thick ring-like disk, 5-celled, with 2–3
ovules in each cell, glabrous ; style about 1½ lin. long ; stigma dilated cushion-like.
Summit of Mount Roraima, 8600 ft., *im Thurn*, 329, 333 ; *McConnell & Quelch*, 79,
494, 642.

Allied to *V. polystachyum*, Benth., but very different in foliage.

Besides the above, there is a specimen belonging to this family which is too imperfect
for identification ; it was collected in the Kotinga Valley, *McConnell & Quelch*, 187.

ERICACEÆ.

PERNETTYA MARGINATA, N. E. Brown, sp. n. Frutex foliosus, ramis gracilibus plus minus
hirtis. Folia breviter petiolata, coriacea, ovata vel elliptica, acuta vel subacuta, basi
rotundata, supra glabra, nitida, infra sæpe parce setulosa, marginibus infra incrassatis
setuloso-denticulatis. Flores axillares, solitares. Pedicelli bracteolati, pubescentes.

Bracteolae ovatae, glanduloso-denticulatae. Calyx glaber, lobis ovatis acutis minute ciliatis. Corolla $3\frac{1}{2}$ lin. longa, urceolata, breviter 5-loba, lobis recurvis. Stamina inclusa, filamentis basi dilatis ciliatis, antheris apicibus 4-aristatis. Bacca globosa, $\frac{1}{4}$ poll. diam.—*P. sp. aff. parvifoliae*, Benth., Oliver, in Trans. Linn. Soc. Ser. II. Bot. ii. p. 278.

A shrub with very leafy slender branches, which are more or less covered with scattered spreading hairs, but are scarcely hispid, and occasionally nearly glabrous. Leaves small, rather crowded, petiolate, rigidly coriaceous; petiole about 1 lin. long; blade 5–8 lin. long, $3\frac{1}{2}$–$4\frac{1}{2}$ lin. broad, ovate or elliptic, acute or subacute, rounded at the base, thickened and slightly recurved along the denticulate margins beneath, the teeth tipped with a minute bristle, usually with a few scattered bristle-like hairs beneath, otherwise glabrous, shining and rugose from depressions (caused by shrinkage in drying?) between the veins above. Flowers axillary, solitary. Pedicels 2–5 lin. long, more or less pubescent, bracteolate. Bracteoles 5 or 6, about 1 lin. long, ovate, acute, gland-toothed, the lowermost crowded. Calyx 5-lobed nearly to the base, not enlarging in the fruiting stage; lobes $1\frac{1}{2}$ lin. long, $\frac{3}{4}$–1 lin. broad, ovate, acute, minutely ciliate, otherwise glabrous. Corolla $3\frac{1}{2}$ lin. long, urceolate, glabrous, with 5 ovate obtuse recurved lobes $\frac{3}{4}$–1 lin. long. Stamens shorter than the corolla, 2 lin. long; filaments ovate-lanceolate, acuminate, ciliate with rather long hairs; anthers tipped with 4 bristles about $\frac{1}{3}$ as long as the cells. Ovary subglobose, glabrous; style $1\frac{1}{2}$ lin. long, glabrous; stigma dilated, discoid. Berry globose, about $\frac{1}{4}$ in. in diam.

Summit of Mount Roraima, 8600 ft., *McConnell & Quelch*, 637; *im Thurn*, 333 A.

Allied to *Pernettya rigida*, DC., but among other characters the more thickened margin of the leaves and more numerous bracteoles serve readily to distinguish it.

Gaultheria setulosa, N. E. Brown, sp. n. Frutex setulis glanduliferis ubique vestitus. Folia brevissime petiolata, late cordato-ovata vel suborbicularia, coriacea, integra, utrinque setuloso-scabrida, ciliata. Racemi solitarii vel 2–3-ni ad apices ramorum, bracteati. Calycis lobi deltoideo-ovati, acuminati. Corolla urceolata, breviter 5-loba, intra glabra. Stamina inclusa, filamentis linearibus ciliatis, antheris obtusis muticis. Ovarium depressum, 5-lobum, pubescens.—*Gaultheria aff. G. vestitae*, Benth., Oliver in Trans. Linn. Soc. Ser. II. Bot. ii. (1887) p. 278.

A shrub, more or less clothed with long setae or gland-tipped hairs on the branches, leaves, and inflorescence. Leaves very shortly petiolate, $\frac{3}{4}$–$1\frac{3}{4}$ in. long, $\frac{2}{3}$–$1\frac{1}{2}$ in. broad, ovate or suborbicular, obtuse or subacute, cordate at the base, entire, rigidly coriaceous, more or less setose or scabrid on both sides, ciliate, with the veins much reticulated and prominent beneath. Racemes solitary or 2–3 together at the apex of the branches, erect, bracteate, 1–4 in. long, 7–15-flowered, rather lax, puberulous and more or less densely covered with gland-tipped bristles on the axis, bracts, pedicels, calyx, and corolla. Bracts $\frac{1}{4}$–$\frac{1}{2}$ in. long, 2–$3\frac{1}{2}$ lin. broad, elliptic subacute, concave, spreading, persistent. Pedicels 3–8 lin. long, ascending or spreading. Calyx 2–$2\frac{1}{2}$ lin. long, 5-lobed to $\frac{3}{4}$ the way down, the lobes $1\frac{1}{2}$–2 lin. long, deltoid-ovate, acuminate. Corolla $3\frac{1}{2}$–4 lin. long, $2\frac{1}{2}$ lin. diam., urceolate, with 5 recurved, ovate, obtuse lobes $\frac{3}{4}$ lin. long, glabrous inside. Stamens 10, included, $\frac{2}{3}$ as long as the corolla; filaments linear, ciliate; anthers $\frac{3}{4}$ lin.

long, oblong, obtuse, shortly bifid at the apex, but not in the least produced into awns or tubes, opening by longitudinal slits nearly to the base. Ovary depressed, 5-lobed, pubescent; style included, rather stout, glabrous; stigma simple, not enlarged. Capsule depressed, 5-angled, pubescent.

Summit of Mount Roraima, 8600 ft., *im Thurn*, 332; *McConnell & Quelch*, 104. 647.

Allied to *Gaultheria cordifolia*, H. B. & K., and *G. restita*, Benth., but differing from both in the scabrid upper surface of the leaves, the stouter gland-tipped setae which clothe it, and by the obtuse, not aristate anthers.

LEDOTHAMNUS SESSILIFLORUS, N. E. Brown, sp. n. Fruticulus nanus, ericoideus. Folia verticillata, 3-na vel 4-na ad nodos posita, imbricata, brevissime petiolata, linearia vel lineari-lanceolata, acuta, minute puberula. Flores solitarii, terminales, sessiles. Sepala 7 vel 6, anguste lanceolata, acuta, puberula vel subglabra, ciliata. Petala 7 vel 6, oblonga obtusa, glabra. Stamina 7 vel 6, filamentis quam antheris multo longioribus. Discus nullus. Ovarium subglobosum vel ovoideum, granulosum, 5-8-loculare; stylus crassus; stigma subinfundibuliforme, minute 5-8-lobulatum.

A dwarf shrublet 4-8 in. high. Stems erect, simple or branched, densely leafy to the apex, at first minutely puberulous, becoming glabrous, and rough from the persistent scars of the fallen leaves. Leaves resembling those of an *Erica*, in densely crowded whorls of 3-4, ascending, imbricating, $1\frac{1}{2}$-$2\frac{1}{2}$ lin. long, $\frac{1}{2}$-$\frac{2}{3}$ lin broad, linear or narrowly linear-lanceolate, acute, narrowed at the base into a very short petiole, thick, flat on the face, grooved down the back, minutely puberulous, ciliate or entire. Flowers terminal, solitary, $\frac{3}{4}$-$1\frac{1}{4}$ in. diam., sessile, surrounded by a few bracts that are intermediate in character between the sepals and leaves. Sepals 7 or occasionally 6, spreading, 3-$1\frac{1}{2}$ lin. long, $\frac{3}{4}$-$\frac{3}{4}$ lin. broad, narrowly lanceolate, acute, minutely puberulous or subglabrous, ciliate. Petals usually 7, very spreading, bright crimson, 5-7 lin. long, 2-3 lin. broad, oblong, obtuse, cuneately narrowed at the base, entire, glabrous. Stamens 7 or 6, shorter than the petals, glabrous; filaments $3\frac{1}{2}$-$4\frac{1}{2}$ lin. long, gradually dilated towards the base; anthers $1\frac{1}{2}$ lin. long, oblong, obtuse. Ovary subglobose or ovoid, granulate-rugose, 5-8-celled, with a stout style $1\frac{1}{4}$-$1\frac{1}{2}$ lin. long, slightly dilated at the apex into a funnel-shaped minutely 5-8-lobed stigma. Capsule sessile, 2-$2\frac{1}{2}$ lin. diam., 5-8-valved, granulate.

Summit of Mount Roraima, 8600 ft., *McConnell & Quelch*, 643.

Var. GLABER, N. E. Brown, var. n. Folia et sepala glabra, ciliata.

Leaves and sepals glabrous, ciliate.

L. guyanensis, Meissn., var. *minor*, Oliver, in Trans. Linn. Soc. Ser. II. Bot. ii. (1887), p. 278, t. 44. f. A.

Mount Roraima, on the upper part of the Ledge and on the summit, *im Thurn*, 308; *McConnell & Quelch*, 99.

This plant is very distinct from *L. guyanensis*, Meissn., with which it has been associated by Oliver, differing not only by its smaller size and smaller leaves, but more especially by its sessile flowers and the long filaments of the stamens. In *L. guyanensis* the flowers have pedicels $\frac{1}{4}$-$\frac{2}{3}$ in. long covered with gland-tipped hairs, and the filaments of the stamens are only about 1 lin. long and shorter than the anthers.

BEFARIA GUIANENSIS. Klotzsch, in R. Schomb. Reisen in Brit.-Guiana, iii. p. 1088; Oliver, in Trans. Linn. Soc. Ser. II. Bot. ii. (1887), p. 278 : Appun, Unter den Tropen, ii. pp. 232, 287, 292.
Upper slopes and Ledge of Mount Roraima, *McConnell & Quelch.* 40.—Endemic.

BEFARIA IMTHURNII. N. E. Brown, sp. n. Fruticulus nanus, ramis pilis glanduliferis vel setulis vestitus. Folia conferta, breviter petiolata, coriacea, elliptico-oblonga vel elliptico-lanceolata, utrinque obtusa vel acuta, supra glabra, subtus glauca et glabra vel costa plus minus setulosa, marginibus integris vel glanduloso-scabridis vel ciliatis. Racemi subumbelliformes, densi. Pedicelli subhispidi. Calyx campanulatus, 7–8-lobus, lobis biseriatis late ovatis obtusis. Petala 6–8. oblonga, obtusa. Stamina 12–16, petalis subæquilonga, basi pilosa.—*Befaria aff. B. resinosæ.* Mutis; Oliver in Trans. Linn. Soc. Ser. II. Bot. ii. (1887), p. 278.

A dwarf shrublet, with the branchlets densely covered with spreading simple or gland-tipped hairs, very leafy. Leaves crowded, very shortly petiolate, coriaceous; petiole ½–1 lin. long; blade ½–1 in. long, ¼–½ in. broad, elliptic-oblong or elliptic-lanceolate, about equally acute or obtuse at each end, with slightly revolute margins, which are either quite entire, minutely gland-scabrid, or ciliate with short gland-tipped bristles or longer simple hairs, glabrous and smooth above, glaucous and either quite glabrous or with some simple or gland-tipped bristles scattered along the midrib beneath. Flowers several, crowded into a short terminal umbel-like raceme or cluster, each flower being solitary in the axil of one of the uppermost leaves. Pedicels 3–7 lin. long, more or less densely covered with stiff spreading hairs. Calyx about 2 lin. long, campanulate, 7–8-lobed to about the middle, with the lobes in two series, broadly ovate, obtuse, glabrous, minutely ciliate. Corolla glabrous, pink; petals 6–8, slightly spreading, 8–9 lin. long, 3 lin. broad, oblong, obtuse, cuneate at the base. Stamens 12–16, about as long as the petals; filaments filiform, slightly thickened and hairy at the base; anthers 1 lin. long, cuneately oblong, obtuse. Ovary depressed, lobulate, glabrous, with a glabrous style 6–8 lin. long, elongating to 1–1¼ in. long in fruit, and a capitate slightly lobed stigma. Capsule about ¼ in. diam., woody, 6 (or more ?)-valved.

Summit of Mount Roraima, 8600 ft., *in Thurn*, 310; *McConnell & Quelch*, 94, 646.
Allied to *B. guianensis*, Klotzsch (*Schomburgk*, 1041), from which it differs in its less elongated, glabrous leaves. In *B. guianensis* the leaves are 1–1½ in. long, and their upper surface is thinly covered with short gland-tipped bristles, tubercular at the base, becoming more or less scabrid after the bristles have fallen or have been rubbed off; on the under side they are more or less densely covered all over with fine gland-tipped hairs, with longer hairs on the midrib, and they appear to be less glaucous than in *B. Imthurnii*.

MYRSINACEÆ.

ARDISIA QUELCHII. N. E. Brown, sp. n. Frutex dioicus, glaber, ramis crassis. Folia alterna, petiolata, coriacea, obovata vel subelliptica, obtusa vel rare subacuta, integra, subtus minutissime rubro-glandulosa. Paniculæ axillares, anguste oblongæ vel pyramidales, minutissime rubro-glandulosæ, floribus parvis ad apices ramorum confertis. Calyx profunde 4-lobus, glanduloso-punctatus, lobis oblongis obtusis. Corolla profunde 4-loba, glanduloso-punctata, lobis oblongis obtusis patentibus. Stamina 4, corollæ lobis breviora et prope basin inserta, filamentis quam antheris paulo brevioribus.

A diœcious shrub, probably of dwarf habit, glabrous in all parts, with branches ¼ in. thick, terete. Leaves chiefly near the apex of the stem, alternate, petiolate, coriaceous ; petiole 2–4 lin. long, rather stout ; blade 1½–2½ in. long, 10–16 lin. broad, obovate or occasionally subelliptic, obtuse, rarely subacute, with revolute margins, entire, more or less densely covered with very minute red glands beneath. Panicles axillary, near the summits of the branches, narrowly oblong or pyramidal, 1–3¼ in. long, ½–1¼ in. broad, covered with minute red glands, with the flowers crowded at the ends of the short, rather distant, simple branches. Bracts ½–1 lin. long, oblong, obtuse, dotted with rather large dark-coloured glands. Calyx 4-lobed nearly to the base ; lobes ½–¾ lin. long, oblong, obtuse, conspicuously gland-dotted. Corolla about 2 lin. diam., 4-lobed nearly to the base ; lobes ¾–1 lin. long, rather more than ½ lin. broad, conspicuously gland-dotted. Stamens 4, shorter than and inserted towards the base of the corolla-lobes, with stout filaments rather shorter than the oblong, ¼ lin. long anthers. Ovary rudimentary, minute, subulate, or none. Female flowers not seen.

Summit of Mount Roraima, 8600 ft., *McConnell & Quelch*, 665.

A very distinct species, unlike any other.

APOCYNACEÆ.

MANDEVILLA GLABRA, N. E. Brown, sp. n. Caules volubiles, glabrescentes. Folia parva, distantia, petiolata, coriacea, lanceolata, acuminata, apice obtusa, glabra. Racemi brevissimi, pauciflori, axillares, glabri. Pedunculi et pedicelli brevissimi. Sepala parva, ovata, acuta, glabra. Corolla infundibularis, 2¼ poll. longa, extra glabra, intra ad insertionem staminum pilis deflexis dense barbata, lobis dolabriformibus. Stamina inclusa, filamentis oblongis apice barbatis, antheris acutis, basi cordatis obtusis.

Stem twining, about 1 lin. thick, glabrous or with a very few short scattered hairs, brown. Leaves opposite, distant, petiolate, coriaceous, glabrous; petiole 2–3 lin long ; blade ¾–1 in. long, 3½–4 lin. broad, lanceolate, acuminate, obtuse at the point, entire, with the midrib impressed above, prominent beneath, and having 5 or 6 small tubercles or glands scattered along it on the upper side, the lateral veins spreading, slightly impressed on both sides in the dried state, not very conspicuous. Racemes axillary, from one axil, very short, about 3-flowered in the specimen seen ; glabrous. Peduncle about 1 lin. long, stout. Pedicels alternate, 1–1¼ lin. long, stout. Sepals 1 lin. long, ¾–⅞ lin. broad, ovate, acute, glabrous, each with a very short, transversely oblong, denticulate scale at its base inside. Corolla about 2¼ in. long. funnel-shaped ; tube curved, cylindrical and about 1½ lin. diam. in the lower half, much enlarged and sub-campanulate in the upper half, glabrous outside and inside, except 5 broad lines that are densely bearded with deflexed white hairs at the insertion of the stamens within; lobes about ¾ in. long, hatchet-shaped, one side being dilated into a large square membranous obtuse lobe. Stamens inserted at the top of the narrow part of the tube included; filaments about 1 lin. long and nearly as broad, flat, oblong, slightly bearded near the apex on the inner face; anthers 3½ lin. long, linear-oblong, acute, shortly cordate at the base, connate, adnate to the stigma. Disk shortly lobed. Ovary glabrous; style about 1½ lin. long, slender, glabrous; stigma conical, 5-winged.

Upper slopes of Mount Roraima, *McConnell & Quelch*, 16.

MANDEVILLA LINEARIS, N. E. Brown, sp. n. Caules volubiles, graciles, puberuli. Folia breviter petiolata, linearia, acuta, supra glabra, subtus tomentosa, marginibus fere vel usque ad costam revolutis. Racemi breves, pauciflori. minute puberuli. Bracteæ parvæ, acuminatæ. Pedicelli brevissimi. Sepala parva, deltoidea, acuminata. Corolla infundibularis, 2¼ poll. longa, recta, extra glabra, intra ad mediam dense barbata. Stamina inclusa, filamentis ellipticis glabris, antheris subacutis basi breviter cordatis vel emarginatis.

Stem twining, slender, puberulous. Leaves opposite, ¾–2½ in. distant, petiolate, thinly coriaceous; petiole 1–1½ lin. long, rather slender, puberulous; blade 1½–2¼ in. long, linear, acute, obtuse at the base, with the margins revolute nearly or quite to the midrib, glabrous and shining, with an impressed midrib above, tomentose, with a prominent midrib beneath, the tomentum usually hidden by the revolute margins. Racemes short, ½–¾ in. long, more than half of which is peduncle, 3-4-flowered, very minutely puberulous. Bracts about ¾ lin. long, ovate, acuminate. Pedicels alternate, about 1 lin. long, rather stout. Calyx-lobes about 1½ lin. long. deltoid, acuminate, sub-glabrous or very minutely puberulous, each with a small ovate scale at the base inside. Corolla about 2¼ in. long, funnel-shaped, straight. 5-lobed, glabrous outside, the middle part of the tube inside densely covered with deflexed white hairs: tube cylindric and about 1½ lin. diam. for ⅔ of its length, upper part much enlarged, subcampanulate; lobes about 5 lin. long, hatchet-shaped, with an incurved apiculus, one side being dilated into a subrectangular, obtuse, membranous lobe. Stamens 5, included, inserted at the top of the narrow part of the tube; filaments about ¾ lin. long, elliptic, glabrous; anthers 2 lin. long, linear-oblong, subacute, slightly narrowed at the emarginate or shortly cordate base. Disk of 5 oblong lobes. Ovary glabrous; style about 1½ in. long, filiform, glabrous; stigma subquadrate when viewed sideways, obtuse, 5-winged.

Kotinga Valley, 3000 ft., *McConnell & Quelch*, 132, 194.

MANDEVILLA SCABERULA, N. E. Brown, sp. n. Caules volubiles, puberuli. Folia distantia, petiolata, oblonga, obtusa, apiculata, basi cordata, supra scaberula, subtus tomentosa, reticulato-venosa. Racemi axillares, multiflori, puberuli. Bracteæ oblongæ vel oblongo-lanceolatæ. Pedicelli brevi. Calycis lobi ovati, acuti, intra squama ovata instructi. Corolla 2 poll. longa, infundibularis, extra pubescens, intra ad insertionem staminum pilis deflexis dense barbata, tubo curvato inferne angusto basi leviter inflato, superne ampliato subcampanulato, lobis dolabriformibus. Stamina inclusa, filamentis linearibus dense barbatis, antheris acutis basi cordatis obtusis.

Stem twining, $1\frac{1}{4}$-$1\frac{3}{4}$ lin. thick, puberulous. Leaves opposite, very distant, $2\frac{1}{2}$-$3\frac{1}{2}$ in. long, $1\frac{3}{4}$-2 in. broad, oblong, obtuse, apiculate, cordate at the base, scaberulous above, finely greyish-tomentose beneath, reticulated with dark veins; petiole $1\frac{1}{2}$-2 lin. long, puberulous. Racemes axillary, from one axil, 2-3 in. long, including the $\frac{3}{4}$ in. long peduncle, many-flowered, densely puberulous in all parts. Bracts about 2 lin. long. $1\frac{2}{3}$-$1\frac{1}{2}$ lin. broad, oblong or oblong-lanceolate, acute, thin, spreading, deciduous. Pedicels alternate, 2-3 lin. long, moderately stout. Calyx-lobes $1\frac{1}{4}$ lin. long and nearly as broad, ovate, acute, each with an ovate acute slightly toothed scale at its base inside. Corolla about 2 in. long, funnel-shaped, curved, 5-lobed, pubescent outside, densely bearded with deflexed white hairs at the insertion of the stamens within, elsewhere glabrous; the lower half of the tube is slightly inflated at its base and there about $2\frac{1}{2}$ lin. diam., narrowed above to $1\frac{1}{2}$ lin. diam.; the upper half much enlarged, funnel-shaped or subcampanulate; lobes about $\frac{3}{4}$ in. long, hatchet-shaped, one side being dilated into a large subquadrate, obtusely rounded, membranous lobe. Stamens 5, included, inserted at the top of the narrow part of the tube; filaments short, flat, linear, densely bearded on the inner face; anthers $2\frac{1}{2}$ lin. long, linear-oblong, acute, shortly cordate at the base, connate, adnate to the stigma. Disk tubular, $\frac{3}{4}$ lin. deep, 5-crenate. Ovary pubescent; style about $1\frac{1}{4}$ in. long, very slender, glabrous; stigma conical, 5-winged.

Tolimbara Creek near Mount Roraima, *McConnell & Quelch*, 146.

ASCLEPIADACEÆ.

DITASSA TAXIFOLIA, Decne. in DC. Prod. viii. p. 578.

Kotinga Valley, *McConnell & Quelch*, 165, 166. Ireng Valley, *McConnell & Quelch*, 323.

LOGANIACEÆ.

BONYUNIA MINOR, N. E. Brown, sp. n. (Plate **9**, figs. 1-5.) Frutex glaber. Folia opposita, approximata, breviter petiolata, coriacea, rotundato-ovata, subacuta, basi rotundata vel leviter cordata. Cymæ subdensæ, ramulis puberulis, floribus sessilibus bracteolatis. Calyx campanulatus, minute puberulus, dentibus deltoideis subacutis. Corollæ tubus subcylindricus, extra pubescens, intra parte inferiore puberulus, superiore glaber; lobi patentes, recurvi, superne carinato-incrassati, superne etiam carina et marginibus puberuli, area basali triangulare glabri. Ovarium breviter pilosum, stylo pubescente, stigmate bilobo.

A shrub. Branches terete, glabrous, dark brown. Leaves opposite, subimbricate, ascending, shortly petiolate, coriaceous, glabrous; petiole 1 lin. long; blade $\frac{3}{4}$-1$\frac{1}{4}$ in. long, $\frac{1}{2}$-1 in. broad, roundish-ovate, subacute, broadly rounded or slightly cordate at the base, with prominent veins beneath. Cymes terminal, rather dense, 1-1$\frac{1}{4}$ in. diam., with puberulous branches 2-4 lin. long. Flowers sessile, bracteolate. Bracteoles $\frac{3}{4}$-1 lin. long, linear or oblong-lanceolate, obtuse, minutely puberulous. Calyx about $1\frac{1}{2}$ lin. long, campanulate, puberulous, with 5 deltoid subacute teeth. Corolla tubular, with 5 spreading recurved lobes; tube $3\frac{1}{2}$ lin. long, subcylindric, pubescent outside, puberulous within in the lower $\frac{2}{3}$, glabrous above; lobes about $2\frac{1}{2}$ lin. long, spreading.

recurved, thickened and keeled in the upper half and along the margins below and there densely puberulous, enclosing a narrowly triangular glabrous basal area. Stamens 5, inserted at the mouth of the tube, glabrous; filaments ¼ lin. long, slender; anthers about 1 lin. long, partly exserted, linear, acute. Ovary shortly hairy; style 1⅜-1¾ lin. long, pubescent; stigma 2-lobed. Capsule 4-6 lin. long, 2½-3 lin. diam., ellipsoidal, sparingly pubescent or nearly glabrous, 2-valved.

    Kotinga Valley, *McConnell & Quelch*, 161.   Ireng Valley, *McConnell & Quelch*, 331.

ANTONIA OVATA, Pohl, Pl. Bras. ii. p. 13, t. 109

    Kotinga Valley, *McConnell & Quelch*, 161.   Upper slopes of Mount Roraima, *McConnell & Quelch*, 324.—Only known from Brazil and Guiana.

GENTIANACEÆ.

SCHULTESIA BRACHYPTERA, Cham. in Linnæa, viii. (1833), p. 8.
    Kotinga Valley, *McConnell & Quelch*, 148.

SCHULTESIA HETEROPHYLLA, Miq. in Linnæa. xix. (1847), p. 136.
    Ireng Valley, *McConnell & Quelch*, 249.

SCHULTESIA BENTHAMIANA, Klotzsch, ex Griseb. in Linnæa, xxii. (1849), p. 34.
    Ireng Valley, *McConnell & Quelch*, 247 (and 224, apparently a starved state).

COUTOUBEA REFLEXA, Benth. in Ann. Nat. Hist. ii. (1839), p. 442.
    Kotinga Valley, *McConnell & Quelch*, 141.

COUTOUBEA SPICATA, Aubl. Pl. Guian. i. p. 72.
    Ireng Valley, *McConnell & Quelch*, 221, 259.

LISIANTHUS IMTHURNIANUS, Oliver. in Trans. Linn. Soc. Ser. II. Bot. ii. (1887), p. 279.
    Summit of Mount Roraima, *McConnell & Quelch*, 101, 682.—Endemic.

LISIANTHUS ULIGINOSUS, Griseb. Gen. et Sp. Gent. p. 181.
    Kotinga Valley, *McConnell & Quelch*, 172.   Ireng Valley, 204, 252.   Upper slopes of Mount Roraima (a small-flowered form), *McConnell & Quelch*, 15.—Widely dispersed in Guiana and Brazil.

LISIANTHUS QUELCHII, N. E. Brown, sp. n. (Plate 9, figs. 6-9.) Fruticulus glaber, ramis tetragonis internodiis 1½-6 lin. longis. Folia opposita, petiolata, oblonga vel elliptico-oblonga vel obovata, subacuta vel obtusa et apiculata, coriacea. Flores 1-3-ni ad apices ramorum, pedicellati. Calyx campanulatus, profunde 5-lobus, lobis oblongis obtusis. Corolla 1-1½ poll. longa, subinfundibularis, curvata, lobis rotundatis obtusis. Stamina inclusa, filamentis apice recurvis, antheris erectis. Ovarium ovoideum, glabrum, in stylum elongatum angustatum, stigmate bilobo.

    A dwarf shrub, glabrous in all parts. Branches 4-angled, 1-1½ lin. thick, with internodes 1½-6 lin. long, leafy at the summit only, minutely tuberculate-rugulose.

Leaves opposite, petiolate, coriaceous; petiole 1–2½ lin. long; blade ¾–1¾ in. long, ½–1 in. broad, oblong, elliptic or obovate, subacute or obtuse and apiculate, more or less acute at the base, slightly revolute along the margins, with the midrib impressed above, prominent beneath, and the veins invisible. Flowers terminal, solitary or in a sessile 3- (or more?) flowered cyme. Pedicels 2–4 lin. long, rather stout, slightly rough from minute tubercles. Bracts and bracteoles ½–1 lin. long, acuminate. Calyx 3½–4 lin. long, campanulate, deeply 5-lobed; lobes 2½–3 lin. long, oblong, obtuse. Corolla 1–1½ in. long, somewhat funnel-shaped, 5-lobed, curved or oblique; lobes 3½–4½ lin. long and broad, suborbicular, contracted at the base. Stamens included; filaments filiform, recurved near the apex and then shortly curved upwards at the very apex; anthers erect, 2–2½ lin. long, oblong subobtuse, cordate at the base. Ovary ovoid, narrowed into the 5 lin. long style, with a shortly 2-lobed stigma.

Summit of Mount Roraima, 8600 ft., *McConnell & Quelch*, 106, 649.

A very distinct species, perhaps nearer to *Lisianthus ovalis*, Ruiz & Pav., than to any other.

LISIANTHUS ELISABETHÆ, Griseb. in Linnæa, xxii. (1849), p. 10.

Lisianthus aff. *L. maranthus*, Oliver, in Trans. Linn. Soc. Ser. II. Bot. ii. (1887), p. 279.
Leiothamnus Elisabethæ, R. H. Schomb. in Verh. des Ver. Beförd. Gartenb. in Preuss. xviii.(1847), p. 155, t. 1; R. Schomb. Bot. Rem. Brit. Guiana, p. 77.

Upper slopes and ledge of Mount Roraima, *im Thurn*, 188; *McConnell & Quelch*, 25.—Endemic.

HYDROPHYLLACEÆ.

HYDROLEA SPINOSA, Linn. Sp. Pl. ed. 1, p. 328.

Ireng Valley, *McConnell & Quelch*, 262. Kotinga Valley, *McConnell & Quelch*, 180. Savannahs generally. *McConnell & Quelch*, 313.

BORAGINACEÆ.

HELIOTROPIUM STRICTISSIMUM, Moric. ?, Pl. Nouv. Am. p. 146, t. 87.

Ireng Valley, *McConnell & Quelch*, 220, 302.

CONVOLVULACEÆ.

IPOMŒA IRENGANA, N. E. Brown, sp. n. Caulis gracilis. volubilis, subpubescens, internodiis ½–1 poll. longis. Folia parva, petiolata, late cordata, obtusa, minute apiculata, supra velutina, subtus albo-tomentosa. Flores axillares, solitarii, pedicellati. Calycis lobi oblongi, obtusi, puberuli. Corolla 1¼–1½ poll. longa, extra pubescens, purpurea.

Stems very slender, twining, woody below, slightly pubescent, with internodes ½–1 in. long. Leaves small; petiole 2–5 lin. long, slender, terete, pubescent; blade ½–1 in. long, ½–¾ in. broad, cordate or roundish-cordate, obtuse, minutely apiculate, velvety-tomentose above, whitish-tomentose beneath. Flowers axillary, solitary. Pedicels 2–2½ lin. long, very minutely bracteolate at the base, pubescent. Sepals subequal, 3½–4 lin. long, 1½ lin. broad, oblong, obtuse, thinly pubescent or puberulous. Corolla 1¼–1½ in. long,

funnel-shaped, pubescent outside, purple. Stamens included; filaments pubescent at their base. Ovary and style glabrous; stigma of 2 globose lobes.
Ireng Valley, on ant-hills, *McConnell & Quelch*, 251, 265.

JACQUEMONTIA EVOLVULOIDES, Meissn. in Mart. Fl. Bras. vii. p. 307.
Ireng Valley, *McConnell & Quelch*, 233.

EVOLVULUS STRICTUS, Benth. in Hook. Lond. Journ. Bot. v. (1846), p. 354.
Ireng Valley, *McConnell & Quelch*, 218, 219, 261.

EVOLVULUS SERICEUS, Sw. Prod. Veg. Ind. Occ. p. 55.
Ireng Valley, *McConnell & Quelch*, 215.

SOLANACEÆ.

SOLANUM CRINITUM, Lam. Illust. ii. p. 20.
Ireng Valley, near Mataruka Mountain, *McConnell & Quelch*, 134.

SCROPHULARIACEÆ.

BEYRICHIA SCUTELLARIOIDES, Benth. Scroph. Ind. p. 9, in nota.

B. ocymoides, Oliver, in Trans. Linn. Soc. Ser. II. Bot. ii. (1889), p. 280, not of Cham.

Upper slopes of Mount Roraima, *McConnell & Quelch*, 5.—Trinidad and Brazil.

HERPESTIS GRATIOLOIDES, Benth. in Hook. Comp. Bot. Mag. ii. (1836), p. 57.
Ireng Valley, *McConnell & Quelch*, 266.

GERARDIA HISPIDULA, Mart. Nov. Gen. & Sp. iii. p. 13, t. 207.
Ireng Valley, *McConnell & Quelch*, 232.

BUCHNERA PALUSTRIS, Spreng. Syst. ii. p. 805.
Ireng Valley, *McConnell & Quelch*, 234.

BUCHNERA, sp. Too imperfect for determination.
Ireng Valley, *McConnell & Quelch*, 236, 238.

LENTIBULARIACEÆ.

UTRICULARIA HUMBOLDTII, R. H. Schomb. in Verh. des Ver. Beförd. Gartenb. in Preuss. xv. (1841), p. 139, t. 3; R. Schomb. Reisen in Brit.-Guiana, ii. p. 263, & iii. p. 1086; im Thurn & Oliver, in Trans. Linn. Soc. Ser. II. Bot. ii. (1889), pp. 256, 262, 265, 267, 269, & 280.

Upper slopes of Mount Roraima, *McConnell & Quelch*, 3.—Also on the Kaieteur Savannah.

UTRICULARIA ALPINA, Jacq. Enum. Pl. Carib. p. 11.

U. montana, Jacq. Select. Stirp. Amer. p. 7, t. 6.

Upper slopes of Mount Roraima, growing on trees, *McConnell & Quelch*, 43.   Roraima

Range, 3500 ft.. *McConnell & Quelch*. 718.—Also in the West Indies, Venezuela, Colombia, Peru, and Ecuador.

UTRICULARIA CAMPBELLIANUM, Oliver, in Trans. Linn. Soc. Ser. II Bot. ii. (1887), p. 280, t. 44. f. B, & pp. 266, 267, & 270.
Upper slopes of Mount Roraima, on trees, *McConnell & Quelch*, 35.—Endemic.

UTRICULARIA QUELCHII, N. E. Brown, sp. n. (Plate 10, figs. 12–16.) Perennis. Folia spathulata, longe petiolata, coriacea, glabra. Caulis 2–5 poll. altus, 1–2-squamosus, 1–2-florus, glaber. Bracteæ et bracteolæ 2–3½ lin. longæ, oblongæ vel elliptico-oblongæ, obtusæ, glabræ. Sepala magna, elliptica, obtusa. Corolla magna, labio superiore ovato et obtuso et apice recurvo, labio inferiore multo majore orbiculare reflexo, calcare ad medium abrupte procurvo subobtuso.— *Utricularia* aff. *U. montana*, Jacq.; Oliver, in Trans. Linn. Soc. Ser. II. Bot. ii. (1887), p. 280.

Perennial. Roots fibrous and tuberous intermixed. Leaves all radical, erect, spathulate, coriaceous. glabrous; petiole ¾–2 in. long; blade ½–1 in. long, 3–5 lin. broad, obovate or narrowly elliptic, obtuse, cuneately narrowed into the petiole. Stem 2–5 in. long, ½–⅔ lin. thick, 1–2-flowered, glabrous, bearing 1–2 lanceolate, acute, glabrous scales 1–2½ lin. long. Bracts and bracteoles subequal, basifixed, 2–3½ lin. long, 1–1½ lin. broad, oblong or elliptic-oblong, obtuse, glabrous, not ciliate. Pedicels 4–6 lin. long, glabrous. Sepals 4½–6 lin. long, 3½–4 lin. broad, elliptic, obtuse, concave, glabrous. Corolla large, glabrous, purple or deep red; upper lip 3–4 lin. long, included in the dorsal sepal, erect, recurved at the apex, ovate, obtuse, with the sides abruptly reflexed around the mouth, then again curved forwards; lower lip 7–9 lin. long, 8–15 lin. broad, abruptly reflexed from the mouth of the spur, suborbicular, very obtuse, entire; spur ¾–1 in. long, gradually tapering from the 2½–3 lin. broad mouth to the obtuse apex, with the basal half hanging straight down and partly embraced by the lower sepal, and the apical half abruptly curved forwards or upwards. Stamens with thick clavate curved filaments, glabrous. Ovary globose, narrowed into a stout style, glabrous; upper lip of the stigma narrow, lower lip very broad, very obtusely rounded or subtruncate.
Summit of Mount Roraima, 8600 ft., *McConnell & Quelch*, 105, 683; *im Thurn*, 293.
Allied to *U. montana*, Jacq., but smaller, with larger petioles to the leaves, broader bracts, and differently coloured flowers, which, to judge from the dried specimens, appear to have been either purple or deep red. Probably it is the plant mentioned by Mr. Quelch in 'Timehri,' vol. ix. p. 178, as " the beautiful crimson *Utricularia montana*," since the flowers of the true *U. montana* (= *U. alpina*), Jacq. are white.

UTRICULARIA CONNELLII, N. E. Brown, sp. n. (Plate 10, figs. 1–6.) Aphylla, 1½–4 poll. alta. Caulis filiformis, 1 2-squamosus, glaber, 1–3-florus. Bracteæ et bracteolæ minutæ, ovatæ vel oblongæ, ciliatæ. Sepala elliptica, multi-nervosa, nervis pubescentibus; sepalum inferius minutum, bilobum. Corolla ringens, glabra, labio superiore erecto, anguste subspathulato-oblongo, labio inferiore suborbiculare obtuso reflexo, calcare leviter curvato subacuto.

Leafless at the time of flowering. Stems 1½–4 in. high, filiform, glabrous, 1–2-flowered and bearing 1–2 minute, peltately attached, very minutely ciliate scales. Bracts ¼ lin. long, ovate, acute, peltately attached, minutely ciliate. Bracteoles slightly shorter than the bracts, basifixed, oblong, acute, minutely ciliate. Pedicels 1–2 lin. long, glabrous. Sepals about 1½ lin. long, the upper nearly 1 lin. broad, ovate, subacute, the lower rather broader, emarginate at the apex, both deeply concave, strongly nerved, with a few short hairs scattered along the nerves. Corolla ringent; upper lip erect, 3–3½ lin. long, ¾–1 lin. broad, subspathulate-oblong, obtuse, with recurved margins, minutely puberulous inside at the base; lower lip 4–5 lin. long, about 4 lin. broad, suborbicular, obtuse, abruptly deflexed from the mouth of the spur, where it is minutely puberulous. Spur 4½–5½ lin. long, nearly in a line with the upper lip, slightly curved forwards, gradually tapering from the 1½ lin. broad base to the subacute apex, compressed. Filaments of the stamens incurved, clavate, glabrous. Ovary ovoid, narrowed into a short style, glabrous; stigma with a narrow acute upper lip and a broadly ovate obtuse lower lip.

Arabapu River, *McConnell & Quelch*, 127.

Allied to *U. cornuta*, Michx., but smaller, more slender, and with a more reflexed lower lip to the corolla.

UTRICULARIA RORAIMENSIS, N. E. Brown, sp. n. (Plate 11. figs. 1–4.) Perennis. Folia radicalia, orbiculato-spathulata, 3–7 lin. longa. Caules simplices vel divisi, 1¼–3 poll. longi, subfiliformi, 1–2-flori, 1–3-squamosi, glabri. Bracteæ minutæ, trifidæ. Flores parvi, pedicellati. Sepala inæqualia, glabra; sepalum superius ellipticum, obtusum, profunde concavum; inferius brevius, subquadratum, truncatum. Corollæ labium posticum ovatum, obtusum, intra minute glandulosum; labium anticum late subreniforme breviter 3-lobum, abrupte reflexum, minute glandulosum; calcar late conicum, obtusum, minute glandulosum.

Perennial. Leaves all radical, spathulate, glabrous: petiole 2–5 lin. long, slender; blade 1–2 lin. long, ½–1¾ lin. broad, obovate or orbicular, obtuse, cuneate at the base. Stems 1–4 to a plant, simple or once branched, 1¼–3 in. high, subfiliform, 1–2-flowered, glabrous, bearing 1–3 minute, oblong, obtuse, glabrous scales. Bracts minute, trifid, with the lateral teeth narrow and acute, and the middle tooth broadly rounded, glabrous, not ciliate. Pedicels 1–2½ lin. long, filiform, erect. Sepals unequal, thin, glabrous; the upper ¾–1 lin. long, elliptic or elliptic-ovate, obtuse, deeply concave, with about 4 rather obscure veins; the lower ½ lin. long, and about the same in breadth, subquadrate, truncate or very slightly emarginate, 4-veined. Corolla small; upper lip 1–1¼ lin. long, ¾–¾ lin. broad, ovate, obtuse, concave, erect or ascending, minutely glandular within; lower lip 1⅓–1½ lin. long, 2 lin. broad, subreniform, shortly 3-lobed, and more or less undulated, abruptly reflexed from the mouth of the spur on which it rests, minutely glandular on the lower part; spur 1½ lin. long, 1¼ lin. broad at the mouth, broadly conical, obtuse, compressed, minutely glandular, directed at a right angle to the pedicel. Stamens with curved clavate filaments, glabrous. Ovary globose, abruptly contracted into a stout style, glabrous; stigma with a minute tooth-like upper lip and a large truncate lower lip.

Summit of Mount Roraima, 8600 ft., *McConnell & Quelch*, 685.

UTRICULARIA CONCINNA, N. E. Brown, sp. n. (Plate 10, figs. 7–11.) Pusilla, glabra. Pedunculus uniflorus, ¾–1 poll. longus. Bracteæ et bracteolæ lanceolatæ, obtusæ. Sepala magna, cordato-ovata. Corolla erecta, labiis calyce paulo longioribus, glabris, labio superiore elliptico vel subrectangulare et apice obscure 3-crenato, labio inferiore elliptico vel subrectangulare undulato-crenato; calcar labiis multo longius, erectum, acutum, prope apicem parcissime pilosulum.

Leaves 2–4. all radical, 3–5 lin. long. lanceolate, elliptic or oblong-lanceolate, obtuse or subacute, tapering into a short petiole at the base, glabrous, erect. Peduncle ¾–1 in. high, 1-flowered, slender, with two distant minute bracts, one near the middle, the other near the base, glabrous. Flowering-bract ¾–1½ lin. long, lanceolate, subobtuse, glabrous, not ciliate. Bracteoles resembling the flowering-bract, but shorter and narrower. Pedicel 2–3 lin. long, glabrous. Sepals 2, erect, large in proportion to the corolla, 2½–3¼ lin. long, 2 2½ lin. broad, cordate-ovate, obtuse, glabrous, not ciliate. Corolla erect, with the lips only slightly exceeding the sepals, and the spur about twice as long; upper lip 1¾–2 lin. long, and about the same in breadth, elliptic or subrectangular, obscurely 3-crenate at the apex, with recurved margins, glabrous; lower lip about 2½–2¾ lin. long, elliptic or subrectangular, crenate and wavy at the apex, with the margins recurved, glabrous; spur about 3¼–3¾ lin. long, erect, acute, with a few scattered hairs on the terminal half. Stamens glabrous. Ovary globose-ovoid, narrowed into a short stout style, glabrous; stigma with a narrow acute upper lip and a broad emarginate lower lip. Capsule about half as long as the sepals, ellipsoidal, obtuse, crowned with the short style and stigma.

Kaieteur Savannah, *Jenman*, 1272; Mazaruni River, 300 ft., *McConnell & Quelch*, 710; and without precise locality, *Schomburgk*, 131.

The flowers of this diminutive species are stated by Messrs. McConnell and Quelch to be "white with purple points." I have only seen one corolla, and am uncertain if my description of it is quite correct in all details, as it was very much flattened; but my drawings of it (figs. 8 & 9) represent its general appearance as nearly as the material would allow, although they may not be accurate. The affinity of *U. concinna* is with *U. Campbelliana*, Oliver, and *U. montana*, Jacq., although it is very much smaller than either of those species.

UTRICULARIA NERVOSA, Weber?, ex Benj. in Mart. Fl. Bras. x. p. 247.

Upper slopes of Mount Roraima, *McConnell & Quelch*, 3 a.

Possibly a distinct species, but the material consists of one flowering stem only, which scarcely admits of proper dissection; externally, however, it much resembles *U. nervosa*, which is a Brazilian species.

UTRICULARIA sp.

Arabapu River, *McConnell & Quelch*, 150 a.

The specimen consists of leafy rhizomes without flowers, which were found entangled amongst the pitchers and false roots of *Genlisea guianensis*, N. E. Brown.

GENLISEA GUIANENSIS, N. E. Brown, in Hooker, Icones Plant. t. 2629.

Arabapu River, *McConnell & Quelch*, 150.

This is the largest species of this genus at present discovered, and more nearly resembles *G. africana*, Oliver, (a native of Angola), than any other with which I am acquainted. The members of the genus *Genlisea* appear to be quite destitute of true roots, their place being supplied by modified leaves, which descend into the soil or water. Some of these modified leaves terminate in the curious tubular two-lobed utricles characteristic of the genus, others being quite simple and root-like; probably all fulfil the functions of roots, and the utricles supply an additional amount of nitrogen to the plants by the absorption of the decomposed remains of the minute animalculæ they capture. The utricles have a very remarkable structure, which will be found well described and illustrated in Darwin's 'Insectivorous Plants,' p. 446, and Goebel's 'Pflanzenbiologische Schilderungen,' ii. p. 121, t. 15-16.

GENLISEA RORAIMENSIS, N. E. Brown, sp. n. (Plate 11, figs. 5-12.) Folia obovato-vel rotundato-spathulata, crassiuscula vel subcoriacea, glabra. Utriculi biformes, alter apice bilobus, alter apice acutus, minute 1-porosi. Caulis 1½-3 poll. longus, 3-6-squamosus, minute glanduloso-hirtellus, 1-4-florus. Bracteæ et bracteolæ minutæ, lanceolatæ, acutæ. Pedicelli minute glanduloso-hirtelli. Calyx 5-lobus, minute pubescens. Corolla parva, lutea, labio superiore late ovato vel elliptico-ovato obtuso concavo glabro, labio inferiore reflexo obtuse triloho glabro, calcari late conico obtusissimo minute glanduloso-hirtello.

A perennial with a very short branching rhizome densely covered with leaves. Leaves rosulate, 3-5 lin. long, ½-¾ lin. broad, obovate or orbicular-spathulate, rather thick or subcoriaceous, glabrous. Utricles 2½-5 lin. long, of two forms, both tubular and ovoid-inflated at the base and descending into the soil among the roots, one (the perfect form) dividing at the mouth into two long twisted lobes, the other (a transition form) acute, with a very minute orifice at the apex and entirely without lobes; a third and imperfect form is sometimes present standing erect among the leaves in which the terminal lobes are very short and scarcely or not at all twisted. Stem simple, 1½-3 in. high, ¼-⅓ lin. thick, 1-4-flowered, minutely and rather sparsely glandular-hairy, bearing 3-6 lanceolate, acute, basifixed, glabrous scales about ⅔ lin. long. Bracts and bracteoles subequal, basifixed, about ¾ lin. long, lanceolate, acute, sparsely pubescent and ciliate. Pedicels 1-2 lin. long, glandular-pubescent. Calyx 5-lobed almost to the base; lobes ¾-1 lin. long, oblong-lanceolate, acute, thinly pubescent and slightly ciliate. Corolla small, yellow; upper lip 1½ lin. long, 1 lin. broad, broadly ovate or elliptic-ovate, obtuse, concave, glabrous; lower lip 2 lin. long and as much in breadth, reflexed, obtusely 3-lobed, glabrous; spur 1¼ lin. long, 1¼ lin. broad at the mouth, stout, conical, very obtuse, compressed, slightly and minutely glandular-hairy, and darker in colour than the rest of the flower. Stamens glabrous; filaments curved, clavate; anthers deep blue. Ovary globose, thinly covered with very minute hairs; style short; stigma oblique. Capsule globose, about 1 lin. diam., minutely and sparsely hairy.

Summit of Mount Roraima, 8600 feet, growing in a somewhat sandy boggy soil, *McConnell & Quelch*, 684.

BIGNONIACEÆ.

TABEBUIA RORAIMÆ, Oliver, in Trans. Linn. Soc. Ser. II. Bot. ii. (1887), p. 280, t. 45.
Upper slopes of Mount Roraima, *McConnell & Quelch*, 33.—Endemic.

ACANTHACEÆ.

RUELLIA VINDEX, Mart. ex Nees in Mart. Fl. Bras. ix. p. 42.
Ireng Valley, *McConnell & Quelch*, 253.

THYRSACANTHUS SCHOMBURGKIANUS, Nees, in Hook. Lond. Journ. Bot. iv. (1845), p. 636.
Upper Essequebo River, *McConnell & Quelch*, 277.

DIANTHERA GUIANENSIS, N. E. Brown, sp. n. Caulis bifariam pubescens. Folia subsessilia, lanceolata vel ovato-lanceolata, acuta, basi angustata rotundata, utrinque glabra vel sparsim pubescentia. Thyrsus terminalis, subspiciformis, pedunculatus. Bracteæ et bracteolæ lineari-lanceolatæ, acutissimæ, subglabræ, ciliatæ. Sepala 5, libera, lineari-lanceolata, acutissima, pubescentia, ciliata. Corolla superne pubescens, labio superiore oblongo marginibus reflexo apice minute bilobo, labio inferiore 3-lobo disco plicato-elevato.—*Justicia* sp., Oliver, in Trans. Linn. Soc. Ser. II. Bot. ii. (1887), p. 280.

Shrubby, with terete, bifariously pubescent branches. Leaves spreading, subsessile, 2–4 in. long, 7–18 lin. broad, lanceolate or ovate-lanceolate, acute, narrowed below the middle to a rounded base, glabrous or sparsely pubescent on both sides. Peduncles terminal, ¾–3½ in. long, naked or bibracteate. Thyrsus spike-like, moderately dense, 1–2½ in. long, 1–1½ in. diam. Bracts and bracteoles 2½–3½ lin. long, linear-lanceolate, very acute, glabrous or slightly pubescent and slightly ciliate. Sepals 5, free, 3–3½ lin. long, ⅔ lin. broad, linear-lanceolate, very acuminate, pubescent, ciliate. Corolla two-lipped, pubescent in the upper part outside, apparently purple or red, spotted with darker; tube ¼ in. long; upper lip 4½ in. long, oblong, with reflexed margins and minutely 2-lobed at the apex; lower lip 5½ lin. long, 3-lobed, with an elevated plicate disk. Stamens 2, inserted at the middle of the tube; anthers 2-celled, with unequal cells, obtuse at each end, separated by a broad connective.

Kotinga Valley, *McConnell & Quelch*, 188; Kukenaam Valley, *im Thurn*, 81; Mount Roraima. *Appun*, 1387.

VERBENACEÆ.

LIPPIA SCHOMBURGKIANA, Schauer, in DC. Prod. xi. p. 577; Oliver, in Trans. Linn. Soc. Ser. II. Bot. ii. (1887), p. 280.
Upper slopes of Mount Roraima, *McConnell & Quelch*. 2; Roraima Range, 3500 ft., *McConnell & Quelch*. 720; Ireng Valley, *McConnell & Quelch*. 235.

I doubt if this Guiana plant is really distinct from the Brazilian *L. glandulosa*, Schauer, described at the same place.

STACHYTARPHETA MUTABILIS, Vahl, Enum. i. p. 208.
    Ireng Valley. *McConnell & Quelch*, 245.

LABIATÆ.

HYPTIS ARBOREA, Benth. in DC. Prod. xii. p. 132.
    Kotinga Valley, *McConnell & Quelch*, 142, 184.

AMARANTACEÆ.

GOMPHRENA GLOBOSA, Linn. Sp. Pl. ed. 1. p. 224.
    At Pelepowta Village in the Ireng Valley, *McConnell & Quelch*, 210.

PHYTOLACCACEÆ.

PHYTOLACCA THYRSIFLORA, Fenzl, ex J. A. Schmidt in Mart. Fl. Bras. ii. p. 343.
    Kotinga Valley, *McConnell & Quelch*, 152.

PROTEACEÆ.

ROUPALA MONTANA. Aubl. Pl. Guian. i. p. 83.
    Savannahs generally, *McConnell & Quelch*, 310.

LORANTHACEÆ.

PHORADENDRON RORAIMÆ. Oliver, in Trans. Linn. Soc. Ser. II. Bot. ii. (1887), p. 281,
    and pp. 267, 269).
    Summit of Mount Roraima, *McConnell & Quelch*, 82, 680.—Endemic.

BURMANNIACEÆ.

BURMANNIA BICOLOR, Mart. Nov. Gen. & Sp. i. p. 10, t. 5; R. Schomb. Reisen in Brit.-
    Guiana, iii. p. 1066.
    Upper slopes of Mount Roraima, *McConnell & Quelch*, 14.—Widely dispersed in
Tropical America from Cuba to Brazil, westward to Peru.

ORCHIDACEÆ. By R. A. ROLFE, A.L.S.

PLEUROTHALLIS RORAIMENSIS, Rolfe, sp. n. Lepanthiformis, caulibus gracilibus, vaginis
    apice ciliatis. Folia elliptica vel obovato-elliptica, minute apiculata, parva. Scapi
    subelongati, gracillimi, pauciflori. Bracteæ spathaceæ. Sepalum posticum basi
    ovatum, apice caudato-acuminatum; sepala lateralia subsimilia, basi angustiora.
    Petala oblonga, obtusa. Labellum trilobum, lobis lateralibus rotundatis, intermedio
    oblongo obtuso.
    Stems slender, ½ in. long, clothed with three or four angular or striate sheaths,
broader and ciliate at the apex. Leaves elliptical or obovate-elliptical, minutely
apiculate, 2½-4 lin. long, 1½-2 lin. broad. Scapes very slender, ¾-1 in. long, about 2- or

3-flowered. Bracts spathaceous, minute. Pedicels 1½ lin. long. Dorsal sepal ovate at the base, caudate-acuminate above, 2 lin. long; lateral similar, but narrower at the base. Petals oblong, obtuse, 1 lin. long, thinly membranaceous. Lip trilobed, 1 lin. long; side lobes spreading, broadly rounded; front lobe oblong, obtuse; disc bearing a pair of thickened nerves. Column clavate, ¾ lin. long.

Roraima, summit, 8600 ft., *McConnell & Quelch*, 687.—Endemic.

Allied to the Colombian *Pleurothallis intricata*, Lindl., but smaller in all its parts, besides being different in structure. The species of the natural group *Lepanthiformes*, to which it belongs, were distributed by Lindley into three sections, owing to the exigencies of an admittedly artificial arrangement, which would place the present one in the section *Acuminatæ*.

STELIS GUIANENSIS, Rolfe, sp. n. Cæspitosa. Caules brevissimi. Folia oblanceolato-oblonga, subobtusa, basi subattenuata. Scapi graciles, multiflori. Bracteæ triangulari-ovatæ, acutæ. Pedicelli breves. Sepala orbiculari-ovata, obtusa, basi connata. Petala suborbicularia, concava. Labellum integrum, suborbiculare, petalis paullo angustius.

A dwarf, densely-tufted plant, with very short stems. Leaves oblanceolate-oblong, subobtuse, somewhat attenuate at the base, 4–9 lin. long, 1½–2 lin. broad. Scapes slender, 2½ in. long, many-flowered. Bracts triangular-ovate, acute, ½ lin. long. Pedicels ¾ lin. long. Sepals orbicular-ovate, obtuse, ¾ lin. long, slightly pubescent, the basal fourth connate. Petals broadly orbicular, somewhat concave, not half as long as the sepals. Lip entire, rather narrower than the petals, but otherwise very similar.

Roraima range, 3500 ft., *McConnell & Quelch*, 703.—Endemic.

A species belonging to Lindley's small group *Monostachyæ apodæ*, and allied to the Peruvian *S. pusilla*, H. B. & K. A specimen collected at the Kaieteur Savannah, Potaro River, British Guiana, by Jenman (1055), is either a form of the same or a closely allied species.

BRACHIONIDIUM BREVICAUDATUM, Rolfe, sp. n. Caulis primarius repens, brevis; secundarius brevissimus. Folia breviter petiolata, elliptico-lanceolata, tridenticulata. Pedunculi filiformes, uniflori. Bracteæ apice acuminatæ. Sepalum posticum ovatum, apice abrupte acuminatum vel brevissime caudatum; sepala lateralia omnino connata et postico subsimilia. Petala ovata, acuminata vel brevissime caudata, margine plus minusve ciliata. Labellum sessile, trilobum, lobis lateralibus falcato-oblongis subobtusis, intermedio reflexo late ovato-rotundato. Columna lata.

Primary stem creeping, with short internodes, clothed with membranaceous sheaths; secondary very short, clothed with about two tubular membranaceous sheaths having a short acuminate apex. Leaves shortly petioled, elliptical-lanceolate, shortly tricuspidate, 8–10 lin. long, 2½–3½ lin. broad; petioles 1½–2 lin. long. Peduncles slender, ¾–1¼ in. long, bearing a short tubular acuminate sheath above the middle. Bract similar to the sheath but rather larger. Dorsal sepal ovate, abruptly acuminate or shortly caudate, 4 lin. long by nearly 3 lin. broad, trinerved; lateral pair united into a body closely resembling the dorsal sepal, but rather broader and 4-nerved. Petals ovate, shortly

I 2

acuminate, 3 lin. long, more or less ciliate, trinerved. Lip sessile, 1½ lin. long, trilobed; side lobes falcate-oblong, subobtuse, suberect; front lobe reflexed, broadly rounded-oblong; disc with a slightly elevated crest between the side lobes. Column broad, ½ lin. long.

Roraima range, 3500 ft., *McConnell & Quelch*, 705.—Endemic.

An interesting addition to this small genus, readily distinguished from its allies by the short secondary stem, and short tails to the sepals and petals.

MASDEVALLIA PICTURATA. Reichb. f. Otia Bot. Hamb. 16; Ridl. in Trans. Linn. Soc. Ser. II. Bot. ii. (1887), p. 281.; Woolw. Masd. p. 87, t. 34.

Roraima, at 3500 ft., *McConnell & Quelch*, 704; Upper slope, *im Thurn*, 279.

In the mountains of Colombia, between 2500 and 6500 ft. elevation; extending along the Coast Andes of Venezuela to Caracas. at 6000 to 6500 ft. ; also in Costa Rica. Roraima seems to be an outlying station for the species.

OCTOMERIA CONNELLII, Rolfe, sp. n. Caules secundarii elongati. Folia subsessilia, oblongo-lanceolata, subobtusa, crasso-coriacea. Flores subfasciculati, mediocres. Sepala et petala ovato-lanceolata, subobtusa. Labellum oblongum, subconcavum, obtusum vel obscure tridentatum, margine minutissime crenulatum.

Secondary stems stout, elongate, 4–12 in. long, clothed with four or five tubular sheaths 1–1½ in. long. Leaf subsessile, thickly coriaceous or somewhat fleshy, oblong-lanceolate, subobtuse, 2–4 in. long, 4–10 lin. broad. Flowers few, or produced mostly in succession, medium-sized, shortly pedicelled. Sepals and petals ovate-lanceolate, subobtuse, 4–6 lin. long. Lip oblong, somewhat concave, obtuse or obscurely tridentate, margin minutely crenulate, 3–4 lin. long. Column clavate, 1½ lin. long.

Roraima, summit at 8600 ft., *McConnell & Quelch*, 700. -Endemic.

A very distinct species. having stems much longer than the leaves, and flowers comparatively large for the genus. It is comparable with *O. grandiflora*, Lindl., but has longer stems, much shorter leaves, and the lip very different in structure.

OCTOMERIA PARVIFOLIA, Rolfe, sp. n. Cæspitosa. Caules secundarii graciles, vaginis tubulosis striatis obtecti. Folia lineari-oblonga, subacuta, parva. Flores fasciculati. Sepala ovato-oblonga, subobtusa. Petala lineari-oblonga, subobtusa. Labellum late deltoideo-trilobum, lobis lateralibus divergentibus anguste triangularibus, intermedio breviter et late triangulari obtuso.

Secondary stems densely tufted, slender, 2½–3 in. long, clothed with about five or six tubular striate sheaths. Leaves linear-oblong, subacute, ? 1¼ in. long, 1–1½ lin. broad, base somewhat attenuate. Flowers fasciculate. Pedicels very short. Sepals ovate-oblong, subobtuse, 1 lin. long. Petals linear-oblong, subobtuse, 1 lin. long. Lip broadly deltoid-triangular, over ½ lin. broad; side lobes narrowly triangular, subobtuse; front lobe broadly triangular, obtuse; disc with a pair of thickened slightly arcuate keels in the centre, and a shorter one in front. Column short.

Roraima, summit, 8600 ft., *McConnell & Quelch*, 696.—Endemic.

In the relatively small proportion which the leaf bears to the rest of the plant, this species approaches the Brazilian *Octomeria breviflora*, Cogn., but the structure of the lip is very different.

BULBOPHYLLUM RORAIMENSE, Rolfe, sp. n. Racemus multiflorus. Bracteæ oblongæ vel ovato-oblongæ, acutæ. Sepala ovato-lanceolata, acuminata, lateralia carinata. Petala ovato-oblonga, subacuta. Labellum velutinum, pandurato-oblongum, obtusum, medio ad basin lateraliter compressum, basi utrinque auriculatum, disco elevato bicarinato. Columna brevis, utrinque bidentata.

Scape moderately slender; raceme 3 in. long, many-flowered. Bracts oblong or ovate-oblong, acute, 2½–3 lin. long. Pedicels 1 lin. long. Sepals ovate-lanceolate, acuminate, 4–5½ lin. long, lateral carinate. Petals ovate-oblong, subacute, 1½ lin. long. Lip 2¾ lin. long, velvety, pandurate-oblong, obtuse; front lobe expanded into an ovate-oblong blade, middle and base laterally compressed, with a rounded-erect basal auricle on either side; disc much elevated and channelled between the pair of obtuse keels. Column stout, 1 lin. long, with two pairs of teeth; upper pair subulate-filiform, incurved, with a broad base, as long as the column, lower pair subulate-oblong, a third as long as the upper.

Roraima, summit, 8600 ft., *McConnell & Quelch*, 103.—Endemic.

Allied to *B. geraense*, Reichb. f., but the scape and raceme more slender, the sepals proportionately broader, and the lip and teeth of the column different in detail. It is described from a single scape.

ELLEANTHUS LINIFOLIUS, Presl, Rel. Haenk. p. 97.

Ireng Valley, *McConnell & Quelch*, 301. Roraima, *Schomburgk*.—Also found in Cuba, Porto Rico, Nicaragua, Panama, Guiana, Brazil, and Bolivia.

DIACRIUM BICORNUTUM, Benth. in Journ. Linn. Soc., Bot. xviii. (1881), p. 312.

Kwaimatta Savannah, *McConnell & Quelch*, 280.—Also found in Guiana, Trinidad, and Tobago.

EPIDENDRUM GRANITICUM, Lindl. in Hook. Journ. Bot. iii. (1841), p. 83.

Kwaimatta Savannah, Rupununi River, *McConnell & Quelch*, 279. Ireng River, *im Thurn*, 13.—Found in British and Dutch Guiana, and Trinidad.

Nearly allied to *E. oncidioides*, Lindl., with which it is made synonymous by Lindley.

EPIDENDRUM SCHOMBURGKII, Lindl. Bot. Reg. (1838), Misc. p. 15; Ridl. in Trans. Linn. Soc. Ser. II. Bot. ii. (1887), p. 281.

Kotinga Valley, *McConnell & Quelch*, 135. " Flowers red, of all shades."—Found in Trinidad, Guiana, Brazil, and Bolivia.

EPIDENDRUM FULGENS, Brongn. in Duperry, Voy. Coquille, Phan. p. 196, t. 43; Rolfe, in Orch. Rev. v. (1897), p. 264.

E. Schomburgkii, var. *confluens*, Lindl. Fol. Orch., Epidendr. p. 70.

E. Schomburgkii, Appun, Unter den Tropen, ii. p. 199 (non Lindl.).

Roraima. upper slopes, *McConnell & Quelch*, 1. North of Roraima, *Appun*, 1202. "Abundant."—Found in British Guiana, and the Brazilian provinces of Rio de Janeiro and Santa Catherina.

EPIDENDRUM ELONGATUM, Jacq. Coll. iii. p. 260; and Ic. Pl. Rar. iii. p. 17, t. 604; Ridl. in Trans. Linn. Soc. Ser. II. Bot. ii. (1887), p. 281.
Roraima, summit, at 8600 ft., *McConnell & Quelch*, 686. South side, at 5500 ft., *im Thurn*, 12.—Found in the Windward Islands, W. Indies, from Antigua to Trinidad, also in Guiana, Brazil, and Bolivia.

EPIDENDRUM ALSUM, Ridl. in Trans. Linn. Soc. Ser. II. Bot. ii. (1887), p. 281.
Roraima, summit, 8600 ft., *McConnell & Quelch*, 90. 699; *im Thurn*, 296.—Endemic.

EPIDENDRUM IMTHURNII, Ridl. in Trans. Linn. Soc. Ser. II. Bot. ii. (1887), p. 282, t. 16. fig. A.
Roraima, summit, 8600 ft., *McConnell & Quelch*, 697: *im Thurn*, 299.—Endemic.

EPIDENDRUM MONTIGENUM, Ridl. in Trans. Linn. Soc. Ser. II. Bot. ii. (1887), p. 282.
Roraima, upper slopes and summit, *McConnell & Quelch*, 37, 694; ledge and top, *im Thurn*, 322.—Endemic.

EPIDENDRUM VIOLASCENS, Ridl. in Trans. Linn. Soc. Ser. II. Bot. ii. (1887), p. 282, t. 16. fig. B.
Roraima, summit, 8600 ft., *McConnell & Quelch*, 84, 695; *im Thurn*, 300.—Endemic.

GALEANDRA JUNCEA, Lindl. Sert. Orch. sub t. 37.
Ireng Valley, *McConnell & Quelch*, 243.—Also found in Guiana and Brazil.

CYRTOPODIUM ANDERSONII, R. Br. in Ait Hort. Kew. ed. 2. v. p. 216.
Kanuku Mts., *McConnell & Quelch*, 276.—Also found in Guiana, Brazil, and Paraguay.

CYRTOPODIUM CRISTATUM, Lindl. Bot. Reg. (1841). sub t. 8.
Kotinga Valley, amid stones on hill, *McConnell & Quelch*, 136. "Flowers yellow and brown."—Also found in Trinidad, Guiana, and Brazil.

ZYGOPETALUM BURKEI, Reichb. f. in Gard. Chron. xx. (1883), p. 684; Ridl. in Trans. Linn. Soc. Ser. II. Bot. ii. (1887), p. 282.
Z. *Mackaii*, R. Schomb. Reisen in Brit.-Guiana, ii. p. 266, iii. p. 1068; Appun, Unter den Tropen, ii. pp. 246, 292 (non Hook.).
Roraima. upper slopes, *McConnell & Quelch*, 26. "Flowers coffee-coloured." South side, at 5500 ft., *im Thurn*, 50. South and east sides, *Appun*, 1390.—Endemic.

ERIOPSIS SCHOMBURGKII, Reichb. f. in Bonplandia, iii. (1855), p. 67.

Pseudoeriopsis Schomburgkii, Reichb. f. in Linnæa, xxii. (1849), p. 853; R. Schomb. Reisen in Brit.-Guiana, iii. p. 1123.

Roraima, upper slopes, *McConnell & Quelch*, 34. "Flowers brown." *Schomburgk*, 1679 a.—Also in the savannah of South Guiana.

HOULLETIA RORAIMENSIS, Rolfe. sp. n. Folia elliptico-lanceolata, magna. Scapus arcuatus. 7–9-florus. Bracteæ oblongæ, subobtusæ, concavæ. Sepala orbiculari-elliptica, concava. Petala orbiculari-elliptica, plana. Labellum profunde trilobum; lobi laterales late oblongi, truncati, oblique apiculatis; intermedius breviter unguiculatus, late trulliformis, apiculatus, callo transverso submembranaceo ad basin unguem sito. Columna clavata.

Leaf petiolate. elliptico-lanceolate, acute, 1½ ft. long, 4½ in. broad. Scape arching (base not seen); raceme 7–9-flowered. Bracts oblong, subobtuse, concave, 6–7 lin. long. Pedicels 1–1¼ in. long. Sepals orbicular-elliptical, concave, 9–11 lin. long, 7–9 lin. broad. Petals orbicular-elliptical, nearly flat, 9–10 lin. long, 7–8 lin. broad. Lip deeply 3-lobed; side lobes broadly oblong. nearly truncate and obliquely apiculate, 6 lin. long, 3½ lin. broad, connected at the base by a suberect, transverse, stout, undulate membrane, and with a somewhat similar connecting callus at the junction of the front lobe, but more distinctly toothed; front lobe shortly and broadly unguiculate. broadly trulliform, abruptly apiculate, and with subacute lateral angles. 5 lin. long by nearly as broad. Column clavate. curved, 5 lin. long.

Roraima, upper slopes, *McConnell & Quelch*, 29.—Endemic.

A very distinct species. nearest *H. Lowiana*, Reichb. f., in structure. but very different in the broad nearly truncate side lobes of the lip, and more like *H. Brocklehurstiana*, Lindl., in habit.

CATASETUM DISCOLOR. Lindl. Bot. Reg. (1844). Misc. p. 34.

Roraima. upper slopes, *McConnell & Quelch*, 6.—Also found in Guiana, Brazil. and Paraguay.

MAXILLARIA CONNELLII, Rolfe, sp. n. Folia oblongo-lanceolata, acuta, basi in petiolum attenuata. Scapus foliis brevior, vaginis ovato-lanceolatis acutis subimbricatis obtectus. Bractea oblongo-lanceolata, acuta. Sepala subobtusa et minute apiculata; sepalum lateralia triangulari-oblonga; posticum oblongo-lanceolatum. Petala oblongo-lanceolata, subacuta. Labellum elliptico-oblongum, obtusum, subundulatum, apice recurvum, callo oblongo apice dilatato truncato. Columna brevis

Leaves oblong-lanceolate, acute, attenuate at the base, 6–8 in. long, 9–12 lin. broad. Scape 3½–4 in. long, covered with ovate-lanceolate acute sheaths, 6–9 lin. long and somewhat imbricate at the base. Bract oblong-lanceolate, acute, 9–12 lin. long. Sepals subobtuse and minutely apiculate, dorsal oblong-lanceolate, 7–8 lin. long; lateral triangular-oblong, 8–9 lin. long. Petals oblong-lanceolate, subacute, 7–8 lin. long. Lip elliptical-oblong, obtuse, somewhat undulate, recurved at the apex, rather fleshy,

5-6 lin. long; callus oblong, dilated and truncate at the apex. Column stout, free part scarcely 2 lin. long, with a much longer foot. Mentum rounded, obtuse, 3 lin. long. Roraima : Kotinga Valley, *McConnell & Quelch*, 137.—Endemic.

Allied to the Colombian *Maxillaria melina*, Lindl., but the leaves smaller, sheaths of the scape shorter, and with various differences in the structure of the flower.

MAXILLARIA QUELCHII, Rolfe, sp. n. Subcaulescens, vaginis imbricatis multistriatis. Pseudobulbi compressi, apice monophylli. Folia oblonga, subobtusa, conduplicata. Scapi foliis subaequales, vaginis lanceolatis subimbricatis obtecti. Bractea lanceolata, acuminata. Sepala oblongo-lanceolata, acuta. Petala lineari-lanceolata, acuta, sepalis breviora. Labellum trilobum, lobis lateralibus erectis rotundato-oblongis membranaceis, intermedio recurvo obovato-orbiculari obscure tricuspidato medio carnoso lateribus incurvo, callo oblongo obtuso concavo.

Subcaulescent, with the stems clothed with conduplicate, triangular-lanceolate, acute, closely striate, imbricating sheaths. 1–2 in. long, and partly enveloping the pseudobulbs. Pseudobulbs compressed, broadly oblong, shining and puncticulate, wrinkled when old, 1 in. long, ¾ in. broad, monophyllous at the apex. Leaves conduplicate, lanceolate-oblong, subobtuse, 3–4 in. long, ¾–1 in. broad. Scapes 3–4 in. long, bearing 5–7 lanceolate, acute, striate, somewhat imbricating sheaths, 6–12 lin. long. Bract resembling the sheaths, 10–12 lin. long. Sepals oblong-lanceolate, acuminate, 1½ in. long. Petals linear-lanceolate, acuminate, 1¼ in. long. Lip ½ in. long, 3-lobed ; side lobes erect, rounded-oblong, membranaceous, 1 lin. long, 1¼ lin. broad ; middle lobe recurved, obovate-orbicular, obscurely tricuspidate at the apex, 2 lin. broad by nearly as long, thickened along the centre and incurved at the sides ; crest oblong, obtuse, concave. Column clavate, incurved, 3 lin. long.

Roraima, summit, at 8600 ft. alt., *McConnell & Quelch*, 690.—Endemic.

Allied to the Peruvian *M. floribunda*, Lindl., but much less scandent, and smaller in all its parts.

ONCIDIUM ORTHOSTATES, Ridl. in Trans. Linn. Soc. Ser. II. Bot. ii. (1887), p. 283.

Kwaimatta Savannah, *McConnell & Quelch*, 281. Ireng River, *im Thurn*, 12.—Also found at Mimatta, on the Rupununi River.

SOBRALIA STENOPHYLLA, Lindl. Fol. Orch., Sobral. p. 2 : Ridl. in Trans. Linn. Soc. Ser. II. ii. (1887), p. 283.

Kotinga River, *McConnell & Quelch*, 117. Ireng Valley, *McConnell & Quelch*, 329. Ipelemouta, Arapu River, *im Thurn*, 19. Roraima. *Appun*, 1076.—Endemic.

EPISTEPHIUM LUCIDUM, Cogn. in Mart. Fl. Bras. iii. pt. iv. p. 141, t. 30.

Roraima, upper slopes, *McConnell & Quelch*, 32.—Also found in Brazil.

EPISTEPHIUM PARVIFLORUM, Lindl. Gen. & Sp. Orch. p. 433.

Kotinga Valley. *McConnell & Quelch*, 160.—Also found in Trinidad and elsewhere in British Guiana.

SPIRANTHES BIFIDA, Ridl. in Trans. Linn. Soc. Ser. II. Bot. ii. (1887), p. 283.
Kotinga Valley, *McConnell & Quelch*, 200. Roraima, summit, 8600 ft. alt., *McConnell & Quelch*, 692. South side at 5500 ft., *im Thurn*, 342.—Endemic.

POGONIA PARVIFLORA, Reichb. f. Xen. Orch. ii. p. 90 ; Ridl. in Trans. Linn. Soc. Ser. II. Bot. ii. (1887), p. 283.
Roraima, upper slopes, *McConnell & Quelch*, 30. " Flowers pink and waxy." South side at 5500 ft., *im Thurn*, 115.—Endemic.

POGONIA TENUIS, Reichb. f. in Griseb. Fl. Brit. W. Ind. p. 637.
Roraima, summit, 8600 ft., *McConnell & Quelch*, 691.—Also found in Trinidad, Venezuela, and on the Upper Amazon.

HABENARIA MORITZII, Ridl. in Trans. Linn. Soc. Ser. II. Bot. ii. (1887), p. 284.
Roraima, upper slopes, *McConnell & Quelch*, 4; at 4000 ft., *im Thurn*, 367.—Also found in Venezuela.

HABENARIA RORAIMENSIS, Rolfe, sp. n. Planta erecta, foliosa. Folia caulina, basi lanceolata, acuta, superiora gradatim in vaginas bracteiformes decrescentia. Bracteæ lanceolatæ, acuminatæ. Sepalum posticum erectum, ovatum, apiculatum ; sepala lateralia patentia, oblique ovato-oblonga, apiculata. Petala bipartita, lobo postico falcato-oblongo apiculato, antico filiformi-lineari arcuato. Labellum tripartitum ; lobi laterales filiformi-lineares divergentes ; lobus intermedius linearis obtusus ; calcar clavatum.

Plant ½-1½ ft. high, somewhat leafy. Leaves cauline, the lower lanceolate, acute, 2-2½ lin. long, 4-5 lin. broad ; upper smaller, decreasing upwards into bract-like sheaths. Bracts lanceolate, acuminate, 6-9 lin. long. Dorsal sepal erect, ovate, apiculate, 2-2½ lin. long, lateral spreading obliquely, ovate-oblong, apiculate, 2-2½ lin. long. Petals bipartite ; upper lobe falcate-oblong, apiculate, 1½-2 lin. long ; lower lobe filiform-linear, curved, shorter than the upper. Lip tripartite ; side-lobes filiform-linear, diverging, 1½-2 lin. long ; front lobe linear, obtuse, 2-2½ lin. long ; spur linear-clavate, 4-5 lin. long. Anther-channels and stigmatic processes short.
Roraima, summit, 8600 ft., *McConnell & Quelch*, 698.—Endemic.
Allied to *H. protensis*, Reichb. f., but readily distinguished by its much smaller flowers.

PHRAGMIPEDIUM KLOTZSCHIANUM, Rolfe, in Orch. Rev. iv. (1896), p. 332.
Cypripedium Klotzschianum, Reichb. f. in Linnæa, xxii. (1849), p. 811 ; Appun. Unter den Tropen, ii. p. 196.
Selenipedium Klotzschianum, Reichb. f. in Bonplandia, ii. (1854), p. 116 ; Ridl. in Trans. Linn. Soc. Ser. II. Bot. ii. (1887), p. 284.
Cypripedium Schomburgkianum, Klotzsch, in R. Schomb. Reisen in Brit.-Guiana, ii. p. 229 ; R. Schomb. Bot. Rem. Brit. Guiana, p. 59.
Arabapu River, *McConnell & Quelch*, 144. Aroic Creek, Kotinga River, *im Thurn*, 5. Ipelemonta, Arapu River, *im Thurn*, 31. Kako River, *Appun*, 1212.—Endemic.

BROMELIACEÆ.

BROCCHINIA REDUCTA, Baker, in Journ. of Bot. xx. (1882), p. 331; Baker, Handb. Brom. p. 88; Mez, in DC. Monog. Phan. ix. p. 341. (Plate 12.)

Roraima Range, 3500 ft., *McConnell & Quelch*, 702.—Also found on the Kaieteur Savannah, *Jenman*, 873.

PUYA FLOCCOSA, E. Morren, in Belg. Hort. xxxv. (1878), p. 81; Mez. in DC. Monog. Phan. ix. p. 478.

P. guianensis, Klotzsch, in R. Schomb. Reisen in Brit.-Guiana, iii. p. 1067.

P. sp., Baker, in Trans. Linn. Soc. Ser. II. Bot. ii. (1887), p. 285.

Roraima Range, 3500 ft., *McConnell & Quelch*, 701.—Also in Venezuela, Colombia, and Bolivia.

CONNELLIA, N. E. Brown, gen. nov.

Flores hermaphroditi, regulares. Sepala libera, oblonga. Petala libera, lata, basi angustata, nuda, sepalis multo longiora. Stamina petalis breviora et iis basi breviter adnata, filamentis filiformibus, antheris oblongis basifixis. Ovarium superum, trigonum, loculis multiovulatis; stylus elongatus; stigmata linearia. Capsula in carpellis 3 septicide separata, carpellis introrsum dehiscentibus. Semina numerosa, parva, linearia, utrinque appendiculata.—Herbæ habitu *Tillandsiæ*. Folia rosulata, integra vel basi denticulata. Inflorescentia terminalis. spiciformis, simplex vel composita. Flores sub quaque bractea solitarii vel plures, pedicellati.

CONNELLIA AUGUSTÆ, N. E. Brown. (Plate 13.) Capsula 6-7 lin. longa, 3 lin. diam., trigona, oblonga, coriacea, glabra, in carpellis 3 septicide soluta, carpellis longe rostratis introrsum dehiscentibus. Semina $1\frac{3}{4}$-2 lin. longa, lineari-teretia, curvata, utrinque membranaceo-appendiculata.—*Encholirium Augustæ*, R. H. Schomb. in Verh. des Ver. Beförd. Gartenb. in Preuss. (1846), p. 18. t. 2; in Bot. Zeitung (1846), p. 454; R. Schomb. Reisen in Brit.-Guiana, ii. p. 271, and iii. p. 1067: & in Bot. Rem. Brit. Guiana, p. 77; De Beer, Brom. p. 27. *Caraguata Augustæ*, Benth. & Hook. f. Gen. Pl. iii. p. 668. *Dyckia Augustæ*, Baker, Handb. Brom. p. 135. *Puya Augustæ*, Mez, in DC. Monogr. Phan. ix. p. 187, partim.

Summit of Mount Roraima, 8600 ft., *McConnell & Quelch*, 670. South slopes of Roraima at 6500 ft., *Schomburgk*, 687, 1021.

The discovery of fruiting specimens of this plant by Messrs. McConnell & Quelch demonstrates that it cannot properly be referred to either of the genera under which it has previously been placed. From *Encholirium* it differs totally in habit, large bracts, broad petals, and seeds. From *Caraguata* it differs in its free petals and in its seeds. From *Dyckia* it differs in habit, in the long-beaked entire (not bifid) carpels into which the ripe fruit separates, and in its seeds. And from *Puya* it differs in habit, in the petals not twisting when the flower fades, in the capsule not dehiscing loculicidally, and in the seeds. The only genus which approaches it in structure is *Lindmania*, Mez, but the habit, branching panicle, small bracts and very small flowers of the species of *Lindmania* are so entirely different from those of *Connellia*, that they cannot naturally be placed in the same genus. Possibly the fruit of *Lindmania*, which I have not seen, and the dorsifixed anthers may afford technical characters to distinguish the two genera, especially if taken in conjunction with the difference in habit.

CONNELLIA QUELCHII, N. E. Brown. (Plate 14.) Folia rosulata 1½-5¾ poll. longa, angusta, convoluta, integra, basi tantum minute denticulata, supra tomentosa, subtus glabra, vel rare utrinque tomentosa, marginibus albo-tomentosis. Scapus simplex, multibracteatus. Bracteae imbricatae, glabrae, nitidae; inferiores steriles amplexicaules, abrupte subulato-cuspidatae; florigerae elliptico-ovatae, apiculatae, valde concavae. Flores sub quaque bractea solitarii, pedicellati, speciosi, rosei.—*Tillandsia stricta*, var. ?, Baker, in Trans. Linn. Soc. Ser. II. Bot. ii. (1887), p. 285. *Puya Augustae*, Mez, in DC. Monog. Phan. ix. p. 187, partim.

Leaves rosulate, 1½-5¾ in. long, 2-4½ lin. broad, linear, convolute-subulate, rather blunt, rigidly coriaceous, minutely denticulate at the base only, densely white-tomentose on the inner face and along the margins, usually glabrous on the convex back, rarely tomentose on both sides. Scape arising from the centre of the rosette, 2-5 in. long to the lowest flower of the 2 3½ in. long raceme, 1-1½ lin. thick, glabrous, clothed with imbricating bracts, which are ¾-1¼ in. long, 6-8 lin. broad, stem-clasping, broadly elliptic-oblong and abruptly contracted into a subulate leafy point at the apex, or broadly ovate and simply acute or acuminate, glabrous, with tomentose margins to the leafy point, brown in the dried state, shining. Raceme moderately dense, 1¼-1¾ in. diam., 7 13-flowered, its bracts ascending or somewhat spreading, 7-10 lin. long, 5-7 lin. broad, elliptic-ovate, acute or obtuse and apiculate, deeply concave, glabrous, brown, shining. Flowers solitary under each bract, pedicellate. Pedicels 2-8 lin. long, glabrous. Sepals free, 5-5½ lin. long, 2½-3 lin. broad, ovate-oblong, acute, glabrous, light brown, with thin rose-pink margins. Petals free, 9 lin. long, 5½ lin. broad, orbicular, obtuse, narrowed into a short broad claw at the base, glabrous, entire, without a scale at their base, bright rose-pink. Stamens about 5 lin. long, glabrous; filaments very shortly adnate to the petals at their base, filiform; anthers ¾ lin. long, oblong, obtuse. Ovary superior, trigonous-ovoid, glabrous, narrowed into a glabrous style 3½ lin. long, with 3 recurving compressed linear stigmas about 1 lin. long, slightly undulated along the stigmatose surface.

Summit of Mount Roraima, 8600 ft., *im Thurn*, 315; *McConnell & Quelch*, 107, 672.

In general appearance this plant bears a slight resemblance to *Tillandsia stricta*, Soland., but in all details is very different. It is considered by Mez to be identical with *C. Augustae*; but although an undoubted congener of that plant, is most certainly very distinct from it specifically, being very much smaller in size, with the upper surface and margins of the leaves tomentose, solitary flowers under each bract, and a glabrous calyx; whilst *C. Augustae* has leaves 8-14 in. long, quite glabrous on both sides, the flowers are in clusters of 3-7 under each bract, and the calyx is thinly covered with short hairs. I have not seen ripe seeds of *C. Quelchii*, but the ovules show that they will be appendaged at each end. It is a very pretty species and well worth cultivating.

K 2

TILLANDSIA RHODOCINCTA, Baker, in Journ. Bot. xxvi. (1888), p. 143, & Handb. Brom.
    p. 178 ; Mez, in DC. Monog. Phan. ix. p. 791. *Tillandsia sp.*, Baker, in Trans. Linn.
    Soc. Ser. II. Bot. ii. (1887), p. 285.
    Summit of Mount Roraima, *McConnell & Quelch*, 671.—Endemic.

IRIDACEÆ.

SISYRINCHIUM ALATUM, Hooker, Icones Plant. t. 219, var.
    Kotinga Valley, *McConnell & Quelch*, 139.

LILIACEÆ.

NIETNERIA CORYMBOSA, Klotzsch, in R. Schomb. Reisen in Brit.-Guiana, iii. p. 1066 ; im
    Thurn & Oliver, in Trans. Linn. Soc. Ser. II. Bot. ii. (1887), pp. 269, 285.
    Upper slopes of Mount Roraima, *McConnell & Quelch*, 12, 36, 328.   Summit of Mount
    Roraima, *McConnell & Quelch*, 83, 656.—Apparently endemic to the region.

TOFIELDIA SCHOMBURGKIANA, Oliver, in Trans. Linn. Soc. Ser. II. Bot. ii. (1887), p. 285,
    t. 49. f. A.

Isidrogalvis guianensis, Klotzsch, in R. Schomb. Reisen in Brit.-Guiana, iii. p. 1065, name only.

    Upper slopes and summit of Mount Roraima, *McConnell & Quelch*, 93, 326, 657 ;
Schomburgk.—Endemic.

XYRIDACEÆ.

XYRIS SEUBERTII, Nilss. in K. Svensk Akad. Handl. xxiv. (1892), No. XIV. p. 51, t. 4.
    f. 1.
    Upper slopes of Mount Roraima, *McConnell & Quelch*, 41.—The locality in which
Schomburgk collected this plant is unknown to me, and the leaves of his specimens are
much smaller than those of the specimens collected by McConnell & Quelch.

XYRIS CONCINNA, N. E. Brown, sp. n.   Planta 3-6 poll. alta, perennis, glabra.   Caudex
¼-½ poll. longus.   Folia disticha, 1-2¾ poll. longa, anguste linearia, acuta.   Pedunculus subteres, uno margine prominente, basi vagina apice breviter foliata
instructus.   Spica ovoidea.   Bracteæ oblongæ vel ellipticæ, obtusæ, castaneæ, late
albo-marginatæ, laceratæ, glabræ.   Sepala lateralia lineari-lanceolata, acuta, carinata,
glabra, carina integra vel ad medium minutissime scabrida.   Petala elliptica, obtusa,
integra, lutea.   Staminodia bibrachiata, brachiis penicillatis luteis.

Perennial.   Caudex ¼-½ in. (or more ?) long, ½ lin. thick, naked below the leaves,
emitting fibrous roots.   Leaves distichous, 1-2¾ in. long, ⅜-⅝ lin. broad, linear, acute,
abruptly dilated into a short, broad, bright brown, clasping base, not twisted, glabrous.
Peduncles 1-6 to a stem, 2½-5½ in. long, ¼-⅓ lin. thick, subterete, with a raised line
along one side, glabrous ; their basal sheaths ¾-1¾ in. long, produced at the apex into a
short compressed or leafy point, keeled, glabrous, often minutely ciliate along the keel or
at its apex.   Spikes 2½-3½ lin. long, ovoid, obtuse.   Bracts 1½-2½ lin. long, 1-1½ lin.

broad, oblong or elliptic, obtuse, chestnut-brown, with a broad white hyaline border, which soon becomes lacerated, glabrous. Lateral sepals 2¾ lin. long, ½ lin. broad, complicate, linear-lanceolate, acute, keeled, yellowish-brown, glabrous, the keel quite entire or very minutely scabrid along the middle. Petals 2 lin. long, 1 lin. broad, elliptic, obtuse, entire, yellow. Staminodes 2-armed, about ½ lin. long, divided into tufts of yellow hairs.

Summit of Mount Roraima, 8600 ft., *McConnell & Quelch*, 496.

Allied to *Xyris Neubertii*, Nilss., but distinguished by its smaller size, lacerated bracts, and the glabrous or very minutely scabrid keel of the lateral sepals. The broad bright brown bases of the leaves give the base of the plant a somewhat bulbous appearance.

XYRIS WITSENIOIDES, Oliver, in Trans. Linn. Soc. Ser. II. Bot. ii. (1887), p. 285, t. 50. f. B.

X. caulescens, Klotzsch, in R. Schomb. Reisen in Brit.-Guiana, iii. p. 1064, name only.

Summit of Mount Roraima, *McConnell & Quelch*, 95, 658.—Endemic.

ABOLBODA SCEPTRUM, Oliver, in Trans. Linn. Soc. Ser. II. Bot. ii. (1887), p. 286, & pp. 258, 259, 262, 267, & 268.

Summit of Mount Roraima, *McConnell & Quelch*, 668.—Endemic on Roraima and the surrounding region.

The specimen collected by McConnell & Quelch consists of adult leaves and young plants, and that collected by im Thurn of the upper part of a flowering stem without leaves, so that this interesting plant is as yet very imperfectly represented in European Herbaria.

RAPATEACEÆ.

STEGOLEPIS GUIANENSIS, Klotzsch, *ex* Koern. in Linnæa, xxxvii. (1871–73), p. 481; im Thurn & Oliver, in Trans. Linn. Soc. Ser. II. Bot. ii. (1887), pp. 265, 267 & 286.

Summit of Mount Roraima, *McConnell & Quelch*, 669.—Endemic.

ERIOCAULACEÆ.

ERIOCAULON TENUIFOLIUM, Klotzsch, in R. Schomb. Reisen in Brit.-Guiana, iii. p. 1116.

Savannahs generally, *McConnell & Quelch*, 307.

PÆPALANTHUS RORAIMÆ, Oliver, in Trans. Linn. Soc. Ser. II. Bot. ii. (1887), p. 286.

Summit of Mount Roraima, *McConnell & Quelch*, 102, 315, 660.—Endemic.

PÆPALANTHUS FLAVESCENS, Koern. in. Mart. Fl. Bras. iii. pt. i. p. 423; im Thurn & Oliver, in Trans. Linn. Soc. Ser. II. Bot. ii. (1887), pp. 263, 286.

P. eriocephalus, Klotzsch in R. Schomb. Reisen in Brit.-Guiana, iii. p. 1064, name only.

Upper slopes of Mount Roraima, *McConnell & Quelch*, 9, 10, 327.—Also in Venezuela and Brazil.

PÆPALANTHUS FRATERNUS, N. E. Brown, sp. n. Acaulis. Folia dense rosulata, linearia, subacuta, basi late dilatata, supra canaliculata, rigida, supra pilis articulatis appressis

tenuiter obtecta et pilis longis paucis laxe ciliata, subtus vel rare utrinque glabra.
in axillis dense lanato-villosa. Pedunculi 8–12 poll. longi, laxe villosi, rare glabri.
Capitula 4½–5 lin. diam., albo-villosa. Bracteæ involucrantes 3–4-seriatæ, late
ovatæ, acutæ, dorso appresse pubescentes, fuscæ. Bracteæ inter flores oblongæ,
subacutæ, apice dense albo-barbatæ. Receptaculum pilosum. Sepala elliptica,
obtusa, hyalino-olivacea, ciliata, apice dense albo-barbata. Petala floris masculini in
tubum infundibuliformem stipitatum connata ; floris fœminei libera, sessilia, anguste
linearia, dense ciliato-barbata.

A stemless perennial. Leaves densely rosulate, 1–1¾ in. long, 1–1½ lin. broad, linear,
tapering to a blunt point, rather abruptly dilated into a broad open sheath at the base,
rigid, concave and thinly covered with adpressed white jointed hairs on the face, convex
and glabrous on the back, rarely glabrous on both sides, veins not prominent, scarcely
striate, often, but not always, thinly ciliate with a few long hairs, densely villose-woolly with
long fine hairs in the axils. Peduncles 1–3 to a plant, 8–12 in. long, slender, obscurely 6–7-
angular, thinly covered with short spreading hairs or rarely glabrous ; their basal sheaths
1–1¾ in. long, with a rigid oblique subacute ciliate mouth, otherwise glabrous. Heads
4½–5 lin. diam., at first hemispherical, afterwards globose, monœcious or rarely unisexual.
Involucral bracts in 3–4 series, the innermost 1¾–2 lin. long, 1½ lin. broad, broadly ovate,
acute, fuscous, adpressed-pubescent on the back, ciliate, the outer gradually smaller.
Flowering-bracts 1½ lin. long, ½ lin. broad, oblong, obtuse or subacute, pale fuscous,
densely bearded with white hairs on the apical part. Receptacle pilose with long white
hairs, as are also the pedicels of the flowers. Male flowers pedicellate ; sepals 3, 1¼ lin.
long, ½ lin. broad, elliptic, obtuse or subacute, fuscous, densely bearded with white hairs
on the apical part ; petals arising ½ lin. above the sepals, all united into a hyaline
funnel-shaped tube ½ lin. long, truncate, with 3 very minute teeth at the apex, glabrous ;
stamens shortly exserted, with white anthers ; rudimentary pistil represented by 3
clavate bodies, minutely papillate at the apex. Female flowers shortly pedicellate ;
sepals 1½ lin. long, ¾–⅞ lin. broad, elliptic, subacute, beautifully reticulated with fuscous,
ciliate from the base and densely bearded on the upper half with long white hairs ;
petals 3, free, arising close to the sepals, 1 lin. long, about ¼ lin. broad, ciliate and
clothed on both sides with long white hairs ; ovary ovoid, trigonous, glabrous, narrowed
into a style about ⅓ lin. long, with 3 linear bifid stigmas, and 3 stout appendages,
papillate at the apex only.

Summit of Mount Roraima, 8600 ft., *McConnell & Quelch*, 96, 659.

Allied to *P. falcatus*, Koern., and *P. flarescens*, Koern. From the former it differs by
its more rigid, channelled leaves, less woolly heads, and more acute involucral bracts,
and from *P. flarescens*, Koern., by the narrower and more acute leaves, which have a
different pubescence, and the very different flower-heads. It also appears to be near
P. Schomburgkii, Klotzsch (which I have not seen), but that plant is described as
having longer and broader leaves, striate, with prominent veins on the upper side, a
subulate point to the peduncular sheath, much shorter peduncles, and glabrous involucral
bracts.

P.EPALANTHUS SUBCAULESCENS, N. E. Brown. sp. n.   Planta 4-8 poll. alta.   Caulis
simplex, dense foliosus.   Folia lineari-lanceolata, acuta, glabra, juniora pilis longis
laxe ciliata.   Pedunculi 2-7-aggregati, obtuse 4-angulati, glabri, vaginis oblique fissis
apice subulato-apiculatis glabris ore ciliatis.   Capitula hemisphærica, albo-villosa.
Bracteæ involucrantes suborbiculares vel late obovatæ, obtusissimæ, minutæ ciliatæ,
fuscæ.   Bracteæ inter flores oblongæ, obtusæ, apiculatæ, apice albo-barbatæ.
Receptaculum glabrum, sed pedicellis laxe pilosis.   Floris masculi sepala obovata,
obtusa, apice albo-barbata ; petala in tubum tridentatum longe stipitatum connata.
Floris fœminei sepala elliptica vel obovata, obtusa, apice albo-barbata; petala
libera, oblonga, obtusa, pilis longis dense ciliata, dorso glabra.

A perennial, with a simple densely leafy stem ½–2½ in. long.   Leaves ¾–1½ in. long,
1–2½ lin. broad, linear-lanceolate, acute, glabrous, striate, green, the younger laxly ciliate
with long white hairs, ascending, becoming deflexed with age.   Peduncles 2–7 to a plant,
2½–5½ in. long, slender, obtusely 4-angled, glabrous ; their basal sheaths 1–1¼ in. long,
glabrous, with an oblique ciliate mouth, acute or subulate-pointed.   Heads 2–3 lin. diam.,
hemispherical, monœcious, white-villous.   Involucral bracts in 3–4 series ; the innermost
¾ lin. long, ¾–1 lin. broad, suborbicular or broadly obovate, very obtuse, glabrous, minutely
ciliate, fuscous, the outer gradually smaller.   Flowering bracts ¾–1 lin. long, ¼ lin. broad,
oblong, obtuse, apiculate, fuscous, densely bearded with short white hairs on the apical
part.   Receptacle apparently glabrous, but with the base of the pedicels pilose with long
hairs.   Male flowers : sepals ¾ lin. long, ¼ lin. broad, obovate, obtuse, brown, bearded
with white hairs at the apex ; petals connate into a hyaline, subtruncate, minutely
3-toothed tube, separated from the sepals by a stipes nearly ½ lin. long, glabrous ; anthers
white.   Female flowers : sepals ¾–1 lin. long, nearly ¼ lin. broad, elliptic or obovate,
obtuse, fuscous or brownish, densely bearded with short white hairs on the apical part ;
petals 3, free, arising close to the sepals, ¾ lin. long, ¼ lin. broad, oblong, obtuse, light
fuscous, densely fringed with very long hairs on the margins and borders of the inner
face, glabrous on the back ; ovary glabrous, trigonous ; style elongated ; stigmas linear,
bifid to halfway down ; appendages rather thick, papillate at the apex.

Kotinga Valley, *McConnell & Quelch*, 153.   Savannahs generally, *McConnell & Quelch*,
300.

A very distinct species, bearing a resemblance to *P. uncinatus*, Gardn., in stem and
foliage, but with very different flower-heads.   It might be placed near *P. plantagineus*,
Koern.

P.EPALANTHUS BIFORMIS, N. E. Brown, sp. n.   Planta pusilla, acaulis, ut videtur annua.
Folia rosulata, 3-4 lin. longa, linearia, acuta, supra arachnoideo-tomentosa, demum
glabra.   Pedunculi 3-4, filiformes, 1¾–2¼ poll. longi, laxe villosi vel subglabri, vaginis
glabris ore obliquis acutis.   Capitula hemisphærica, 2–2½ lin. diam., pallide luteo-
alba.   Bracteæ involucrantes oblongæ vel ovato-oblongæ, acutæ, glabræ.   Bracteæ
inter flores nullæ.   Receptaculum et pedicelli lanati.   Flores masculi quam fœminei
multo minores, oblique deltoidei, acuti, sepalis inæqualibus ad medium barbatis,
petalis in tubum minutum stipitatum connatis.   Flores fœminei recti ; sepala

corum 3, libera, anguste lanceolata, acuminata, carinata, glabra, ad medium ciliata; petala 3, cuneato-obovata, prope apicem obtusum incurvum leviter connata, dorso pilis longis dense vestita.

A small stemless annual ? Leaves rosulate, very spreading, 3–4 lin. long, ¼–½ lin. broad, linear, acute, thinly cobwebby-tomentose above, becoming glabrous, glabrous beneath, woolly in the axils. Peduncles 3–4 to a plant, 1¾–2¼ in. long, filiform, thinly villose or nearly glabrous. Heads simple, monœcious, 2–2½ lin. diam., very pale straw-coloured in all parts. Involucral-bracts in 3–4 series, much shorter than the flowers, the innermost ¾ lin. long, ¼–⅓ lin. broad, oblong or ovate-oblong, acute, quite glabrous, thin, semi-transparent. Flowering-bracts none. Receptacle and pedicels very woolly. Male flowers much smaller than the female flowers, with rather longer pedicels, very oblique; sepals 3, two of them ½ lin. long, ¼ lin. broad, obliquely semiovate, straight along one margin, very much curved along the other, acute, the third smaller, rhomboid-lanceolate, acute, all bearded with short hairs at about the middle, transparent; petals connate into a very minute, stipitate, funnel-shaped cup, glabrous; anthers white. Female flowers straight, projecting much beyond the males; sepals 3, free, 1 lin. long, ¼ lin. broad, narrowly lanceolate, acuminate, boat-shaped, keeled, glabrous, ciliate at the middle only, trans-parent; petals arising a little above the sepals, scarcely ½ lin. long, about ⅓ lin. broad, cuneate-obovate, obtuse and inflexed at the apex, and apparently slightly connate there, densely clothed with long hairs on the back; ovary trigonous, glabrous, with a glabrous style, divided at the apex into 3 simple stigmas and 3 slender clavate appendages. Capsule scarcely ¼ lin. diam. Seeds ellipsoidal, faintly ribbed, glabrous, brown.

Kotinga Valley, near Mount Roraima, *McConnell & Quelch*, 126.

This species much resembles *Pœpalanthus simplex*, Miq., but is readily distinguished by the very unequal size and dissimilar form of the male and female flowers, the females conspicuously projecting much beyond the males, so that the heads have a somewhat echinate appearance.

PÆPALANTHUS UMBELLATUS, Kunth, Enum. Pl. iii. p. 537.
Kotinga Valley, *McConnell & Quelch*, 129.

PÆPALANTHUS SUBTILIS, Miq. Stirp Surin. Sel. p. 221.
Savannahs generally, *McConnell & Quelch*, 312.

PÆPALANTHUS CAPILLACEUS, Klotzsch, in R. Schomb. Reisen in Brit.-Guiana, i. p. 377, ii. p. 5, & iii. p. 1063; Koern. in Mart. Fl. Bras. iii. pt. I. p. 415, t. 53. f. 2.
Kukennam River, *McConnell & Quelch*, 314. Roraima, *Appun*, 1217.—Endemic to the region.

CYPERACEÆ.

CYPERUS UNCINATUS, Poir. Encycl. vii. p. 247.
Kotinga Valley near Roraima, *McConnell & Quelch*, 128. Savannahs generally, *McConnell & Quelch*, 321.

FUIRENA UMBELLATA, Rottb. Descr. et Ic. Pl. p. 70, t. 19. f. 3.
Ireng Valley, *McConnell & Quelch*. 254.

HYPOLYTRUM PUNGENS, Vahl. Enum. ii. p. 283.
Kotinga Valley, *McConnell & Quelch*. 179.

EVERARDIA ANGUSTA, N. E. Brown, sp. n. Folia linearia, acuta, laxe pilosa. Culmi basi vaginati, aphylli, valde compressi, leviter concavo-convexi, parce pilosi vel fere glabri. Panicula elongata, linearia, stricta, ramis gracilibus erectis 1- (rare 2-)spiculatis in axillis vaginorum aggregatis. Spiculæ masculæ lanceolatæ, glumis 5-7 coraceis oblongis acutis mucronatis brunneis sterilibus et glumis 4-6 membranaceis oblongis obtusis fertilibus instructæ; stamina sub quaque gluma 6-12. Spiculæ fœmineæ omnes ad apicem paniculi dispositæ, glumis 5 oblongo-lanceolatis acutis mucronatis ovarium solitarium stipitatum circumdatis: stigmata 3, dense villosa; pili hypogyni copiosi.

Leaves in tufts of 3-6, distinct from the flowering culms, 8-12 in. long, 1¼-1¾ lin. broad, linear, acute, often folded, but when expanded channelled down the face, with an acute ridge on each side of the channel, flat on the back, thinly pilose, usually slightly recurving. Flowering culms 14-18 in. high, including the panicle, ½-⅝ lin. broad, flattened, slightly concave on one side, convex on the other, sparingly pilose or nearly glabrous, produced on distinct leafless shoots, embraced by a long glabrous leafless sheath at the base. Panicle 7-12 in. long, strictly erect, linear, composed of 4-5 distant tufts of erect, simple or once umbellately divided, filiform branchlets, clustered in the axils of close-fitting brown sheaths ½-¾ in. long, which have spreading leafy points ½-1 in. long. Spikelets solitary or very rarely 2 at the end of the branchlets, light brown. Male spikelets 3-4 lin. long, 1-1¼ lin. thick, lanceolate, with 5-7 coriaceous, oblong, acute, mucronate, brown empty glumes, thinly and minutely pubescent on the back, and 4-6 membranous, oblong, obtuse, fertile glumes; stamens 6-12 under each glume; anthers 2 lin. long, linear, tipped with a minute tuft of stiff hairs. Female spikelets all at the apex of the panicle, more slender than the males, 3 lin. long, about ¾ lin. thick, with about 5 oblong-lanceolate, acute, mucronate, minutely ciliate glumes surrounding the solitary pubescent ovary; stigmas 3, densely villose; hypogynous hairs copious.

Summit of Mount Roraima, 8600 ft., *McConnell & Quelch*. 676.

This species is easily distinguished from the following by its very much narrower leaves and less floriferous panicles.

EVERARDIA MONTANA, Ridl. in Trans. Linn. Soc. Ser. II. Bot. ii. (1887), p. 287.
Summit of Mount Roraima. *McConnell & Quelch*, 674.—Endemic.

GRAMINEÆ.

PANICUM ELIGULATUM, N. E. Brown, sp. n. Folia erecta, linearia, attenuato-acuta, rigida, cinereo-glauca, supra ad basin longe villosa et ad basi vaginorum villoso-tomentosa; ligula nulla. Culmi 10-13 poll. longi, stricti, striati, glabri, ad nodos subglauci, bivaginati, vagina inferiore foliosa. Panicula 2-3 poll. longa, oblonga, multiflora. Spiculæ ellipsoideæ, 1-2-floræ. Glumæ 3 inferiores vacuæ, glabræ, brunneæ vel atro-fuscæ ; gluma infima parva ; secunda et tertia subæquales ellipticæ, obtusæ, profunde concavæ 6–7-nerves. Gluma florens elliptica, obtusa, profunde concava, lævis, 5-nervis, glabra, albida. Palea elliptica, obtusa, concava, 2-nervis, glabra, albida.

Leaves, excluding the sheaths, 6–9 in. long, 2½-3 lin. broad, linear, tapering to a very acute subpungent point, with involute margins, rigid, erect, greyish-glaucous, striate, more or less densely pilose on the upper side at the base, and densely villose-tomentose at the very base of the sheaths ; ligule none. Culms 10–13 in. long, straight, striate, glabrous, more or less glaucous at the nodes, bearing two sheaths, the lower of which bears a short leaf. Panicle 2–3 in. long, ¾ 1 in. diam., oblong-lanceolate, moderately compact, with semiverticillate, erect, glabrous branchlets and pedicels. Spikelets 1¼–1½ lin. long, ellipsoidal, 1–2-flowered. Empty glumes 3, glabrous, brown or blackish ; the lowest ¾-1 lin. long, ½ lin. broad, oblong or elliptic-oblong, obtuse, 2-nerved ; the 2 inner 1¼ lin. long, ½ lin. broad, elliptic, obtuse, deeply boat-shaped, 6–7-nerved. Flowering glume 1 lin. long, elliptic, obtuse, deeply concave, 5-nerved, glabrous, smooth, whitish. Pale similar to the flowering glume, but smaller and flatter, 2-nerved, whitish. Anthers ¾ lin. long, very dark purplish brown. Stigmas 2, densely plumose, brown or fuscous.

Summit of Mount Roraima, 8600 ft.. *McConnell & Quelch*, 675.

Allied to *Panicum loreum*, Trin., but the leaves and panicle are shorter than they are in that species, the spikelets rather larger, and the leaves quite destitute of a ligule, the absence of which is its most remarkable character, since there are few grasses in which all trace of a ligule is absolutely wanting.

PANICUM CHNOODES, Trin. Gram. Panic. p. 211.

Roraima Range, 3500 ft., *McConnell & Quelch*. 709. Also in Brazil.

ECHINOLÆNA HIRTA, Desv. Journ. Bot. i. (1813), p. 75.

E. scabra, H. B. & K. Nov. Gen. & Sp. i. p. 118, t. 38 ; Oliver, in Trans. Linn. Soc. Ser. II. Bot. ii. (1887), p. 288.

Upper slopes of Mount Roraima, *McConnell & Quelch*, 74.—Throughout Guiana and Brazil. The only other species of this genus is a native of Madagascar.

OLYRA MICRANTHA, H. B. & K. Nov. Gen. & Sp. i. p. 199.

Roraima Range, 3500 ft., *McConnell & Quelch*, 708. Widely dispersed in Brazil and Guiana.

ARUNDO RORAIMENSIS, N. E. Brown, sp. n. Planta ½-3 ped. alta, culmo ad apicem laxe folioso glabro. Folia linearia, complicata, apice oblique subacuta, subrigida, glabra vel minutissime scaberula, rare supra ligulam laxe pilosa, intra microscopice papillosa ; ligula ad annulum dense pilosum reducta. Panicula 4–6 poll. longa, ramis pedicellisque scaberulis vel villosis. Spiculæ 3–5-floræ, rhachilla breviter pilosa inter flores articulata. Glumæ 2 inferiores vacuæ, subæquales, lineares, acutæ vel minute trifidæ, 1-nerves, submembranaceæ, glabræ; glumæ florentes oblongæ, longe aristatæ, basi longe pilosæ, 5-nerves. Palea lineari-oblonga, bifida vel emarginata, 2-nervis, membranacea, marginibus inflexis.

Perennial, 1½–3 ft. (or more?) high. Stems laxly leafy to the top, glabrous. Lower leaves 9–20 in. long, the upper gradually shorter, 1½–3 lin. broad, erect, slightly rigid, linear, complicate, very obliquely subacute, glabrous or occasionally very minutely and thinly scaberulous on the back, microscopically papillate on the upperside, sometimes pilose and ciliate with long hairs just above the ligule, which is reduced to a dense ring of hairs. Panicle slightly nodding, 4–6 in. long, 1½–2½ in. broad, not very dense, its branches and pedicels scaberulous or villose. Spikelets 8–9 lin. long, 3–5-flowered, the rhachilla readily disarticulating between the flowers, which are hermaphrodite. Empty glumes 2, subequal, 3–3½ lin. long, linear, acute and mucronate or shortly bifid at the apex, 1-nerved, membranous, glabrous. Flowering glume (excluding the awn) 3 lin. long, oblong-lanceolate, very concave, villose on the basal part with white hairs 2 lin. long, 5-nerved, trifid at the apex, with the middle tooth (or nerve) running out into a straight scabrid awn about 4 lin. long. Pale 2½ lin. long, oblong-linear, with inflexed margins, bifid or emarginate at the apex, 2-nerved, scabrous on the nerves, otherwise glabrous. Lodicules ¼ lin. long, broad and oblique, subentire or crenately 2-lobulate, glabrous. Stamens 3. Ovary about 1 lin. long, slightly fusiform, or subterete, glabrous. Styles 2, plumose for ⅔ of their length, yellow or brown.

Summit of Mount Roraima, 8600 ft., *McConnell & Quelch*, 673.

Allied to *A. pilosa*, D'Urv.

ARUNDINARIA DEFLEXA, N. E. Brown, sp. n. Culmi superne ramosi, ramis erectis teretibus glabris foliosis. Folia deflexa, lanceolata, acuminata, glabra, marginibus scaberulis; ligula brevis, subtruncata; vagina ad apicem longe setosa. Panicula terminalis, erecta, angusta, laxa, glabra. Spiculæ angustæ, paucifloræ. Glumæ inferiores 3 vacuæ, gluma extima minimus, 2 sequentes florentibus subsimiles sed minores; glumæ florentes ovato-lanceolatæ, obtusæ, concavæ, 7-nerves, glabræ, minutissime ciliatæ. Palea angusta, brevissime bifida, bicarinata, carinis ciliatis.

Stems branching in the upper part. Branches very erect, close to and parallel with the main stem, terete, glabrous, leafy, nearly concealed by the leaf-sheaths. Leaves deflexed, 5–5½ in. long, 9–11 lin. broad, lanceolate, tapering to a very acute point, glabrous on both sides, scabrid on the margins, probably slightly glaucous beneath; primary veins not very distinct from the rest; sheaths closely embracing the stem, glabrous, striate, with a fringe of long bristles at the apex; ligule short, subtruncate, glabrous. Panicle 5–11 in. long, 1–2 in. broad, lax, with slender erect glabrous branches. Spikelets about 3-flowered, 5–6 lin. long, narrow, with the 3 lower glumes empty, the lowest of which is about 1 lin. long, the second and third 2–2½ lin. long, oblong, obtuse, concave, glabrous, not ciliate, obscurely 5–7-nerved. Flowering glume 3½–3¾ lin. long, ovate-lanceolate, obtuse, concave, glabrous, very minutely ciliate, 7-nerved. Pale 3 lin. long, linear-oblong, with inflexed sides, slightly bifid at the obtuse apex, with 2 keel-like ciliate nerves. Anthers 1½ lin. long, linear.

Summit of Mount Roraima, 8600 ft., *McConnell & Quelch*, 678.

The spikelets on the specimens seen are imperfect, most of them consisting of empty bracts only, and none that I have examined contain a perfect ovary.

CHUSQUEA LINEARIS, N. E. Brown, sp. n.   Culmi graciles, internodiis ¾–2¼ poll. longis, ramulis brevibus ad nodos aggregatis.   Folia 6–10 lin. longa, 1–1½ lin. lata, lanceolata, acutissima, glabra, secus unum marginem minute scaberula; vaginæ striatæ, pubescentes, ligula brevi subtruncati.   Racemi ad nodos aggregati, lineares, spiculis 3–6, unifloris.   Glumæ inferiores 4 vacuæ, gluma infima minima, sequentes majores pubescentes; gluma florens convoluta, obtusa, apicem tantum pubescens, 7–8-nervis.   Palea oblongo-ovata, obtusa, convoluta, glabra, apice ciliata, 4-nervis

Stems slender, terete, glabrous, with internodes ¾ 2¼ in. long, concealed by the striated sheaths, bearing at the nodes clusters of 4–10 simple leafy or flowering branches 1½–3 in. long.   Leaves distichous, those on the branches 1½–2 lin. distant, 6–10 lin. long, 1–1½ lin. broad, lanceolate, tapering to a very acute mucronate point, abruptly narrowed into a very short petiole at the base, glabrous, minutely ciliate-scabrid along one margin, striate beneath from the numerous closely placed prominent nerves; sheaths striate, pubescent; ligule short, subtruncate, no bristles.   Racemes linear, with 3–6 pedicellate, adpressed, 1-flowered spikelets, or the terminal one with 14–15 spikelets. Outer 4 glumes empty; the lowest ¼–¾ lin. long, broadly oblong, obtuse, 1-nerved; the second 1¼–1¾ lin. long, oblong, obtuse, with or without a short awn, 1-nerved; the two others subequal, 2½–2¾ lin. long, oblong-lanceolate, acute, very concave, 5–6-nerved, all more or less pubescent on the back and ciliate, at least at the apex.   Flowering glume 2¾ lin. long, ovate-lanceolate, obtuse, convolute, pubescent and ciliate at the apex only, with 7–8 slender nerves.   Pale 2 lin. long, oblong-ovate, convolute, obtuse and ciliate at the apex, membranous, with 4 slender nerves.   Lodicules 3, narrowly oblong, obtuse, ciliate at the apex. ⅔–¾ lin. long.   Stamens 3: anthers 1 lin. long, linear.   Ovary narrowly ovoid, glabrous; styles 2, narrowly plumose nearly to the base.

Summit of Mount Roraima, 8600 ft., *McConnell & Quelch*, 677.

Allied to *C. abietifolia*, Griseb., but among other characters is easily distinguished by its linear racemes.

———————

II. PTERIDOPHYTA.

By C. H. Wright. A.L.S.

1. Gleichenia pubescens, H. B. & K. Nov. Gen. & Sp. i. p. 29. *Mertensia pubescens.* Willd.; R. Schomb. Reisen in Brit.-Guiana, ii. p. 272; Appun. Unter den Tropen, ii. p. 594.
Roraima range, 3500 ft., *McConnell & Quelch*, 610, 619.
British Guiana: Kwating Creek; also Mexico and West Indies to Chili.

2. Cyathea vestita, Mart. in Denkschr. Regensb. ii. (1822), p. 146. *C. hirtula*, Mart.; R. Schomb. Reisen in Brit.-Guiana, ii. p. 272; Appun. Unter den Tropen, ii. p. 594.
Roraima range, 3500 ft., *McConnell & Quelch*, 605.
Humirida Mountains, Brazil.

3. Hemitelia subincisa, Kunze, in Bot. Zeit. ii. (1844), p. 296.
Roraima range, 3500 ft., *McConnell & Quelch*, 620.
British Guiana: Kwating Creek; also Central and Tropical South America.

Alsophila marginalis, Klotzsch. in Linnæa, xviii. (1844), p. 542; Appun. Unter den Tropen, ii. 594.
Roraima range, 3500 ft., *McConnell & Quelch*, 604.
Mexico.

5. Alsophila villosa. Presl. ex Hook. Sp. Fil. i. p. 43; Appun. Unter den Tropen, ii. p. 594; Baker, in Trans. Linn. Soc. Ser. II. Bot. ii. (1887). p. 289. *Cyathea villosa*, H. B. & K. Nov. Gen. & Sp. i. p. 24, and vii. t. 670.
Roraima range, 3500 ft., *McConnell & Quelch*, 621.
British Guiana: Arapu River; also throughout Tropical South America.

6. Alsophila microphylla, Klotzsch, in Linnæa, xviii. (1844), p. 541.
Roraima range, 3500 ft., *McConnell & Quelch*, 606.
Venezuela and New Granada.

7. Dicksonia conifolia, Hook. Sp. Fil. i. p. 70, t. 24. fig. A.
Summit of Roraima, 8600 ft., *McConnell & Quelch*, 564.
Jamaica, Venezuela, New Granada, and South Brazil.

8. Hymenophyllum crispum, H. B. & K. Nov. Gen. & Sp. i. p. 26.
Summit of Roraima, 8600 ft., *McConnell & Quelch*, 563.
Cuba, Jamaica, Mexico, Venezuela, New Granada, Ecuador, Peru, and Bolivia.

9. HYMENOPHYLLUM DEJECTUM, Baker, in Trans. Linn. Soc. Ser. II. Bot. ii. (1887), p. 289; Hook. Ic. Pl. t. 1610.

Roraima: upper slopes, *McConnell & Quelch*, 46; summit, *McConnell & Quelch*, 110, 113.

Endemic. Mr. im Thurn gathered it on the summit, as stated on p. 269 of Trans. Linn. Soc. Ser. II. Bot. ii. (1887).

10. HYMENOPHYLLUM POLYANTHOS, Sw. Syn. Fil. p. 149; R. Schomb. Reisen in Brit.-Guiana, iii. p. 1044. *H. elaratum*, Sw.; R. Schomb. Reisen in Brit.-Guiana, ii. p. 272, iii. p. 1044; Appun, Unter den Tropen, ii. p. 594. *H. Pœppigianum*, Presl; R. Schomb. Reisen in Brit.-Guiana, iii. p. 1044; Appun, Unter den Tropen, ii. p. 594.

Roraima range, 3500 ft., *McConnell & Quelch*, 611; upper slopes, *McConnell & Quelch*, 50 p.p., 73; summit, 8600 ft., *McConnell & Quelch*, 624.

British Guiana: Kwating Creek, Potaro River and Mazaruni River; also West Indies, Central America, the entire South American continent, Tropical and Subtropical Asia, New Zealand, Mascarene Islands, and Tropical Africa.

11. HYMENOPHYLLUM MICROCARPUM, Desv. in Mém. Soc. Linn. Paris, vi. (1827), p. 333.

Roraima: upper slopes, *McConnell & Quelch*, 44, 69.

Portorico, Guatemala, New Granada, Ecuador, Peru, Bolivia, and South Brazil.

12. HYMENOPHYLLUM SERICEUM, Sw. Syn. Fil. p. 146.

Summit of Roraima, 8600 ft., *McConnell & Quelch*, 628.

West Indies, Guatemala, French Guiana, New Granada, Ecuador, Peru, Bolivia, and South Brazil.

13. HYMENOPHYLLUM LINEARE, Sw. Fl. Ind. Occ. iii. p. 1749.

Roraima: upper slopes, *McConnell & Quelch*, 55 pro parte; summit, 8600 ft., *McConnell & Quelch*, 562.

Tropical America from the West Indies and Mexico southward to Peru and Brazil, Tropical and South Africa, and Mascarene Islands.

14. HYMENOPHYLLUM sp., *H. multifido*, Sw., affinis.

Mazaruni, between 250 and 3000 ft., *McConnell & Quelch*, 596, 598.

15. TRICHOMANES ELEGANS, Rudge, Pl. Guian. Rar. 1c. p. 24. *Hymenostachys elegans*, Presl; R. Schomb. Reisen in Brit.-Guiana. ii. p. 272; Appun, Unter den Tropen, ii. p. 594.

Roraima range, 3500 ft., *McConnell & Quelch*, 615; Mazaruni River, under 3000 ft., *McConnell & Quelch*, 594.

Central America, Trinidad, New Granada, Venezuela, and Northern Brazil.

In no. 594 the upper part of one of the fertile fronds is barren, and about six pairs of pinnæ have grown out in a similar manner to those of the barren fronds.

16. TRICHOMANES MACILENTUM, Van den Bosch, Hymenophyll. Nov. p. 12; Baker in Trans. Linn. Soc. Ser. II. Bot. ii. (1887). p. 289.

Mazaruni River. 250 ft., *McConnell & Quelch*, 578; between 250 and 3000 ft., *McConnell & Quelch*, 597.

British Guiana: upper slopes of Roraima; forests near the Kaieteur Savannah, Potaro River; Amutu, below the Kaieteur Fall, Potaro River: Macouria River; also in Trinidad and Brazil, especially the northern provinces.

This is regarded by Mr. Baker (Trans. Linn. Soc. *loc. cit.*) as a variety of *T. Bancroftii*, Hook. & Grev.

17. TRICHOMANES BANCROFTII, Hook. et Grev. Ic. Fil. t. 204; R. Schomb. Reisen in Brit.-Guiana, iii. p. 1043; Appun. Unter den Tropen, ii. p. 594.

Mazaruni River, between 250 and 3000 ft., *McConnell & Quelch*, 587.

British Guiana: Amutu and below the Kaieteur Fall on the Potaro River; also in the West Indies, Guatemala, French Guiana, Northern Brazil, and Peru.

18. TRICHOMANES BRACHYPUS, Kunze, in Linnæa, ix. (1834), p. 105; R. Schomb. Reisen in Brit.-Guiana, ii. p. 272, iii. p. 1043; Appun. Unter den Tropen, ii. p. 594.
T. Ankersii, Parker; R. Schomb. *loc. cit.*: Appun. *loc. cit.*

Roraima range. 3500 ft., *McConnell & Quelch*, 609.

British Guiana: in the forest just below the Kaieteur Fall, Potaro River; Amutu, Potaro River; Tumbana-Capra; also in St. Vincent, Trinidad, Guatemala, French Guiana, Venezuela, New Granada, and Brazil.

19. TRICHOMANES PYXIDIFERUM, Linn., var. EMARGINATUM, Hook. et Baker. Syn. Fil. p. 81.

Mazaruni, between 250 and 3000 ft., *McConnell & Quelch*, 599.

British Guiana: upper slopes of Roraima; also in the Andes of Quito. The type occurs throughout the tropics of both hemispheres.

20. TRICHOMANES RADICANS. Sw. Fl. Ind. Occ. iii. p. 1736.

Roraima range, 3500 ft., *McConnell & Quelch*, 612.

Extending from the Southern United States, through Central America and the West Indies, to Southern Brazil and Bolivia; also in Western Europe, Atlantic Islands, West Africa, Mascarene Islands, Northern India, China, Japan, and Polynesia.

21. TRICHOMANES RORAIMENSE, Jenm. in Gard. Chron. Ser. III. xx. (1896), p. 716.

Summit of Roraima, 8600 ft., *McConnell & Quelch*, 108, 561.

22. TRICHOMANES CRISPUM, Linn. Sp. Pl. ed. 2. p. 1560; Baker, in Trans. Linn. Soc. Ser. II. Bot. ii. (1887), p. 289.

Roraima: upper slopes, *McConnell & Quelch*, 63; Roraima range, 3500 ft., *McConnell & Quelch*, 616.

British Guiana: Essequibo River; Berbice (coast); Corentyne River; forests near
Kaieteur Savannah; Kaieteur Ravine; also West Indies, Central America, French
Guiana, Venezuela, New Granada, Ecuador, Peru, Bolivia, Paraguay, throughout Brazil,
and West Tropical Africa.

23. TRICHOMANES PINNATUM, Sw. Syn. Fil. p. 142.   *Neurophyllum pinnatum*, Presl;
   R. Schomb. Reisen in Brit.-Guiana, iii. p. 1044.
   Mazaruni, between 250 and 3000 ft., *McConnell & Quelch*, 585; Roraima range,
3500 ft., *McConnell & Quelch*, 614.
   British Guiana: Potaro River, below the Kaieteur Fall; Kanaku Mountains; Karawanu
Mountains; Corentyne River; Berbice; also in the West Indies, Guatemala, French
Guiana, Venezuela, New Granada, Peru, Northern Brazil, and Chili.

24. TRICHOMANES PRIEURII, Kunze, Analect. Pterid. p. 48; R. Schomb. Reisen in
   Brit.-Guiana, ii. p. 272. iii. p. 1043.   *T. rigidum*, Appun, Unter den Tropen. ii.
   p. 594.
   Roraima range, 3500 ft., *McConnell & Quelch*, 613.
   British Guiana: Kaieteur Ravine; Potaro River, below the Kaieteur Fall; also in
the West Indies, French Guiana, Venezuela, New Granada, Ecuador, and Brazil from
the Amazon region southward to Santa Catherina.

25. TRICHOMANES GEMMATUM, J. Sm. in Hook. Journ. Bot. iii. (1841), p. 417.   *T. cellu-
losum*, Klotzsch in Linnaea. xviii. (1844), p. 531; R. Schomb. Reisen in Brit.-
Guiana, ii. p. 272, iii. p. 1043.
   Roraima range, 3500 ft., *McConnell & Quelch*, 608.
   British Guiana: Kanaku Mountains; Amutu, Potaro River; Pacatout, below the
Kaieteur Fall, Potaro River; also in Venezuela, Northern Brazil, Polynesia, the Philip-
pines, Borneo and the Malay Peninsula.

26. LINDSAYA DUBIA, Spreng. Syst. Veg. iv. p. 79; R. Schomb. Reisen in Brit.-Guiana,
   iii. p. 1048.
   Mazaruni, between 250 and 3000 ft., *McConnell & Quelch*, 593.
   British Guiana: Roraima; Pacatout, below the Kaieteur Fall, Potaro River; Amutu,
Potaro River; also in French Guiana.

27. LINDSAYA TRAPEZIFORMIS, Dryand. in Trans. Linn. Soc. iii. (1797), p. 42, var.
   Roraima range, 3500 ft., *McConnell & Quelch*, 617.
   Intermediate between var. *laxa*, Baker, and var. *arcuata*, Baker (in Mart. Fl. Bras. i.
II. p. 355).   The type is widely diffused in Tropical America, Asia, and Australia.

28. LINDSAYA STRICTA, Dryand. in Trans. Linn. Soc. iii. (1797), p. 42; im Thurn and
   Oliver, in Trans. Linn. Soc. Ser. II. Bot. ii. (1887). pp. 269, 290.
   Roraima: upper slopes, *McConnell & Quelch*, 55, 62, 76; summit. 8600 ft., *McConnell
& Quelch*. 197, 557.

British Guiana: Kaieteur Savannah; Head of Iteribisci Lake; also in the West Indies, Central America, French Guiana, Venezuela, New Granada, Peru, Bolivia, and throughout Brazil.

29. PTERIS AQUILINA, Linn., var. CAUDATA, Hook. Sp. Fil. ii. p. 196; im Thurn, in Trans. Linn. Soc. Ser. II. Bot. ii. (1887), p. 266.
Summit of Roraima, 8600 ft., *McConnell & Quelch*, 553.
Humirida Mountains: Florida, West Indies, Central America, Venezuela, Brazil, China, Malay Peninsula, and East Africa. The type is cosmopolitan.

30. PTERIS PALMATA, Willd. Sp. Pl. v. p. 357.
Kanuku Mountains, 1000 ft., *McConnell & Quelch*, 273.
British Guiana: Rupununi and Watu Ticaba; also in the West Indies, Central America, Venezuela, New Granada, Ecuador, Peru, Bolivia, Brazil, and New Guinea.

31. PTERIS INCISA, Thunb. Fl. Cap. ed. Schdlt. p. 733; Baker, in Trans. Linn. Soc. Ser. II. Bot. ii. (1887), p. 290.
Roraima: upper slopes, *McConnell & Quelch*, 75.
Also at the bottom of the cliff, Roraima. West Indies, Central America, Venezuela, New Granada, Galapagos Islands, Ecuador, South Brazil, Juan Fernandez, Chiloe, Polynesia, Himalaya, Formosa, Ceylon, Tasmania, Mascarene Islands, South Africa, and West Tropical Africa.

32. LOMARIA PROCERA, Spreng. Syst. Veg. iv. p. 65; Baker, in Trans. Linn. Soc. Ser. II. Bot. ii. (1887), p. 290.
Summit of Roraima, 8600 ft., *McConnell & Quelch*, 124, 566.
Throughout Tropical America from the West Indies and Mexico to Chili; also in Polynesia, Malaya, New Zealand, Tasmania, Southern Australia, Mascarene Islands, and South Africa.

33. LOMARIA BORYANA, Willd. Sp. Pl. v. p. 292; Baker, in Trans. Linn. Soc. Ser. II. ii. (1887), p. 290. *Lomaria Schomburgkii*, Klotzsch, in R. Schomb. Reisen in Brit.-Guiana, ii. p. 272, iii. p. 1050, and in Linnaea, xx. (1846), p. 346; Appun, Unter den Tropen, ii. p. 594.
Summit of Roraima, 8600 ft., *McConnell & Quelch*, 124.
West Indies, Venezuela, New Granada, Ecuador, Bolivia, South Brazil, Chili, Patagonia, Tristan d'Acunha, Tropical and South Africa, and the Mascarene Islands.

34. ASPLENIUM SERRATUM, Linn. Sp. Pl. ed. 1, p. 1078.
Roraima range, 3500 ft., *McConnell & Quelch*, 601.
British Guiana: Berbice; Kuyuni Creek; Oreala; also in Florida, West Indies, Central America, French Guiana, Venezuela, New Granada, Ecuador, Galapagos Islands, Peru, Bolivia, Paraguay, Brazil, and the Society Islands.

35. ASPLENIUM LUNULATUM, Sw., var. ERECTUM, Baker, in Mart. Fl. Bras. i. ii. p. 135
Oliver, in Trans. Linn. Soc. Ser. II. Bot. ii. (1887), p. 290.   *A. harpeodes*, Kunze, in
Linnaea, xviii. (1844), p. 329 ; R. Schomb. Reisen in Brit.-Guiana, iii. p. 1051 ;
Appun, Unter den Tropen, ii. p. 595.
Upper slopes of Roraima, *McConnell & Quelch*, 45.

West Indies, Central America, Venezuela, New Granada, Ecuador, Peru, Bolivia,
Argentine, Paraguay, Brazil, New Caledonia, India, Mascarene Islands, Tropical Africa,
South Africa, and the Atlantic Islands.

36. ASPLENIUM SERRA, Langsd. et Fisch. Pl. Voy. Russes, i. p. 16, t. 19 ; R. Schomb.
Reisen in Brit.-Guiana, ii. p. 272, iii. p. 1051 ; Appun, Unter den Tropen, ii.
p. 595.
Summit of Roraima, 8600 ft., *McConnell & Quelch*, 623.

British Guiana : Kwating Creek ; also in Brazil, Venezuela, New Granada, Ecuador,
Peru, New Caledonia, Tropical and South Africa, and the Mascarene Islands.

37. ASPLENIUM AURITUM, Sw. Fl. Ind. Occ. iii. p. 1616 ; R. Schomb. Reisen in Brit.-
Guiana, ii. p. 272, iii. p. 1051.
Roraima range, 3500 ft., *McConnell & Quelch*, 607.

West Indies, Central America, Venezuela, New Granada, Ecuador, Galapagos Islands,
Peru, Bolivia, Brazil, South India, Madagascar, and East Tropical Africa.

38. ASPIDIUM MENISCIOIDES, Willd. Sp. Pl. v. p. 218.
Roraima range, 3500 ft., *McConnell & Quelch*, 618.

British Guiana : Mazaruni Bush ; Potaro River ; Kabalebo River ; Berbice ; Essequibo
River ; also in Trinidad, French Guiana, Brazil, and Peru

39. NEPHRODIUM CONTERMINUM, Desv. in Mém. Soc. Linn. Paris, ii. (1827), p. 255 ;
Baker, in Trans. Linn. Soc. Ser. 11. Bot. ii. (1887), p. 290.
Summit of Roraima, 8600 ft., *McConnell & Quelch*, 627.

British Guiana : upper slopes of Roraima ; also in Florida, West Indies, Central
America, and South America southward to Chili and the Argentine.
This form has the ultimate segments more obtuse than the type.

40. NEPHRODIUM DENTICULATUM, Hook. Sp. Fil. iv. p. 147 ; Baker, in Trans. Linn. Soc.
Ser. 11. Bot. ii. (1887). p. 290.
Summit of Roraima, 8600 ft., *McConnell & Quelch*, 622.

Roraima : on the upper slopes and near the base of the cliff ; also in the West Indies,
Central America, Venezuela, New Granada, and Brazil.

41. POLYPODIUM (§ GRAMMITIS) CONNELLII, Baker, n. sp. ; ad *P. gramineum*, Sw., accedit ;
differt frondibus glabris longioribus margine revolutis, soris haud contiguis regulariter
biseriatis.
A densely caespitose herb.   Rhizome scarcely creeping ; paleae lanceolate, brown,

membranous. Frond linear, simple, entire, 3–4 in. long. 1–1½ lin. wide, rigidly coriaceous, glabrous, gradually contracted into a very short, but distinct, stipe; veins immersed, concealed. Sori oblong, superficial, parallel with the midrib, often confluent.
Summit of Roraima, 8600 ft., *McConnell & Quelch*, 111, 118, 570.

42. POLYPODIUM MARGINELLUM, Sw. Fl. Ind. Occ. iii. p. 1631 ; Baker, in Trans. Linn.
Soc. Ser. II. Bot. ii. (1887), p. 291.   *Mecosorus marginellus*, var. *major*, Klotzsch ;
R. Schomb. Reisen in Brit.-Guiana, iii. p. 1054.
Roraima: upper slope, *McConnell & Quelch*, 51 ; summit, 8600 ft., *McConnell & Quelch*, 117, 119, 568.
West Indies, Venezuela, Peru, Brazil, Samoa, and St. Helena.
Swartz (Fl. Ind. Occ. iii. p. 1631) says this species has "venis bifidis"; subsequent authors describe the veins as simple, which is the case in all the specimens at Kew.

43. POLYPODIUM LEPTOPODON, C. H. Wright, n. sp.; ad *P. marginellum*, Sw. accedit :
differt fronde membranacea, marginibus ciliatis, venis unifurcatis, stipite elongato tenui piloso.
Rhizome shortly creeping, 2 lin. in diam., with brown lanceolate scales near the apex.
Frond oblanceolate, obtuse, up to 2 in. long by 3 lin. broad, glabrous except for a few cilia on the margin when young, edged with a black line ; veins once forked, conspicuous ; sori few, near the apex of the frond, often confluent ; stipe up to 2½ in. long, slender, pilose.
Summit of Roraima, 8600 ft., *McConnell & Quelch*, 569.

44. POLYPODIUM FURCATUM, Mett. in Abhandl. Senck. naturf. Ges. ii. (1858), p. 34 ;
Baker, in Trans. Linn. Soc. Ser. II. Bot. ii. (1887), p. 291.
Mazaruni, 250 ft., *McConnell & Quelch*, 576 ; between 250 and 3000 ft., *McConnell & Quelch*, 584.
British Guiana : upper slope of Roraima ; below and above the Kaieteur. Potaro River ; also in French Guiana, North Brazil, and the Island of Grenada.

45. POLYPODIUM SERRULATUM, Mett. Fil. Hort. Bot. Lips. p. 30 ; Baker, in Trans. Linn.
Soc. Ser. II. Bot. ii. (1887), p. 291.   *Xiphopteris serrulata*, Kaulf. ; R. Schomb.
Reisen in Brit.-Guiana, ii. p. 272, iii. p. 1056.
Mazaruni, between 250 and 3000 ft., *McConnell & Quelch*, 592.
British Guiana : upper slopes of Roraima ; also in the West Indies, Central America, Venezuela, New Granada, Ecuador, Peru, Bolivia, Brazil, Sandwich Islands, Mascarene Islands, and West Tropical Africa.

Var. STRICTISSIMUM, Hook. Sp. Fil. iv. p. 175.
Summit of Roraima, 8600 ft., *McConnell & Quelch*, 555.
Ecuador.

46. POLYPODIUM TOVARENSE, Klotzsch, in Linnæa, xx. (1846), p. 374; Baker, in Trans.
Linn. Soc. Ser. II. Bot. ii. (1887), p. 291.
Roraima: upper slopes, *McConnell & Quelch*, 67.
Venezuela. New Granada, and Ecuador.

47. POLYPODIUM MONILIFORME, Lag. in Sw. Syn. Fil. p. 33; Baker, in Trans. Linn. Soc.
Ser. II. Bot. ii. (1887), p. 291.
Roraima : upper slopes, *McConnell & Quelch*, 47, 66; summit, 8600 ft., *McConnell &
Quelch*, 558
West Indies, Central America, Andes of New Granada, Ecuador, and Bolivia.

48. POLYPODIUM HARTII, Jenm. in Journ. Bot. xxiv. (1886), p. 272.
Mazaruni, between 250 and 3000 ft., *McConnell & Quelch*, 591.
Jamaica, Dominica, and Island of Grenada.

49. POLYPODIUM TRICHOMANOIDES, Sw. Prodr. Veg. Ind. Occ. p. 131 ; R. Schomb. Reisen
in Brit.-Guiana, iii. p. 1052 ; Appun, Unter den Tropen, ii. p. 595 ; Baker, in
Trans. Linn. Soc. Ser. II. Bot. ii. (1887), p. 291.
Roraima : upper slopes, *McConnell & Quelch*, 49; Mazaruni, *McConnell & Quelch*, 575.
British Guiana : Kaieteur Ravine and Savannah; also in the West Indies, Central
America, French Guiana, Brazil (Prov. Bahia), Ecuador, Peru. Juan Fernandez.
Ascension Island, Northern India, and East Tropical Africa.

50. POLYPODIUM CULTRATUM, Willd. Sp. Pl. v. p. 187 ; R. Schomb. Reisen in Brit.-Guiana,
ii. p. 272, iii. p. 1052 ; Baker, in Trans. Linn. Soc. Ser. II. Bot. ii. (1887), p. 292.
Roraima : upper slopes, *McConnell & Quelch*, 54, 56, 71.
British Guiana : Kaieteur Savannah; also in the West Indies, Central America,
Venezuela, New Granada, Peru, Bolivia, Brazil, West Tropical Africa, and the Mascarene
Islands.

51. POLYPODIUM XANTHOTRICHIUM, Klotzsch, in Linnæa, xx. (1846), p. 376; Baker, in
Trans. Linn. Soc. Ser. II. Bot. ii. (1887), p. 292.
Roraima : upper slopes, *McConnell & Quelch*, 64, 68.
Endemic.

52. POLYPODIUM CAPILLARE, Desv. in Berl. Ges. naturf. Freunde, Mag. v. (1811), p. 316 ;
Baker in Trans. Linn. Soc. Ser. II. Bot. ii. (1887), p. 292.
Roraima : upper slopes, *McConnell & Quelch*, 53, 58.
British Guiana : in woods near the Kaieteur Savannah; also in the West Indies,
Venezuela, Ecuador, Peru, and Brazil.

53. POLYPODIUM KALBREYERI, Baker, in Trans. Linn. Soc. Ser. II. Bot. ii. (1887), p. 291.
Roraima : upper slopes, *McConnell & Quelch*, 65, 72.
New Granada.

54. POLYPODIUM RIGESCENS, Bory. in Willd. Sp. Pl. v. p. 183; Baker, in Trans. Linn. Soc. Ser. II. Bot. ii. (1887), p. 292.

Roraima: upper slopes, *McConnell & Quelch*, 18, 70; summit, 8600 ft., *McConnell & Quelch*, 559.

British Guiana: Kwating Creek; also in the West Indies, Venezuela, New Granada, Ecuador, Peru, Brazil, Solomon Islands, Mascarene Islands, and Tropical Africa.

55. POLYPODIUM ELASTICUM, Bory, in Willd. Sp. Pl. v. p. 183.

Makarapan Mt. on the north of Kwaimatta, 2000 ft., *McConnell & Quelch*, 278.

British Guiana: Kwating Creek; Berbice; also in Florida, the West Indies, Central America, New Granada, Ecuador, Peru, Bolivia, Paraguay, and Brazil.

56. POLYPODIUM MERIDENSE, Klotzsch. in Linnæa, xx. (1846), p. 380.

Summit of Roraima, 8600 ft., *McConnell & Quelch*, 498, 499, 560.

Venezuela, New Granada, South Brazil.

7. POLYPODIUM INCANUM, Sw. Syn. Fil. p. 35.

Kanaku Mts., 500 ft., *McConnell & Quelch*, 271.

British Guiana: Savannah Bush; Rupununi; Corentyne River; also in the Southern United States, West Indies, Central America, French Guiana, Venezuela, New Granada, Peru, Brazil, Paraguay, Uruguay, Chili, South Africa, and the Zambesi.

58. POLYPODIUM CRASSIFOLIUM, Linn. Sp. Pl. ed. 1, p. 1083; R. Schomb. Reisen in Brit.-Guiana, iii. p. 1053; Appun, Unter den Tropen, ii. p. 595.

Roraima range, 3500 ft., *McConnell & Quelch*, 603.

West Indies, Central America, French Guiana, Surinam, Venezuela, New Granada, Ecuador, Galapagos Islands, Peru, Bolivia, Brazil.

59. GYMNOGRAMME CYCLOPHYLLA, Baker, in Trans. Linn. Soc. Ser. II. Bot. ii. (1887), p. 293, t. 53.

Summit of Roraima, 8600 ft., *McConnell & Quelch*, 116, 120, 567.

Endemic.

60. GYMNOGRAMME ELAPHOGLOSSOIDES, Baker, in Trans. Linn. Soc. Ser. II. Bot. ii. (1887), p. 293, t. 54.

Summit of Roraima, 8600 ft., *McConnell & Quelch*, 112, 551.

Endemic.

61. GYMNOGRAMME PUMILA, A. Spreng. Tent. Suppl. ad Syst. Veg. p. 31; R. Schomb. Reisen in Brit.-Guiana, iii. p. 1054.

Mazaruni, 250 ft., *McConnell & Quelch*, 191.

British Guiana: Rupununi River; also in the West Indies, Central America, New Granada, and Brazil.

62. GYMNOGRAMME FLEXUOSA, Desv. in Mém. Soc. Linn. Paris, ii. (1827), p. 215'; Baker, in Trans. Linn. Soc. Ser. II. Bot. ii. (1887), p. 293.

Roraima: upper slopes, *McConnell & Quelch*, 59; summit, 8600 ft., *McConnell & Quelch*, 629.

Central America, Venezuela, New Granada, Ecuador, Peru, Bolivia, and Brazil.

63. ACROSTICHUM SIMPLEX, Sw., var. MARTINICENSE, Hook. et Baker, Syn. Fil. ed. 1, p. 400.

Mazaruni, between 250 and 3000 ft., *McConnell & Quelch*, 581.

British Guiana: Essequibo River and on the coast; also in the West Indies, New Granada, Ecuador, Peru, and Brazil.

64. ACROSTICHUM CONFORME, Sw. Syn. Fil. pp. 10, 192, t. 1. fig. 1.

Mazaruni, 250 ft., *McConnell & Quelch*, 577.

British Guiana: Essequibo River and on the coast; also in the West Indies, Central America, Venezuela, New Granada, Ecuador, Peru, Chili, Brazil, Polynesia, Queensland, India, Mascarene Islands, Tropical and South Africa.

The form of this polymorphic species represented in this collection has been named *Acrostichum alatum*, Fée (Mém. Fam. Fougèr. ii. p. 35, t. 5. fig. 2).

65. ACROSTICHUM LATIFOLIUM, Sw. Fl. Ind. Occ. iii. p. 1589; Baker, in Trans. Linn. Soc. Ser. II. Bot. ii. (1887), p. 294.

Summit of Roraima, 8600 ft., *McConnell & Quelch*, 571.

British Guiana: upper slopes of Roraima; Asabaru Creek; Sheenabowa and Kaieteur Ravine, Potaro River; Demerara River and on the coast; also throughout the West Indies and Tropical America, and widely diffused in Polynesia, Java, Mascarene Islands, Tropical and South Africa.

66. ACROSTICHUM SQUAMOSUM, Sw. in Schrad. Journ. Bot. iv. (1800), p. 11; Baker, in Trans. Linn. Soc. Ser. II. Bot. ii. (1887), p. 295.

Roraima: upper slopes, *McConnell & Quelch*, 57.

British Guiana: Kaieteur Savannah and Essequibo River; also in the West Indies, Central America, Venezuela, Ecuador, Brazil, Sandwich Islands, Ceylon, South India, Mascarene Islands, Tropical Africa, and the Atlantic Islands.

67. ACROSTICHUM DECORATUM, Kunze, in Linnæa, ix. (1834), p. 25; Baker, in Trans. Linn. Soc. Ser. II. Bot. ii. (1887), p. 294.

Roraima range, 3500 ft., *McConnell & Quelch*, 602.

West Indies, Peru, and South Brazil.

68. ACROSTICHUM PELTATUM, Sw. Fl. Ind. Occ. iii. p. 1593; Appun, Unter den Tropen, ii. p. 595; Baker, in Trans. Linn. Soc. Ser. II. Bot. ii. (1887), p. 295.

Roraima: upper slopes, *McConnell & Quelch*, 61; Mazaruni, between 250 and 3000 ft., *McConnell & Quelch*, 582.

West Indies, Central America, Venezuela, New Granada, Ecuador, and Brazil.

69. ACROSTICHUM OLIGARCHICUM, Baker, in Hook. et Baker, Syn. Fil. ed. 1, p. 418.
Roraima range, 3500 ft., *McConnell & Quelch*, 600.
North Peru.

70. SCHIZÆA FLUMINENSIS, Miers, in Mart. Fl. Bras. i. pars ii. p. 184, t. 15. fig. 2.
Mazaruni, between 250 and 3000 ft., *McConnell & Quelch*, 580.
British Guiana : Kukenaam, and woods at the side of the Kaieteur Savannah ; also in
Venezuela and Brazil.

71. SCHIZÆA ELEGANS. Sw. Syn. Fil. p. 151 ; Baker, in Trans. Linn. Soc. Ser. II. Bot.
ii. (1887), p. 295.
Mazaruni, between 250 and 3000 ft., *McConnell & Quelch*, 589.
British Guiana: Essequibo River ; Epiro Creek, Corentyne River ; Demerara River,
and on the coast ; also in the West Indies, Central America, Surinam, Venezuela, New
Granada, and Brazil.

72. SCHIZÆA PENNULA, Sw. Syn. Fil. pp. 150, 379. *Actinostachys pennula*, Hook. ;
R. Schomb. Reisen in Brit.-Guiana, iii. p. 1045.
Mazaruni, between 250 and 3000 ft., *McConnell & Quelch*, 588.
British Guiana : Roraima ; Kukuya Creek ; Kaieteur Savannah ; Serra Mey and
Demerara River; also in the West Indies, Surinam, Brazil, and New Caledonia.

73. ANEMIA TOMENTOSA, Sw. Syn. Fil. p. 157 ; Baker, in Trans. Linn. Soc. Ser. II.
Bot. ii. (1887), p. 295.
Kanuku Mountains, 1000 ft., *McConnell & Quelch*, 272, 274.

Var. FULVA, Hook. et Baker, Syn. Fil. ed. 1, p. 433.
Ireng Valley, *McConnell & Quelch*, 201.
British Guiana : Roraima and Rupununi ; also in the West Indies, Central America,
Venezuela, New Granada, Peru, Paraguay, Brazil, and Uruguay.

74. LYCOPODIUM ALOPECUROIDES, Linn. Sp. Pl. ed. 2, p. 1565; Baker, in Trans. Linn.
Soc. Ser. II. Bot. ii. (1887), p. 295 ; Jenman, in Timehri, v. (1886), p. 44.
Roraima : upper slopes, *McConnell & Quelch*, 60.
Southern United States, Venezuela, New Granada, Peru, Brazil, Bolivia, and Uruguay.

75. LYCOPODIUM CERNUUM, Linn. Sp. Pl. ed. 2, p. 1566 : Jenman, in Timehri, v. (1886)
p. 45.
Ireng Valley, *McConnell & Quelch*, 206.
British Guiana : Corentyne, Pomeroon and Macouria Rivers and at Berbice; also
throughout the tropics and extending a short distance on either side.

76. LYCOPODIUM CONTIGUUM, Klotzsch, in Linnæa, xviii. (1844), p. 519.
Summit of Roraima, 8600 ft., *McConnell & Quelch*, 572.
Higher parts of the Andes in Venezuela, New Granada, Ecuador, and Bolivia.

77. LYCOPODIUM CLAVATUM, Linn. Sp. Pl. ed. 2, p. 1564; Jenman, in Timehri, v. (1886), p. 44.

Roraima range, 3500 ft., *McConnell & Quelch*. 707.

Arctic and alpine zones of both hemispheres, also on the mountains throughout the tropics.

78. LYCOPODIUM CAROLINIANUM, Linn. Sp. Pl. ed. 2, p. 1567; Jenman, in Timehri, v. (1886), p. 43.

Roraima : upper slopes, *McConnell & Quelch*. 52.

British Guiana: Kaieteur Savannah ; Corentyne River; Kako Creek ; Demerara ; also in Florida, Guadeloupe, Brazil, Paraguay, Hongkong, Ceylon, Mascarene Islands, and South Africa.

79. SELAGINELLA VERNICOSA, Baker, in Trans. Linn. Soc. Ser. II. Bot. ii. (1887), p. 295, t. 56. f. A.

Summit of Roraima, 8600 ft., *McConnell & Quelch*, 574, ex parte.

Also found by im Thurn at the base of the cliff.

Var. OLIGOCLADA, Baker, *l. c.* fig. B.

Summit of Roraima, 8600 ft., *McConnell & Quelch*, 574, ex parte.

80. SELAGINELLA FLABELLATA, Spring, Monogr. Lycopod. p. 174.

Essequibo River, *McConnell & Quelch*, 115.

British Guiana : foot of the Kaieteur. Tropics and subtropics of America, Asia, and Polynesia.

81. SELAGINELLA ANCEPS, A. Br. in Ann. Sc. Nat. Sér. V. iii. (1865), p. 278.

Roraima range, 3500 ft., *McConnell & Quelch*, 706.

British Guiana : Potaro River; also in Guatemala, Venezuela, New Granada, Ecuador, and Peru.

III. BRYOPHYTA.

MUSCI by V. F. BROTHERUS, Ph.D.

DICRANACEÆ.

DICRANUM LONGISETUM, Hook. Musc. Exot. t. 139.

Mount Roraima, *McConnell & Quelch*, 343.

Found in the mountains of Venezuela, New Granada, and Quito.

Var. LAXIFOLIUM, Broth. n. var. Folia laxius disposita, apice argutius serrulata.

Mount Roraima, Ledge, 7500–8000 ft., *McConnell & Quelch*, 344.

DICRANODONTIUM PULCHRO-ALARE, Broth., n. sp. *Dioicum*, cæspitosum, cæspitibus densiusculis lutescentibus nitidis; *caulis* 8 cm., sterilis usque ad 12 cm. altus, arcuato-flexuosus, fusco-tomentosus, densiuscule foliosus, sæpe innovationibus elongatis gracilibus. *Folia* falcata, canaliculato-concava, e basi lanceolata longe subulata, usque ad 1 cm. longa, superne dense et argute serrulata, nervo basi folii latitudinis tertiam partem vel paulum ultra occupante et superne dorso serrulato ibidemque folium totum occupante; cellulæ superiores angustæ; basilares ad nervum laxæ, rectangulares, hyalinæ; exteriores angustissimæ, limbum multi-seriatum efformantes; alares in ventrem magnum fugacem dispositæ, laxæ, teneræ, fuscæ. *Bracteæ perichætii* internæ e basi vaginante subito in subulam integram attenuatæ, cellulis omnibus elongatis angustis teneris. *Seta* 2·5 cm. alta, tenuis, serpentino-flexuosula, lutea, apice cygnea, rubra. *Theca* sicca erecta, plicata, humida ob setam apice cygneam horizontalis, lævis, oblonga, c. 2·5 mm. alta, leptodermis, fuscidula. *Peristomium* simplex; *exostomii* dentes 16, aurantiaci, c. 0·37 mm. longi et c. 0·075 mm. lati, usque ad basin in cruribus duobus filiformi-bus inæqualibus articulatis dense papillosis divisi; *spori* 0·017 mm., fusci, papillosi. *Cetera* ignota.

Mount Roraima, Ledge, 7500–8000 ft., *McConnell & Quelch*, 345, 346.
Endemic.

CAMPYLOPUS CHIONOPHILUS, Mitt. in Journ. Linn. Soc., Bot. xii. (1869), p. 81. *Dicranum chionophilum*, C. Muell. Syn. i. 398.
Mount Roraima, Ledge, 7500–8000 ft., *McConnell & Quelch*, 342.
Found in the mountains of New Granada.

CAMPYLOPUS RORAIMÆ, Broth., n. sp. *Dioicus*, cæspitosus, cæspitibus densis nigrescentibus superne lutescentibus etiamque nitidiusculis; *caulis* ad 3 cm. usque altus, tomentosus, dense et per totam longitudinem æqualiter foliosus, ramosus. *Folia* homomallula, erecto-patentia, canaliculato-concava, e basi oblongo-lanceolata, breviter subulata, c. 5 mm. longa et c. 0·75 mm. lata, marginibus summo apice serratis, nervo basi dimidiam partem folii latitudinis occupante, lamina usque ad apicem folii distincta; cellulæ basilares subrectangulares, inter se porosæ, marginem versus angustiores, dein rhomboideæ; superiores rhombeæ, incrassatæ; alares numerosæ, subquadratæ, rubræ, basin totam occupantes. *Cetera* ignota.

Mount Roraima, Ledge, 7500–8000 ft., *McConnell & Quelch*, 347.
Endemic.
Species *C. concolori*, Brid. affinis, sed foliis multo brevioribus primo visu digno-scenda.

CAMPYLOPUS ATRATUS, Broth., n. sp. *Dioicus*, robustus, ater, apice lutescens, niti-diusculus. *Caulis* 10 cm. altus, erectus, haud tomentosus, dense et per totam longitudinem æqualiter foliosus, parce ramosus; *folia* sicca suberecta, humida recurvulo-patentia, canaliculato-concava, superne tubulosa, e basi lanceolata longe et anguste subulata, pilo stricto tenui hyalino longiusculo serrato terminata,

c. 10 mm. longa et c. 1·1 mm. lata, marginibus integris superne conniventibus, nervo basi tertiam partem folii latitudinis occupante, lamina usque ad apicem folii distincta; cellulæ elongatæ, angustæ, marginem versus incrassatæ, lumine angustissimo, limbum inferne latiusculum hyalinum superne tenuiorem, ultra medium evanidum efformantes, alares numerosæ, subquadratæ, rubræ, in ventrem distinctum dispositæ. *Cætera* ignota.

Summit of Mount Roraima, 8600 ft., *McConnell & Quelch*, 527.
Endemic.

Species cum *Campylopode griseo*, Hornsch., comparanda, sed statura multo robustiore, foliis strictipilis, integris, tubulosis, limbatis facillime dignoscenda.

LEUCOBRYACEÆ.

LEUCOBRYUM MEGALOPHYLLUM, Mitt. in Journ. Linn. Soc., Bot. xii. (1869), p. 112. *Dicranum megalophyllum*, Raddi, Critt. Bras. p. 3. *Leucobryum giganteum*, C. Muell. Syn. i. p. 79, ii. p. 536. *Leucobryum robustum*, Sull. in Proc. Amer. Acad. (1861), p. 279.

Mount Roraima, Ledge, 7500–8000 ft., *McConnell & Quelch*, 351 (forma).
Found in Cuba, Jamaica, Trinidad, Barbados, New Granada, Venezuela, and Brazil.

LEUCOBRYUM CRISPUM, C. Muell. Syn. i. p. 78.
Roraima range at 3500 ft., *McConnell & Quelch*, 546.
Found in the West-Indian Islands, Venezuela, New Granada, and Brazil.

LEUCOBRYUM LÆVIFOLIUM, Broth. *Dioicum*, robustiusculum, cæspitosum, cæspitibus mollibus dilabentibus lutescenti-albidis ætate fuscescentibus nitidis; *caulis* usque ad 6 cm. altus, erectus, dense foliosus, plerumque fasciculatim ramosus, ramis fastigiatis. *Folia* sicca et humida suberecta, stricta vel rarius homomallula, canaliculato-concava, e basi oblongo-lanceolata sensim acuminata, acuta, 5–6 mm. longa et c. 0·66 mm. lata, dorso sicca et humida lævissima, marginibus superne involutaceis integerrimis, limbata, limbo hyalino, inferne e seriebus cellularum 7–8 formato, superne angustiore, apice obsoleto, lamina e stratis cellularum æqualium duobus composita. *Cætera* ignota.

Summit of Mount Roraima, 8600 ft., *McConnell & Quelch*, 505, 536.

Species *L. Martiano*, Hampe, affinis, sed statura robustiore, nitore foliisque strictis, raro indistincte homomallulis oculo nudo jam dignoscenda.

OCTOBLEPHARUM MITTENII, Jaeg. Adumbr. i. p. 169. *Octoblepharum longifolium*, Mitt. in Journ. Linn. Soc., Bot. xii. (1869), p. 110.
Summit of Mount Roraima, 8600 ft., *McConnell & Quelch*, 517.
Found in Brazil.

TORTULACEÆ.

LEPTODONTIUM CIRRHIFOLIUM, Mitt. in Journ. Linn. Soc., Bot. xii. (1869), p. 52.
Summit of Mount Roraima, 8600 ft., *McConnell & Quelch*, 511.
Found in the mountains of Quito.

GRIMMIACEÆ.

MACROMITRIUM MUCRONIFOLIUM, Schwaegr. Suppl. ii. II. t. p. 167. t. 172.
Roraima range. 3500 ft., *McConnell & Quelch*, 544.
Found in Florida, in the West-Indian Islands, Guiana, Surinam, and Brazil.

ZYGODON SUBDENTICULATUS, Hampe, Ann. Sc. Nat. Sér. V. iv. (1863-67), p. 326.
Summit of Mount Roraima. *McConnell & Quelch*, 540.
Found in New Granada.

FUNARIACEÆ.

FUNARIA CALVESCENS, Schwaegr. Suppl. i. II. p. 77, t. 65.
Mount Roraima, Ledge, 7500-8000 ft., *McConnell & Quelch*, 338.
Found in South Europe and in the tropical and subtropical regions of Asia, Africa, America, and Australia.

BARTRAMIACEÆ.

BREUTELIA SCOPARIA, Besch. in Ann. Sc. Nat. Sér. VI. iii. (1876), p. 209. *Bartramia scoparia*, Schwaegr. Suppl. iii. l. t. 211.
Summit of Mount Roraima, 8600 ft., *McConnell & Quelch*, 514.
Found in the West-Indian Islands.

MNIACEÆ.

RHIZOGONIUM LINDIGII, Mitt. in Journ. Linn. Soc., Bot. xii. (1869), p. 328. *Mnium Lindigii*, Hampe, in Ann. Sc. Nat. Sér. V. iv. (1863–67), p. 345.
Summit of Mount Roraima, 8600 ft., *McConnell & Quelch*, 502, 537.
Found in Costa Rica and in the mountains of New Granada.

MNIUM ROSTRATUM, Schrad. in Linn. Syst. Nat. 13 ed. Gmel. ii. pars ii. p. 1330.
Roraima, Ledge, 7500-8000 ft., *McConnell & Quelch*, 339.
Found in all parts of the world.

NECKERACEÆ.

RHACOCARPUS HUMBOLDTII, Lindb. in Öfvers. Svensk. Vet.-Ak. Förh. (1862). *Harrisonia Humboldtii*, Spreng. Syst. Veg. iv. i. p. 115.
Mount Roraima, Ledge, 7500-8000 ft., *McConnell & Quelch*, 336, and summit of Mount Roraima, 519, 534 (var. *fusco-viridis*).
Found in the mountains of New Granada.

PILOTRICHUM BIPINNATUM, Brid. Bryol. Univ. ii. p. 283.
Roraima range, 3500 ft., *McConnell & Quelch*, 548.
Found in the West-Indian Islands, in Guiana, Brazil, and in the mountains of Quito and Peru.

N 2

HOOKERIACEÆ.

HOOKERIA (§ HYLOTAPIS) PILOTRICHELLOIDES, Broth.. n. sp. *Robustiuscula*, mollis, fusco-aurea, nitida; *caulis* usque ad 15 cm. longus, flexuosus, complanatulus, dense foliosus, per totam longitudinem pinnatim ramosus, ramis vix ultra 1 cm. longis patentibus strictis vel arcuatulis complanatulis dense foliosis obtusis. *Folia* sicca imbricata, humida suberecta, cymbiformi-concava, oblonga vel ovato-oblonga, in apiculum acutum, recurvulum subito contracta, marginibus inferne revolutis, integerrimis vel apice minutissime crenulatis, nervis binis elongatis vix divergentibus longe infra apicem evanidis dorso lævibus; cellulæ angustissimæ lineares, seriatim papillosæ; basilares læves; infimæ laxæ, breves, fusco-aureæ. *Cætera* ignota.

Mount Roraima, Ledge, 7500–8000 ft.. *McConnell & Quelch*, 337.
Endemic.

Species pulcherrima, mollitie necnon caule longissimo *Pilotrichellis* nonnullis similis, cum nulla alia commutanda.

HOOKERIA (§ OMALIADELPHUS) RORAIMÆ, Broth., n. sp. *Dioica*, robusta, lutescenti-viridis, ætate fusco-aurea, nitida; *caulis* usque ad 20 cm. longus, complanatulus, dense foliosus, dense pinnatim ramosus, ramis patulis, 1–1·5 cm. longis, strictis, complanatulis, dense foliosis, obtusis: *folia* sicca laxe imbricata, valde undulata, humida erecto-patentia, concaviuscula; *lateralia* oblongo-lanceolata, breviter acuminata, acutiuscula, marginibus inferne revolutis dein erectis minute serrulatis, nervis binis tenuibus parce divergentibus infra apicem evanidis dorso superne denticulatis; cellulæ elongatæ, angustissime lineares; basilares infimæ laxæ, fusco-aureæ, omnes lævissimæ; *bracteæ periclætii* internæ e basi ovata sensim subulatæ, minute denticulatæ, enerves; *seta* 1·5 cm. vel paulum ultra alta, sat tenuis, rubra, lævissima; *theca* horizontalis, e collo brevi ovalis, sicca deoperculata sub ore haud constricta, fusca; *peristomium* duplex; *exostomii* dentes e basi lanceolata longissime subulati, c. 0·95 mm. longi et c. 0·14 mm. lati, latiuscule exarati, dense et alte lamellati, aurantiaci; *endostomium* sordide luteum, minute papillosum; *processus* carinati, vix perforati; *operculum* longe et anguste subulatum; *calyptra* ad medium thecæ producta, basi multifida, apice fusca, glabra.

Roraima range, 3500 ft.. *McConnell & Quelch*, 490, 550.
Endemic.

Species pulcherrima, statura robusta ab omnibus speciebus sectionis oculo nudo jam dignoscenda.

STEREODONTACEÆ.

ECTROPOTHECIUM AMABILE, Mitt. in Journ. Linn. Soc., Bot. xii. (1869), p. 514.

Mount Roraima, Ledge, 7800–8000 ft., *McConnell & Quelch*, 341, and summit of Mount Roraima, 8600 ft., 516, 542.

Found in the mountains of New Granada.

CTENIDIUM MALACODES, Mitt. in Journ. Linn. Soc. Bot. xii. (1869), p. 509.
Mount Roraima, Ledge, 7500–8000 ft., *McConnell & Quelch*, 340.
Found in the mountains of New Granada and Quito.

LESKEACEÆ.

THUIDIUM ANTILLARUM, Besch. in Ann. Sc. Nat. Sér. VI. iii. (1876), p. 244.
Roraima range, 3500 ft., *McConnell & Quelch*, 549.
Found in Costa Rica and the West-Indian Islands.

THUIDIUM PSEUDO-PROTENSUM, Mitt. in Journ. Linn. Soc., Bot. xii. (1869), p. 578.
Hypnum pseudo-protensum, C. Muell. in Bot. Zeit. vi. (1848), col. 779.
Mount Roraima, Ledge, 7500–8000 ft., *McConnell & Quelch*, 348.
Found in Venezuela.

SPHAGNACEÆ.

SPHAGNUM SANGUINALE, Warnst. in Bot. Centralbl. lxxvi. (1898), p. 385.
Mount Roraima, Ledge, 7500–8000 ft., *McConnell & Quelch*, 350, 541 in part.
Endemic.

SPHAGNUM MEDIUM, Limpr. in Bot. Centralbl. vii. (1881), p. 313.
Mount Roraima, Ledge, 7500–8500 ft., *McConnell & Quelch*, 349, 541 in part.
Found in Europe and in America from Labrador to Patagonia.

HEPATICÆ. By F. STEPHANI.

The collection of Liverworts made by Messrs. McConnell and Quelch is a small one, but is of particular interest from a geographical point of view. Many plants were found which hitherto had been only observed in the Andes of South America; their unexpected appearance on the top of Mount Roraima is quite startling: the curious *Frullania mirabilis*, Jack et Steph., is of particular interest, as well as the very rare and beautiful *Pleurozia paradoxa*, Jack, both of which up to this time had not been elsewhere collected.

It is possible that some of these plants may have intermediate stations of which we are at present ignorant; but a similar surprising collection was made by Mr. Ule (of the Botanic Garden of Rio Janeiro) in the Serra do Mar and the Serra Itaiaia, where Andine forms were collected, though stations forming connecting-links are altogether missing.

There are also several new species, amongst which *Metzgeria inflata* is one of the most curious in the genus, being quite hairless and almost without any rootlets, lying like a small inflated cylindric pouch amongst other mosses.

As cryptogamic plants, and in particular Liverworts, with few exceptions, have very small spores and live in sheltered and moist places from where the wind cannot easily carry away the spores, they are a better indication than phaenogamic plants as to the Flora we must regard as the remnant of another, which, like that of South America, once covered a wide area, and is now separated by intermediate barren plains or treeless Llanos and Pampas of enormous extension where no Liverworts can live.

That the spores are not able to propagate a Liverwort beyond, perhaps, a small area, no better example can show than the very interesting flora of Killarney, where—doubtless for many centuries—a few species of Hepaticæ of tropical origin have been preserved without being able to reach the Continent.

The present condition of the literature of Liverworts seldom allows one to make geographical speculations ; but when my "Species Hepaticarum " is finished, and the number and relation of known liverworts, as also their distribution, settled, we may be able to draw conclusions which, I think, will be of value to all who study the geographical distribution of plants.

The following Liverworts have been collected, viz. :—

A. ANACROGYNÆ.

1. DUMORTIERA HIRSUTA, Nees, Hep. Eur. iv. p. 163. *Marchantia hirsuta*, Sw. Prodr. Fl. Ind. Occ. p. 115.
Roraima, Ledge, 7500–8000 ft., *McConnell & Quelch, 334/6.*
Common in Tropical and Subtropical America, England, Italy, Africa.

2. ANEURA SCHWANECKEI, Steph. in Hedwigia xxvii. (1888), p. 278.
Summit of Roraima, *McConnell & Quelch,* 512.
Found also in the West-Indian Islands.

3. ANEURA ALGOIDES, Steph. in Bull. Herb. Boiss. vii. (1899), p. 682. *Metzgeria algoides,* Taylor, in Hook. Lond. Journ. Bot. v. (1846), p. 410.
Summit of Roraima, *McConnell & Quelch,* 529.
An Andine plant, collected by Jameson near Quito.

4. ANEURA RORAIMENSIS, Steph., n. sp. *Dioica*, minor, pallide olivacea, aliis hepaticis consociata. *Frons* ad 5 mm. longa, exalata, irregulariter bipinnata, sæpe subfasciculata. *Truncus* primarius angustus, biconvexus, ramis trunco latioribus minus convexis. *Cuticula* ubique lamellata, lamellis denticulatis margine bene prominulis. *Cellulæ* frondis internæ corticalibus multo majores, fronde in adspectu itaque optime reticulata. *Rami feminei* in trunco solitarii, breves, margine latissime alati, alis profunde inciso-lobatis, lobis lanceolatis vel ligulatis obtusis, squama basali similiter lobata ramulum ♀ a tergo tegente. *Reliqua* desunt.

A very good and most distinct species, easily to be recognized by the rough cuticula of the cortical cells.

In the monograph of the genus *Aneura* (' Species Hepticarum,' p. 736) it is to be placed after No. 81, *Aneura scabra*, Steph.

Summit of Roraima, *McConnell & Quelch,* 350.   Mixed with *Micropterygium pterygophyllum*, Spruce.

5. ANEURA BREUTELII, Steph. in Bull. Herb. Boiss. vii. (1899), p. 759.
Summit of Roraima, *McConnell & Quelch*, 533.
Collected before by Breutel in the West-Indian Island of St.Kitts.

6. ANEURA FUCOIDES, Steph. in Bull. Herb. Boiss. vii. (1899), p. 680. *Jungermannia fucoides*, Sw. Prodr. fl. Ind. occ. p. 45.
Roraima, Ledge, 7500–8000 ft., *McConnell & Quelch*, 334-6 in part.
Common in Tropical America.

7. METZGERIA INFLATA, Steph., n. sp. *Dioica*, spectabilis, brevis, flaccida, pallide lurida, optime nitida, muscis consociata. *Frons* furcata, ad 3 cm. longa, omnino nuda, basi tantum paucis radicellis affixa. *Costa* tenuis, cellulis corticalibus utroque latere biseriatis tecta et in sectione transversa late ovalis ; cellulæ antice et postice magnæ, æquales, internæ multo minores triseriatæ. *Alæ* apice cucullatæ, ubique maxime irregulariterque revolutæ, in sectione transversa valde asymmetricæ, uno latere quadruplo latiores, re vera itaque sinuatim lobatæ, lobis bulloso inflatis ob flexuram tamen haud discretis. *Cellulæ* alarum 36–54 μ, parietibus validis, trigonis parvis. *Rami feminei* parvi, fere conduplicati, margine breviter setosi.
Summit of Roraima, *McConnell & Quelch*, 524.
This plant is well adapted to retain the water which it takes up from the mosses on which it is growing in rather exposed places on the very summit of the mountain ; it may be compared to the Tasmanian species *M. saccata*, Mitt., which prefers to grow on the uppermost twigs of trees, where it has a similar exposed situation and shows a similar adaptation to retain the water within the inflated lobes of the thallus.

8. METZGERIA HAMATA, Lindb. Monogr. Metzg. p. 25.
Roraima, Ledge, 7500–8000 ft., *McConnell & Quelch*, 334/4 and 5.
Common in all parts of the globe.

9. MONOCLEA GOTTSCHEI, Lindb. in Rev. Bryol. xiii. (1886), p. 102, in adnot.
Roraima, at 3500 ft., *McConnell & Quelch*, 551.
West-Indian Islands and the northern part of South America, Chile, Peru.
This plant has been distributed by Gottsche and others under the name of *Monoclea Forsteri*, a very different plant and altogether antarctic (New Zealand and Patagonia).

10. PALLAVICINIUS WALLISII, J. B. Jack & Steph. in Hedwigia, xxxi. (1892), p. 23.
Summit of Roraima, *McConnell & Quelch*, 501.
Collected before by Wallis in the mountains of New Granada near Antioquia, 8000 ft.

B. ACROGYNÆ.

11. JAMESONIELLA COLORATA, Spruce, in Journ. Bot. xvi. (1876), p. 30. *Jungermannia colorata*, Lehm. in Linnæa, iv. (1829), p. 366.

Summit of Roraima, *McConnell & Quelch*, 539 in part.

America, Australia, South Africa. Very common.

12. SYZYGIELLA QUELCHII, Steph., n. sp. *Sterilis* magna, fusco-purpurascens, tenera et flaccida, aliis hepaticis sparsim consociata. *Caulis* ad 8 cm. longus simplex (semper?). *Folia* opposita, conferta, assurgentia, si alam decurrentem anticam excipis oblique falcato-ovata, apice duplo angustiora quam basi, oblique truncata vel lenissime emarginata, omnino integerrima, angulis solum dentiformibus; *margine postico* valde arcuato, basi folii opposti brevissime coalito ibidemque *hamatim auriculato, margine antico* substricto breviter recurvo, longe decurrente, folia tamen antice haud attenuata sed oblique truncata et abrupte desinentia, folio opposito minime coalita. *Cellulæ* foliorum nodulose incrassatæ, nodulis maximis nusquam confluentibus, multo majores quam in *S. manca*, Steph.

Roraima, Ledge, 7500–8000 ft., *McConnell & Quelch*, 334/11 in part.

A most beautiful and very curious plant ; the two opposite leaves are quite erect and touch each other, the stem being perfectly hidden when seen from above. At the postical base these two leaves are united for a very short space ; just above this point they are rounded off and much projecting, and have a large incurved acuminate lobule.

13. SYZYGIELLA PERFOLIATA, Spruce, in Trans. Edinb. Bot. Soc. xv. (1885), p. 500, in adnot. *Jungermannia perfoliata*, Sw. Prodr. Veg. Ind. Occ. p. 143.

Summit of Roraima, *McConnell & Quelch*, 524 in part.

Found in Venezuela and the West Indies.

14. PLAGIOCHILA AËREA, Taylor, in Hook. Lond. Journ. Bot. v. (1846), p. 263.

Roraima, Ledge, 7500–8000 ft., *McConnell & Quelch*, 334.

Found before in Venezuela and Mexico.

15. PLAGIOCHILA GAYANA, Steph., n. sp. *Dioico*, spectabilis, pallide glauco-virens, ætate flavo-virens, effuse cæspitans. *Caulis* ad 10 cm. longus, longe remoteque pauci-ramosus, ramis late divergentibus, apice sæpe fasciculacis ubique æqualiter foliatis. *Folia* magna, tenera, remotiuscula, basi tantum imbricata, subrecte patula, breviter inserta, *i. e.* basi antica et postica fere opposita, breviter decurrentia, ceterum ovato-oblonga, apice fere triplo angustiora quam basi, margine antico substricta recurva subintegerrima, margine postico arcuata versus basin ampliata, rotundata ibidemque cum folio opposito ad cristam erectam conniventia, longe spinosa, spinis sub 30 magnis approximatis angustis longe acuminatis recte patulis 7 cellulas longis basi 2–4 cellulas latis. Folii *cellulæ* $34 \times 50 \mu$, trigonis majusculis ; basales $34 \times 80 \mu$, parietibus æqualiter incrassatis. *Perianthia* in caule terminalia, geminatim innovata, foliis parum longiora, plus duplo angustiora quam longa, antice late alata,

apice recte truncata ut in ala longe spinosa, spinis ut in folio sed magis confertis. *Folia floralia* caulinis simillima. *Andraeia* in caule terminalia, longe spicata, spicis ad 2 vel 3 subfasciculatis erectis; bracteæ ad 16 jugæ, e basi longe saccata parum recurvo-patulæ, apice truncatæ et paucidenticulatæ.

Roraima, Ledge, 7500–8000 ft., *McConnell & Quelch*, 334/3 in part.

In *Plagiochila superba*, Wahlenb., the leaf-cells are much larger, the spines very stout, very much longer and less numerous. Lindenberg says (Monogr. Plag. p. 80) that Sieber had given him this species as coming from Australia; but this is a mistake of Sieber, who had not marked his packets and did not know on his return whence he had procured the plants; many errors of the same kind have been previously pointed out by me.

16. PLAGIOCHILA REMOTIFOLIA, Hampe & Gottsche in Linnæa. xxv. (1852), p. 340.
Roraima, Ledge, 7500–8000 ft., *McConnell & Quelch*, 334·3.
Pretty common in the West Indian Islands.

17. PLAGIOCHILA RUTILANS, Lindenb. Spec. Hep. ii. & iii. (Monogr. Hep. Gen. Plag.) p. 47.
Roraima, Ledge, 7500–8000 ft., *McConnell & Quelch*, 334/2 in part.
Common in Tropical America.

18. LEIOSCYPHUS FRAGILIS, J. B. Jack & Steph. in Hedwigia, xxxi. (1892), p. 20.
Summit of Roraima, *McConnell & Quelch*, 524 in part.
Also in New Granada.

19. LOPHOCOLEA BREUTELII, Gottsche, in Syn. Hep. p. 154.
Roraima, Ledge, 7500–8000 ft., *McConnell & Quelch*, 334/14 in part.
Common in the West Indian Islands.

20. MASTIGOBRYUM RORAIMENSE, Steph., n. sp. *Dioica*, mediocris, apice dilute flavo-virens, inferne brunneola, erecta, laxe intricata. *Caulis* ad 4 cm. longus, repetito furcatus, postice flagellis numerosis capillaceis instructus. *Folia* conferta, valde decurva, in plano subrecte patula, oblonga, parum falcata, antice parum ampliata, caulemque haud superantia, apice triplo angustiora quam basi, acute bidentula sinu lunato parum profundo vel truncata, angulis acutis. *Cellulæ* foliorum magnæ, apice 27 μ, trigonis maximis contiguis vel late confluentibus, medio infero multo majores, 37–56 μ, incrassatio parietum grosse trabeculata. *Amphigastria* caulina caule triplo fere latiora, imbricata, transverse inserta, late obcuneata, tertio supero inciso biloba, lobis similiter sed brevius bilobis; cellulæ amphigastriæ caulinis simillimæ, parum minores. *Folia floralia* quadrijuga, intima caulinis æquilonga, profundissime bifida, laciniis late lanceolatis, marginibus externis crenatis vel crenato-dentatis, internis subintegerrimis. *Amphigastrium florale* foliis suis æquale. *Perianthium* (juvenile) ore longe fimbriatum, ciliis triangulariter articulatis hic illic ramosis. Reliqua desunt.

Summit of Roraima, *McConnell & Quelch*, 523.

21. MASTIGOBRYUM DISSODONTUM, Steph. n. nomen; *Bazzania bidens* var. *dissodonta*,
    Spruce, in Trans. Edinb. Bot. Soc. xv. (1885), p. 371.
    Summit of Roraima, *McConnell & Quelch*. 532.
    Found in Colombia.

22. MASTIGOBRYUM PORTORICENSE, Hampe & Gottsche in Linnæa, xxv. (1852), p. 318.
    Roraima at 3500 ft., *McConnell & Quelch*, 545.
    Common in the West Indian Islands and northern South America.

23. MASTIGOBRYUM VINCENTINUM, Lehm. & Lindenb. Syn. Hep. p. 226.
    Roraima, Ledge, 7500–8000 ft., *McConnell & Quelch*, 334/10, 15, & 16.
    Common in the West Indian Islands.

24. MASTIGOBRYUM KRUGIANUM, Steph. in Hedwigia, xxvii. (1888), p. 300.
    Roraima, Ledge, 7000–8000 ft., *McConnell & Quelch*, 334/14 in part.
    Found before in the island of Santo Domingo.

25. MASTIGOBRYUM GRACILE, Hampe & Gottsche, in Linnæa, xxv. (1852), p. 346.
    Roraima, Ledge, 7500–8000 ft., *McConnell & Quelch*, 334/11 in part.
    Known from different places in the West Indian Islands.

26. MICROPTERYGIUM GRANDISTIPULUM, Steph., n. sp. *Sterilis*, minor, dilute brunnea
    vel flavo-rufescens, muscicola, valde intricatim cæspitans. *Caulis* tenuis, ad 2 cm.
    longus, irregulariter ramosus. *Folia* conferta, decurvula, semiamplexicaulia, ex
    angusta basi ovato-oblonga, longe acuminata, apice abrupte attenuata ibidemque
    paucidenticulata vel integerrima. *Folii* lobulus posticus integerrimus, brevi spatio
    (ad ¼) carinatim coalitus, folium subinde oblique percurrens, attenuatus, longe sub
    folii apice desinens. *Cellulæ* foliorum leves, 8×12 μ, basales 8×17 μ, sub-
    rectangulatæ, maxime æqualiterque incrassatæ. *Amphigastria* magna, imbricata,
    foliis parum breviora, transverse inserta, plana, integerrima, medio infero fere
    circularia, superne abrupte angustata, lanceolata, acuta.
    Roraima, Ledge, 7500–8000 ft., *McConnell & Quelch*, 334/14 in part.
    There is not a species of this genus which does not have some of its leaves merely
    conduplicate, the wing being entirely wanting; where the latter is developed it is part
    of the antical lobe, which can easily be observed if a transverse cut of the leaf is made;
    the same occurs sometimes in *Scapania*, and is best developed in *Schistochila*.

27. MICROPTERYGIUM PTERYGOPHYLLUM, Spruce, in Trans. Edinb. Bot. Soc. xv. (1885),
    p. 384. *Jungermannia pterygophylla*, Nees, in Mart. Fl. Bras. vol. i. pars prior,
    Algæ, Lichenes, Hepaticæ, p. 377.
    Summit of Roraima, *McConnell & Quelch*, 530 in part.
    Common in Tropical America.

28. LEPIDOZIA COMMUTATA, Steph. in Hedwigia, xxvii. (1888), p. 293.
    Summit of Roraima, *McConnell & Quelch*, 521.
    Very common in the West Indian Islands.

29. LEPIDOZIA LAXEPINNATA, Spruce, in Trans. Edinb. Bot. Soc. xv. (1885), p. 360.
Roraima at 3500 ft.. *McConnell & Quelch*, 552.
An Andine species not found anywhere else before.

30. SCHISMA JUNIPERINUM, Nees, Hep. Eur. iii. p. 575. *Jungermannia juniperina*, Sw.
Veg. Ind. Occ. iii. p. 1855.
Summit of Roraima, *McConnell & Quelch*, 522, 528, 538, 539; in the last associated
to *Jamesoniella colorata*, Spruce.
Very common in Tropical America.

31. SCHISMA PENSILIS, Steph., n. nomen. *Scutlaera pensilis*, Taylor, in Hook. Lond.
Journ. Bot. v. (1846), p. 372.
Roraima, Ledge, 7500-8000 ft.. *McConnell & Quelch*, 334·2 in part.
A pretty rare Andine species.

32. SCHISMA DURANDII, Steph., n. sp. *Sterilis* longissima, gracilis, lurida, longe
lateque stratificata et dense caespitosa. *Caulis* ad 20 cm. longus, fragilis, simplex
superne saepe fasciculatim ramosus, apice breviter circinatus, postice flagellifer,
flagellis brevibus approximatis parvifoliis. *Folia* pro planta parva, triplo longiora
quam lata, ad $\frac{2}{3}$ bifida, laciniis lanceolatis apice longe setaceis valde hamatis
valdeque divergentibus. *Cuticula grosse verrucosa*. *Cellulæ* foliorum subapicales
$17 \times 25 \mu$, parietibus longioribus et marginalibus trabeculatim incrassatis. Cellulæ
basales $25 \times 70 \mu$, oblongo-hexagonæ, trigonis magnis saepe trabeculatim confluentibus. *Flagellorum* folia multoties minora, ovato-oblonga, laxe accumbentia,
porrecta, ad $\frac{2}{3}$ bifida, laciniis late lanceolatis vix setaceis.
Roraima, Ledge, 7500-8000 ft.. *McConnell & Quelch*, 334·2, 334·11 & 334·14, all
in part.
This plant has been found before by Pittier in the higher mountains of Costa Rica.

33. SCHISMA SUBDENTATUM, Steph., n. sp. *Sterilis*, mediocris, fusco-purpurascens,
optime nitens, densissime depresso-caespitosa. *Caulis* ad 6 cm. longus, simplex vel
furcatus, furcis divergentibus. *Folia* confertissima, maxime decurvo-hamata,
angusta, plus 3-plo longiora quam lata, ad $\frac{2}{3}$ bifida, laciniis parum divergentibus,
longe acuminatis, acutis. *Cellulæ* foliorum subapicales $17 \times 25 \mu$, parietibus
longioribus valde incrassatis; incrassatio marginalis, praecipue *ad angulos cellularum,
grosse nodulose- vel subdentatim prominula*. *Cellulæ* basales folii longe hexagonæ,
$25 \times 68 \mu$, parietibus longioribus maxime trabeculatim incrassatis.
Roraima, Ledge, 7500-8000 ft.. *McConnell & Quelch*, 334·1.

34. TRICHOCOLEA SPHAGNOIDES, Steph., n. nomen. *Leiomitra sphagnoides*, Spruce, in
Trans. Edinb. Bot. Soc. xv. (1885), p. 350.
Roraima, Ledge, 7500-8000 ft.. *McConnell & Quelch*, 334·9 in part, 11 in part,
and 13.
Andes of Quito.

35. Scapania portoricensis, Hampe & Gottsche, in Linnæa, xxv. (1852), p. 342.
Summit of Roraima, *McConnell & Quelch*, 573.
Not rare in the West Indian Islands, and found by Spruce also on the top of Mount Abitagua, 2000 m. (his *Scapania splendida*).

36. Pleurozia paradoxa, Steph., n. nomen.—*Physiolium paradoxum*, J. B. Jack, in Hedwigia, xxvii. (1886), p. 85.
Summit of Roraima, *McConnell & Quelch*, 543.
Known before from Pasto, collected by F. C. Lehmann.

37. Harpalejeunea tenax, Steph., n. sp.   *Sterilis*, minor, fusco-olivacea, rigida, dense cæspitosa. *Caulis* ad 15 mm. longus, capillaceus, parum ramosus. *Folia* remotiuscula, caule vix latiora, parum patula, cauli fere parallela, valde concava, in plano cordiformia, tertio supero abrupte angustata acuminata acuta vix incurva, *lobulo* duplo angustiore, valde inflato, in acumen folii attenuato. *Cellulæ* foliorum parvæ, ad 12 μ, trigonis late confluentibus. *Amphigastria* parva, transverse inserta, caulem vix superantia subrotunda, appressa, integerrima.
Roraima, Ledge, 7500–8000 ft., *McConnell & Quelch*, 334.
A much reduced form, rigid and evidently well adapted to a dry climate, the leaves being very small, little projecting from the stem, the cell-walls very thick. This plant is almost unique in the great number of species of *Lejeunea*, which always live in damp and well sheltered places, and disappear where a dry atmosphere can reach them.

38. Frullania mirabilis, J. B. Jack & Steph. in Hedwigia, xxxi. (1892), p. 15.
Summit of Mount Roraima, *McConnell & Quelch*, 510.
Collected before by Wallis in New Granada, near Antioquia.

39. Frullania atrata, Nees, in Syn. Hep. p. 463.   *Jungermannia atrata*, Sw. Prodr. Fl. Ind. Occ. p. 144.
Summit of Roraima, *McConnell & Quelch*, 535.
Very common in Tropical America.

40. Frullania longicollis, Lindenb. & Gottsche, in Syn. Hep. p. 783.
Summit of Roraima, *McConnell & Quelch*, 335.
An Andine species, found also in Mexico.

IV. THALLOPHYTA.

FUNGI. By G. MASSEE, F.L.S.

PHOMA PSAMMISIÆ, Massee, n. sp. Maculæ nullæ; perithecia epidermide tecta, gregaria, 500 μ diam., atra, ostiolo papillato pertusa; sporæ ellipticæ, 2-guttulatæ, 10-11 × 3 μ.

Spots absent; perithecia gregarious, covered by the grey raised epidermis, lenticular, averaging 500 μ in diameter, black, glabrous; ostiolum minute, papillate; texture parenchymatous, dense, olive; spores hyaline, elliptical, ends obtuse with two minute polar guttulæ, 10-11 × 3 μ.

On dead branch of *Psammisia coriacea*, N. E. Brown. Summit of Roraima, *McConnell & Quelch*.

Allied to *P. stictica*, Berk. et Broome.

ECHINOBOTRYUM ROSEUM, Massee, n. sp. Mycelium tenuissimum vix manifestum, album; hyphæ fertiles erectæ, septatæ, hyalinæ, 4 μ crassæ. Conidia in apicibus hypharum fertilium densius aggregata, sessilia, fusoidea, 15-17 × 6 μ, roseo-tincta.

Sterile hyphæ prostrate, hyaline, septate, branched, about 4 μ thick, loosely interwoven into a very thin white layer; fertile hyphæ erect, septate, simple, hyaline, 4 μ thick, apex minutely nodulose and producing numbers of sessile spindle-shaped, pale rose-coloured conidia measuring 15-17 × 6 μ.

Parasitic on *Oelomeria parvifolia*, Rolfe. Summit of Roraima, *McConnell & Quelch*, 696.

Allied to *E. hercc*, Sacc., from which the present differs in the form and colour of the spores.

STEMPHYLIUM ERICOCTONUM, A. Br. & de Bary, Krankh. d. Pflanz. (1854), p. 18, tab. 2.

On living branches of *Leitgebia lathraeiana*, Oliver. Summit of Roraima, *McConnell & Quelch*.

Europe.

MACROSPORIUM RAMULOSUM, Sacc. Fung. Ital. tab. 854 (1881).

On fading leaves of *Tofieldia Schomburgkiana*, Oliver. Summit of Roraima. *McConnell & Quelch*.

Europe, and in the Andes of Colombia.

CAPNODIUM FIBROSUM, Berk. in Hook. Fl. Nov. Zel. ii. (1855), p. 209.

Forming a black bristly pile on living twigs of *Psammisia*. Summit of Roraima, *McConnell & Quelch*, 662.

N. Zealand.

RHIPIDONEMA MEMBRANACEUM, Sacc. Syll. vi. (1888), p. 688.

On bark. Roraima, 8000 ft., *McConnell & Quelch*, 508, 526.

Amazon Valley; Marianne Islands.

LICHENES.   By G. MASSEE, F.L.S.

SPHÆROPHORON COMPRESSUM, Ach. Meth. Lich. (1803), p. 135.
   On stones.   Summit of Roraima, *McConnell & Quelch*, 506.
   Cape Horn; Chili; W. Indies; Europe; India; Ceylon.

CLADONIA RANGIFERINA, Hoffm. Flor. Germ. (1795), p. 114.
   On the ground.   Summit of Roraima, *McConnell & Quelch*, 507 & 520.
   Cosmopolitan.

PARMELIA DICTYORHIZA, Massee, n. sp.   Thallus membranaceo-cartilagineus, substellatus,
   repetito dichotomo-laciniatus, cretaceus, subtus niger, spongiosus.   Apothecia
   ignota.
   Thallus thin, cartilaginous, radiating from a centre in an irregularly stellate manner,
repeatedly dichotomously divided, chalk-white above, black and spongy below, the
spongy stratum composed entirely of closely septate brown hyphæ 11–12 μ thick,
arranged in the form of an irregular network.   Apothecia unknown.   Laciniæ about
2 mm. wide.
   On the ground.   Summit of Roraima, *McConnell & Quelch*, 53.
   Allied to *P. hypotropa*, Nyl., but separated from this and every other described species
in the reticulate structure of the spongy lower surface of the thallus.

PARMELIA PERFORATA, Ach. Lich. Univers. (1810), p. 110.
   On branches.   Summit of Roraima, *McConnell & Quelch*, 503 & 513.
   Central and N. America; Central Africa; Polynesia.

ALECTORIA OCHROLEUCA, Nyl. Prod. Lich. (1857), p. 46.
   On branches.   Summit of Roraima, *McConnell & Quelch*, 504.
   Mexico; United States; Europe; Himalaya; Japan; Australia.

EXPLANATION OF THE PLATES.

PLATE 1.

Ilex apicidens. (Figs. 1 to 6.)

Figs. 1 & 2. Branches with lax and dense inflorescences, natural size.
Fig. 3. Flower, × 4.
   4. Flower with petals and stamens removed, × 4.
   5. Stamen, dorsal view, × 4.
   6. Stamen, front view, × 4.

Cyrilla brevifolia. (Figs. 7 to 16.)

Figs. 7 & 8. Two branches, natural size.
Fig. 9. Fragment of a raceme with one flower, × 5.
  10. Sepal, seen from within, × 7.
  11. Petal, seen from within, × 7.
  12. Stamens, front and side views, × 7.
  13. Flower, with the outer parts removed to show the ovary, × 7.
  14. A trifid stigma, × 7.
  15. Ovary, longitudinal section, × 12.
  16. Ovaries, transverse sections, × 12. The ridges on the ovaries may be due to shrinkage, but they are represented as seen after long boiling.

PLATE 2.

Macairea aspera.

Fig. 1. Branch, natural size.
   2. Fragment of leaf, upper surface, × 4.
   3. Flower, with the petals and six stamens removed, × 5.
   4. Petal, × 5.
   5. Transverse section through the calyx-tube and ovary, × 5.
Figs. 6 & 7. Long and short stamens from another specimen (no. 24, *McConnell & Quelch*), × 5.

PLATE 3.

Passiflora Quelchii.

Fig. 1. Branch, natural size.
   2. Inflorescence, natural size.
   3. Longitudinal section of a flower, × 2.
   4. Filament of the lower corona, × 5.

PLATE 4.

Henriquezia Jenmani.

Fig. 1. Leaf and inflorescence, natural size.
    2. Flower, with the corolla removed, natural size.
    3. Corolla, laid open, natural size.
    4. Ovary after the sepals have fallen, × 3.
    5. Ovary, longitudinal section, × 3.
    6. Ovary, transverse section, × 3.

PLATE 5.

Didymochlamys Connellii.   (Figs. 1 to 9.)

Fig. 1. Part of a plant seen from above, natural size.
    2. Part of a plant seen from beneath, natural size.
    3. Inflorescence, with one bract removed, × 2.
    4. Flower with 2 sepals and the corolla removed, × 5.
    5. Corolla, laid open, × 2.
    6. A lobe of the corolla, × 4.
    7. Ovary, with glands and calyx-lobes, longitudinal section, × 5.
    8. Ovary, longitudinal section, showing placentas, × 5.
    9. Ovary, transverse section, × 5.

Chalepophyllum Connellii.   (Figs. 10 to 17.)

Figs. 10 & 11. Two branchlets showing the range of variation in different specimens, natural size,
    but the stems are not stout enough.
Fig. 12. Calyx and ovary, natural size.
    13. Part of a corolla laid open, natural size.
    14. Stamens, dorsal and front views, × 2.
    15. Ovary, longitudinal section, × 4.
    16. Ovary, transverse section, × 4.
    17. Ovule, × 12.

PLATE 6.

Retiniphyllum laxiflorum.

Fig. 1. Branch, natural size.
    2. Flower, × 2.
    3. Apex of a pedicel, × 5.
    4. Longitudinal section through the lower part of a flower, × 5.
    5. Three views of a stamen, × 5.
    6. Ovary, transverse section, × 5.
    7. Longitudinal section of an ovarian cell, × 20.
    8. Transverse section of an ovarian cell, × 20.
    9. Oblique dorsal view of the cap-shaped placenta and ovules, × 20.
    10. Oblique front view of the placenta and one ovule, the other ovule removed, × 20.
    11. Fruit, × about 2½.
    12. Fruit, transverse section, × 3.

PLATE 7.

Heterothalamus densus. (Figs. 1 to 7.)

Fig. 1. Branch of a male plant, natural size.
2. Branch of a female plant, natural size.
3. Involucre of a male head of flowers, × 5.
4. Involucre of a female head of flowers, × 5.
5. Male floret, × 5.
6. Bract from the receptacle of a female head, × 5.
7. Female floret, × 5.

Quelchia conferta. (Figs. 8 to 14.)

Figs. 8 & 9. Two branches, showing variation in the length of the peduncles, natural size.
Fig. 10. A flower-head, × 4.
11. A flower-head, longitudinal section, × 4.
12. Corolla laid open, with four stamens removed, × 4.
13. Anthers, dorsal view, with three filaments cut off, × 4.
14. Fruit, × 2.

PLATE 8.

Stiftia Connellii.

Fig. 1. Branch, natural size.
2. Bract from the receptacle, × 2.
3. Floret, with part of the pappus removed, × 2.
4. Stamens, × 2.
5. Apex of style, × 2.

PLATE 9.

Bonyunia minor. (Figs. 1 to 5.)

Fig. 1. Branch, with flowers and fruit, natural size.
2. Branchlet of an inflorescence, × 4.
3. Part of a corolla laid open, × 4.
4. Longitudinal section of a flower, with the corolla removed, × 4.
5. Transverse section of an ovary, × 12.

Lisianthus Quelchii. (Figs. 6 to 9.)

Figs. 6 & 7. Portions of different plants, natural size.
Fig. 8. Flower with two sepals and the corolla removed, natural size after boiling.
9. Corolla laid open, natural size.

PLATE 10.

Utricularia Connellii. (Figs. 1 to 6.)

Fig. 1. Three entire plants, natural size.
2. Part of inflorescence, showing bract and bracteoles, × 5.
3. Flower, × 2.
4. Calyx, dorsal view, × 5.
5. Stamens, × 5.
6. Pistil, × 10.

Utricularia concinna. (Figs. 7 to 11.)

Fig. 7. Three entire plants, natural size.
    8. Inflorescence, × 3.
    9. Flower, viewed from above, with the dorsal sepal turned back, × 3.
   10. Stamens, × 10.
   11. Pistil, × 10.

Utricularia Quelchii. (Figs. 12 to 16.)

Fig. 12. Two entire plants, natural size.
   13. Bract, bracteoles, and calyx, natural size.
   14. Corolla, natural size.
   15. Stamens, × 5.
   16. Pistil, × 5.

PLATE 11.

Utricularia roraimensis. (Figs. 1 to 4.)

Fig. 1. Group of plants, natural size.
    2. Part of a raceme, with the corolla removed, × 5.
    3. Corolla, × 5.
    4. Stamen, × 10.

Genlisea roraimensis. (Figs. 5 to 12.)

Fig. 5. Plant, natural size.
    6. Fragment of the base of a stem, with leaf (+ +), false roots, and an imperfect utricle standing erect among the leaves, × 10.
    7. Perfect utricle, × 5.
    8. Imperfect utricle, transition form between the ordinary false root and the perfect utricle, × 5. This form has a very minute pore at the apex.
    9. Imperfect utricle, erect form, × 5.
   10. Part of a raceme, with the corolla removed, × 5.
   11. Corolla, × 5.
   12. Stamen, × 5.

PLATE 12.

Brocchinia reducta.

Fig. 1. Rosette of leaves, natural size.
    2. Inflorescence, natural size.
    3. Flower, with a sepal and two petals removed, × 5.
    4. Sepal, × 5.
    5. Petal, × 5.
    6. Style and stigmas, × 5.
    7. Transverse section of unripe capsule, seeds not shown, × 5.
    8. Seed, × 5.

PLATE **13.**

Connellia Augustæ.

Fig. 1. Leaf, natural size.
 2. Inflorescence in flower, natural size.
 3. Inflorescence in fruit, natural size.
 4. Sepal, natural size.
    Petal, natural size.
 6. Ovary, the other parts of the flower being removed, natural size.
 7. Ovule, × 30.
 8. Ripe fruit and bracteole, natural size.
 9. Seeds, × 10.
   Figs. 1, 3, 8, & 9 are from McConnell & Quelch's specimen, the rest are from
   Schomburgk's specimen.

PLATE **14.**

Connellia Quelchii.

Figs. 1 & 2. Plants natural, size.
Fig. 3. A large tuft of leaves, natural size.
 4. A leaf, tomentose on the back, natural size.
 5. Sepal, × 2.
 6. Petal, × 2.
 7. Ovary, × 2.
 8. Young fruit, × 2.
 9. Transverse section of an ovary, × 5.

1. ILEX APICIDENS N.E.Brown. 2-6 CYRILLA BREVIFOLIA BRITTON.

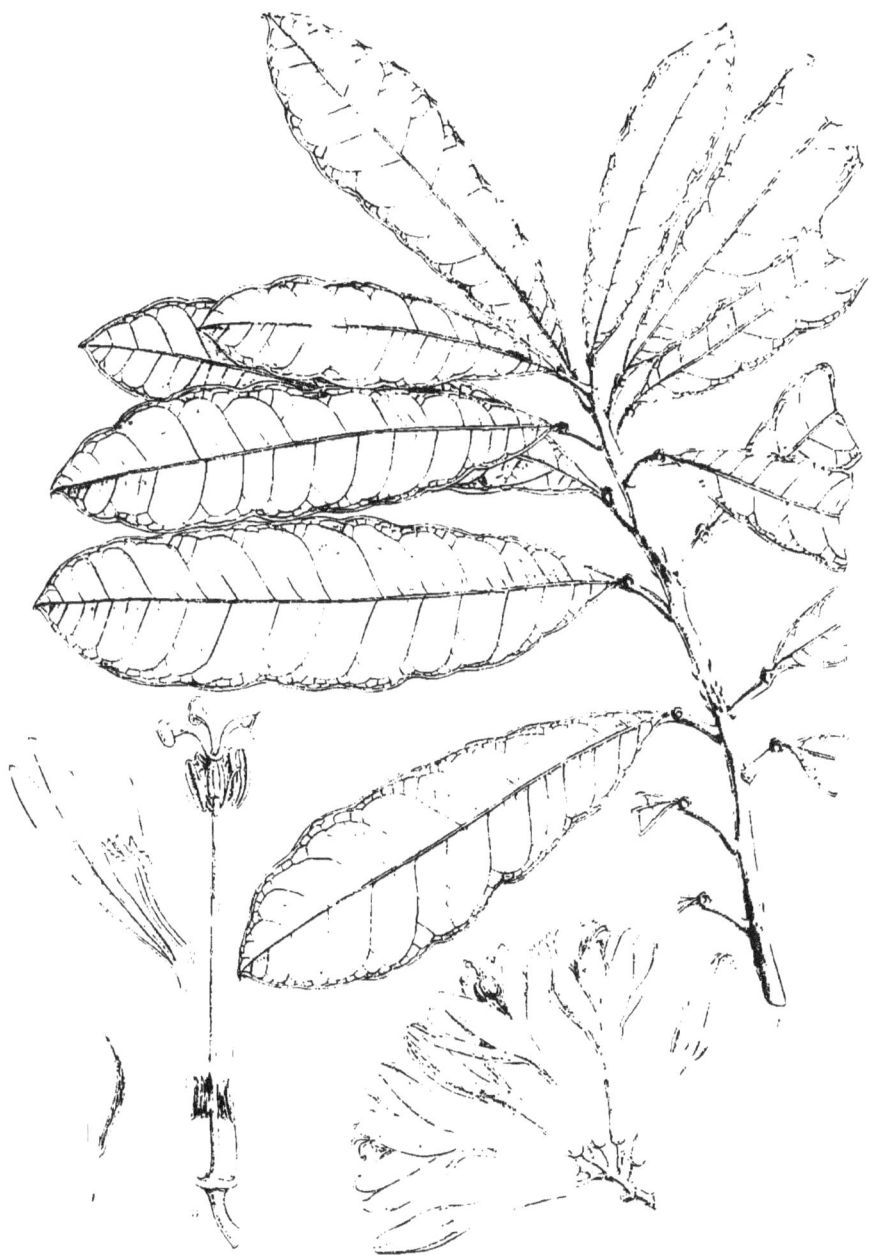

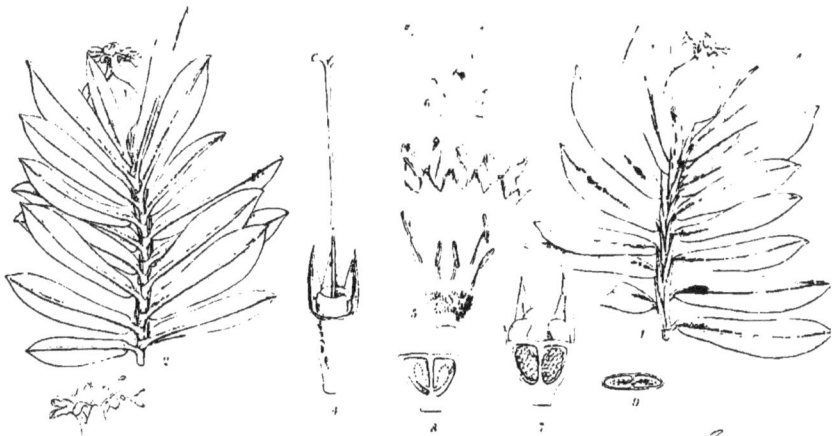

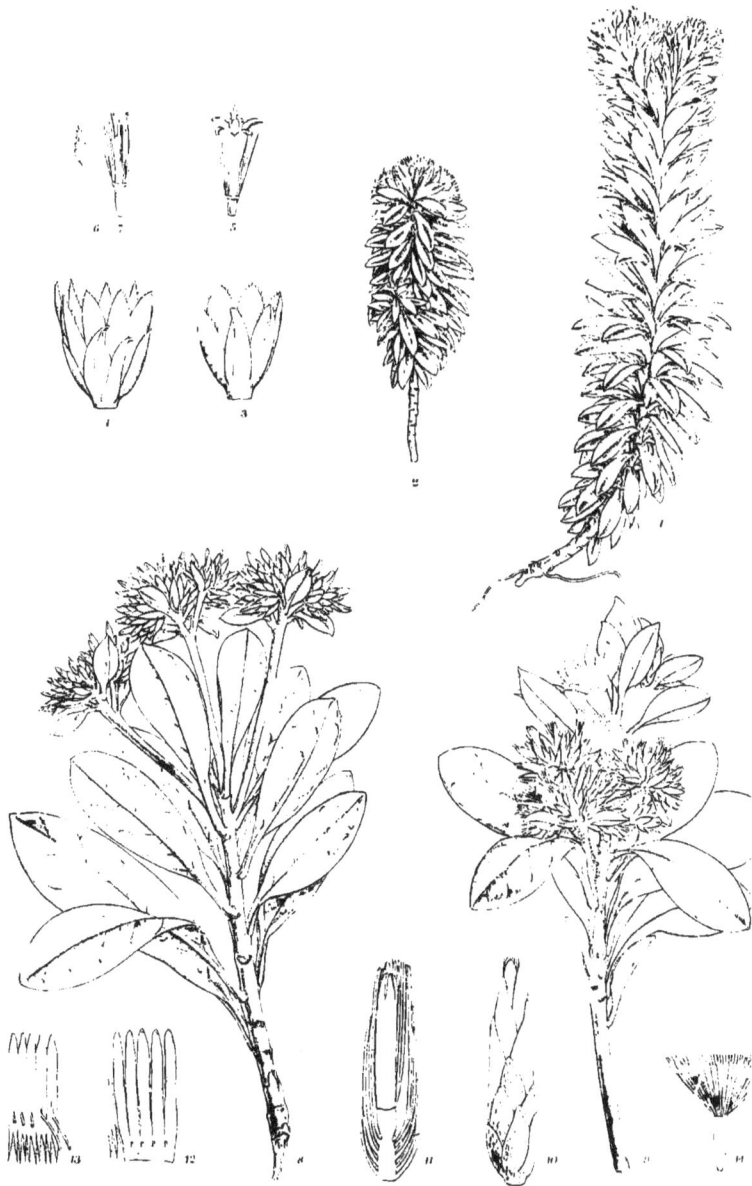

J.N.Fitch del. N.E.Brown ad.

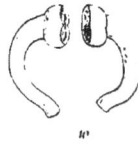

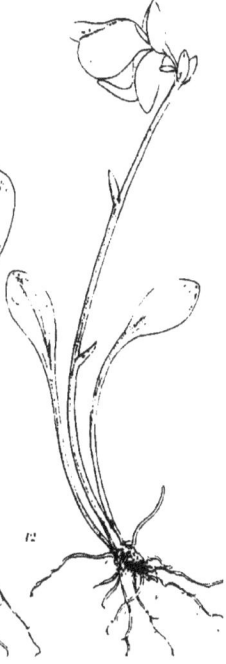

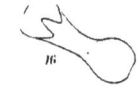

LINNEAN SOCIETY OF LONDON.

MEMORANDA CONCERNING TRANSACTIONS.

The First Series of the Transactions, containing both Botanical and Zoological contributions, has been completed in 30 Vols., and a few entire sets are still for sale. Only certain single volumes, or parts to complete sets, may be obtained at the original prices. The price of the Index to Vols. 1–25 is 8s. to the public, and 6s. to Fellows; to Vols. 26–30, 4s. to the public, and 3s. to Fellows.

The Second Series of the Transactions is divided into Zoological and Botanical sections. The prices of the Botanical parts of these which have been published are as undermentioned. (For the Zoological parts see Zoological wrapper.)

SECOND SERIES.—BOTANY.

Volume.	When Published.	Price to the Public. £ s. d.	Price to Fellows. £ s. d.
I. Part I.	1875.	0 8 0	0 6 0
Part II.	1875.	0 16 0	0 12 0
Part III.	1876.	0 12 0	0 9 0
Part IV.	1876.	0 10 0	0 7 6
Part V.	1878.	1 4 0	0 18 0
Part VI.	1879.	1 6 0	0 19 6
Part VII.	1880.	1 4 0	0 18 0
Part VIII.	1880.	1 1 0	0 16 0
Part IX.	1880.	1 0 0	0 15 0
II. Part I.	1881.	0 12 0	0 9 0
Part II.	1882.	0 5 0	0 3 9
Part III.	1883.	0 10 0	0 7 6
Part IV.	1883.	0 3 0	0 2 3
Part V.	1883.	0 3 0	0 2 3
Part VI.	1884.	0 13 6	0 10 0
Part VII.	1884.	0 9 6	0 7 0
Part VIII.	1884.	0 10 0	0 7 6
Part IX.	1886.	0 7 0	0 5 0
Part X.	1887.	0 3 4	0 2 6
Part XI.	1886.	0 6 0	0 4 6
Part XII.	1886.	0 8 0	0 6 0
Part XIII.	1887.	1 7 0	1 0 0
Part XIV.	1887.	0 7 0	0 5 0
Part XV.	1887.	0 10 0	0 7 6
Part XVI.	1888.	0 2 6	0 2 0
III. Part I.	1888.	3 12 0	2 14 0
Part II.	1891.	0 5 0	0 3 9
Part III.	1891.	0 7 0	0 5 0

SECOND SERIES.—BOTANY (continued).

Volume.	When Published.	Price to the Public. £ s. d.	Price to Fellows. £ s. d.
III. Part IV.	1891.	0 6 0	0 4 6
Part V.	1891.	0 6 0	0 4 6
Part VI.	1891.	0 3 6	0 2 8
Part VII.	1892.	0 6 0	0 4 6
Part VIII.	1893.	0 6 0	0 4 6
Part IX.	1893.	1 8 0	1 1 0
Part X.	1894.	0 10 0	0 7 6
Part XI.	1894.	0 3 4	0 2 6
IV. Part I.	1894.	1 0 0	0 15 0
Part II.	1894.	2 0 0	1 10 0
Part III.	1895.	2 10 0	1 17 6
Part IV.	1895.	0 3 4	0 2 6
V. Part I.	1895.	0 9 0	0 6 9
Part II.	1895.	0 12 0	0 9 0
Part III.	1896.	0 6 0	0 4 6
Part IV.	1896.	1 0 0	0 15 0
Part V.	1896.	0 14 0	0 10 6
Part VI.	1896.	0 4 0	0 3 0
Part VII.	1897.	0 4 0	0 3 0
Part VIII.	1897.	0 6 0	0 4 6
Part IX.	1899.	0 12 0	0 9 0
Part X.	1899.	0 6 0	0 4 6
Part XI.	1899.	0 7 0	0 5 0
Part XII.	1899.	0 12 0	0 9 0
Part XIII.	1900.	0 1 6	0 1 2
Part XIV.	1900.	0 3 0	0 2 3
Part XV.	1901.	0 6 0	0 4 6
VI. Part I.	1901.	1 10 0	1 2 6

www.ingramcontent.com/pod-product-compliance
Lightning Source LLC
Chambersburg PA
CBHW030733280326
41926CB00086B/1356